R
Ross 13

S
S Class

Sailfish

Sunfish

SS
Sea Shell

Seminole

Shamrock

S
Shields Class

6
Six Meter

Snipe

S
Snowbird

Southeaster

 Sprite

Star

 Tallstar

Teal

Tech Dinghy

NY
Thirties

Thistle

Town Class

Turnabout

12
Twelve Meter

210
210 Class

 Vixen

Wayfarer

Windmill

Wood Pussy

Y
Y Flyer

Zephyr

Z
Zip

Cruising Classes

 Amphibi-Con

Amphibi-ette

A30
Annapolis 30

B20
Barnegat 20

Bay Lady

 Bear

B
Bounty II

20
California 20

24
California 24

CV
Cap Vert

32
Chesapeake 32

 Chinook

CC
Coastwise Cruiser

C29
Columbia 29

 C/27
Controversy 27 (Mt. Desert 27)

C
Corsaire

Cutlass

D32
Dickerson 32

Dolphin

Electra

Frisco Flyer

H
Holiday Classes

I
Idler

K
Kestrel

K40
K 40 (Kettenburg 40)

King's Cruiser

 Lion

Marauder

CC
Marlin and Fish Class

M
Maya

M
Meridian

New Horizons

N7
Nomad

Orion

P
Polaris

RR
Ranger

Catamaran Classes

S25
Schock 25

Seawitch

RS
Swiftsure

T27
Tartan 27

Thunderbird

20
Triangle 20

I
Tripp 30

Triton

WE
Week Ender

Catalina Catamaran

Cougar Catamaran III
Mark III One-design

DC-14

Malibu Outrigger

P
Pacific Catamaran

Scamper

Shearwater III

Tiger Cat

Tiki II

Wildcat II

R. C. Dobbyn

THE SAILBOAT CLASSES
OF NORTH AMERICA

Other books by Fessenden S. Blanchard

CRUISING GUIDE TO THE NEW ENGLAND COAST
(with R. F. Duncan)

CRUISING GUIDE TO THE CHESAPEAKE

CRUISING GUIDE TO THE INLAND WATERWAY AND FLORIDA

LONG ISLAND SOUND

BLOCK ISLAND TO NANTUCKET

GHOST TOWNS OF NEW ENGLAND

MAKE THE MOST OF YOUR RETIREMENT

SNIPES racing on Long Island Sound in 1961. Snipes are the largest sailboat class in the world. *Photo by Morris Rosenfeld.*

INTERNATIONAL ONE DESIGN class. *Photo by Morris Rosenfeld.*

THE
SAILBOAT CLASSES
OF NORTH AMERICA

MORE THAN TWO HUNDRED

RACERS, CRUISERS, AND

CATAMARANS

IN STORIES AND PICTURES

BY FESSENDEN S. BLANCHARD

EXPANDED AND UPDATED

BY THEODORE A. JONES

ASSOCIATE EDITOR,

ONE-DESIGN & OFFSHORE YACHTSMAN

1968

DOUBLEDAY & COMPANY, INC.

GARDEN CITY, NEW YORK

ACKNOWLEDGMENTS

So many people helped me on this book that it is impossible to note here more than a few, though many of their names are scattered through these pages in the accounts of the various sailboat classes. Class secretaries, yacht designers, boat builders, editors of boating magazines and writers for these magazines, dealers, racing skippers, yachtsmen from many parts of the United States and abroad contributed information and opinions for this book.

Besides the many articles in yachting magazines from which information was gleaned, of especial help was the list and information compiled annually for *Yachting's Boat Owners Buyers Guide* under the heading "One Design Class Boats." Another valuable source of information was *The Sailing Cruisers of 1962—being a catalogue of Stock Boats from 18' to 45' available in U.S.A.* This was brought out by the *Skipper* (Second St. at Spa Creek, Annapolis, Md.). *One Design Sailboat Classes*, published by the National Association of Engine and Boat Manufacturers, also provided much useful information, as did the yearbook of the Yacht Racing Association of Long Island Sound.

Among the books which proved helpful, besides the numerous class yearbooks and other publications, was the most interesting *Forty Years among the Stars*, by Commodore George W. Elder (Schanen and Jacque, publisher, Port Washington, Wisconsin; obtainable through the International Star Class Yacht Racing Association, 51 East 42nd St., New York 17, N.Y.). Another was *Modern Sailing Catamarans*, by Robert B. Harris (Charles Scribner's Sons, New York, N.Y.).

Magazines from which much was learned included *Motor Boating, Popular Boating, One Design Yachtsman, Rudder, The Skipper, Sports Illustrated,* and *Yachting.*

In closing I should like especially to express my appreciation to the following for their help: Joseph H. Choate, William S. Cox, William J. H. Dyer, W. H. de Fontaine, Donald K. Evans, Walter C. Hadley, Robert B. Harris, James M. and Allegra K. Mertz, James T. Northrop, Donald G. Parrot, Philip L. Rhodes, Critchell Rimington, Drake Sparkman, Roderick Stephens and Olin J. Stephens II, William H. Taylor, Ralph Thacher, Mrs. John C. White, Jr., and Peter Wilson.

TO WILLIAM H. TAYLOR

*with gratitude for his valued aid and advice on
this and other books—and because he is Bill Taylor*

CONTENTS

PREFACE

The purpose of this book is to tell factually, but with interesting history and anecdote, the fascinating story of the sailboat classes of North America —and of countries overseas when substantial numbers of boats have been imported.

I have not separated the one-design from the development classes as a group, but when a class comes in the latter category, I have stated the fact in the description of the class.

Sailboats belong to a class, as I interpret it, when a number of them are alike or their differences are under sufficient restrictions to enable them to race against each other as a class without the necessity of handicap allowances. *The Sailboat Classes of North America* covers both one-design and development classes together, but is divided into two principal categories: Part I—Racing Classes, in which racing and/or day sailing is the primary objective, and Part II—Cruising Classes, in which cruising is the principal objective, though the boats may sometimes race as a class, as in the case of the Tritons or Concordias. The fact that many of the cruising boats also compete in such events as the Bermuda Race or on club cruises does not make them part of a class, as I shall consider it. I am including here among cruising classes only those classes which have been built on a one-design or restricted class basis in sufficient numbers, as I see it, to justify their inclusion. Whether they race as a class is not the important factor; primary consideration, rather, is given to their number, importance, and, if they have been sailing a long time, to their reputation among yachtsmen. There are too many new—and old—so-called cruising classes to include more than a few in this category. While I have had helpful advice, the classes selected are "up to me" and all brickbats should be thrown in my direction. Part III is a brief section covering some of the principal catamaran classes.

Dimensions are not a primary consideration in my decision on whether to include a class with the racers or the cruisers; the consideration is the purpose for which the boats are primarily used. For instance, 12 Meters are included among the racing classes where 8-foot dinghies are also included. Neither is the number a deciding factor; there are over three hundred

Tritons and they race against each other, but I believe the primary interest in the class is in its cruising capabilities. There are hundreds of sailboat classes in the United States. They come and they go and no one can do justice to them all, nor is there room to include them all here.

However, this is more than a book on "The Stars and Snipes Forever," as someone irreverently suggested that I call it. I have tried to include *all* the classes which are important today or seem likely to become significant. I also have included those which may not be considered important now but which have had an interesting history. For this is not a handbook of racing classes with a mere listing of a few facts about each. It is rather an attempt, when information is available, to go behind the better-known facts and delve into the history of the classes we describe. Why, when, and how did they come into being? What are some of the yarns which are told about them? I am hoping to make this book interesting as well as informative.

Most of the leading classes have associations, a few with paid secretaries or other executives, and permanent offices run on a businesslike basis. More frequently the secretaries or class managers rotate in office and affairs are run on a somewhat informal basis. These associations play a vital part in class affairs and many a class owes its success to the association which guides it. Besides organizing races, these associations maintain class standards and rules; register boats in the classes, assigning numbers; maintain records of boat owners, fleets, races; answer questions about the class; try to keep everyone reasonably happy; and stimulate social activities of many kinds. I have tried herein to list the association connected with each class and the address of the Secretary or correspondent. As explained in the Introduction to "Racing Classes: Single Hull," I have suggested ways of obtaining information in cases when secretarial addresses change.

As the facts regarding the classes included in this book have been obtained from many sources and could not be personally checked, I cannot guarantee the accuracy of what is contained herein. I have, however, done the best I could to make the information reliable and have enlisted experienced advice to this end. I shall welcome comments, corrections, and additions which can be taken into consideration in future editions.

FESSENDEN S. BLANCHARD
23 Robin Hill Road
Scarsdale, New York

INTRODUCTION

On September 7, 1890, an article appeared in the Boston *Globe* with an alarming heading:

"Is Racing Dying Out? Committees Have Hard Work to Fill Classes."

The article then went on to say that yacht racing had become largely an expensive competition in which only the wealthy could afford to engage. Rather than a competition between boats in which sailing skill determined the result, it had become a competition between designers.

"Considering its great fleet," said the *Globe,* "the New York Yacht Club has been lamentably weak in its racing events this summer and many other clubs have experienced a dearth of yachts on race days.

"The reason for this state of affairs seems to be that racing is being reduced to a scientific basis and the old boats are being rapidly outbuilt. Few of our yacht owners can order a new boat every year, so the advent of a new flyer gradually thins out the ranks of her class."

At the time that article was written only a single one-design class had appeared on the American yachting scene and that class was located at a small port far away from the main centers of yachting. While there may have been other attempts at establishing one-design classes in other isolated areas, there is little doubt that the North Haven dinghies (which began sailing in 1887) represent the oldest one-design class in the nation—at least the oldest in continuous existence and still racing. As indicated in the section on these dinghies, this was vouched for by the editors of *Yachting* after considerable research. So far as the great yachting areas of Long Island Sound and Massachusetts Bay were concerned, one-design classes had not yet appeared.

The first of the other one-design classes arrived a year after the *Globe* article burst into print and four years after the North Haven dinghies had begun racing on the waters of Fox Island Thorofare. In 1891 four small catboats were built by the Seawanhaka Corinthian Yacht Club of Oyster Bay, Long Island, long a leader in yachting progress since its founding in 1871. Each boat was painted a different color and given a number instead of a name. In 1895 and 1896, two larger one-design classes, both designed by Nathanael Herreshoff, took to the water: five 21-foot-waterline fin-keel sloops and the so-called Newport Thirties, which were 42 feet over-all and 30 feet on the waterline. Among the owners of these boats were a number of men who were to become well known in the yacht-racing world, as they were in other fields: W. S. Douglas, W. Butler Duncan, H. B. Duryea, Ralph N. Ellis, W. S. Gould, J. B. McDonough, E. D. Morgan, James A. Stillman, Cornelius Vanderbilt, and Harry Payne Whitney. The owners and racers of the first North Haven dinghies were not so well known, though their names should be enshrined in somebody's yachting Hall of Fame. Among them should be Miss Ellen Hayward, later to become Mrs. Henry Wheeler, winner in 1887 of the first official race held by the first one-design class of which we have any record. It took a long time for women to take a leading place in some of the great yachting centers. Not so at North Haven! Other pioneers among these early North Haven dinghy owners and racers were Dr. C. G. Weld, Alfred Bowditch, Tucker Deland, and Charles K. Cobb.

One of the earliest of all one-design classes has an unusually appropriate name which all who have studied Latin will recognize: Idem. The first boats were built about 1897–98 by the St. Lawrence Boat Company. According to George K. Earle IV (writing on April 13, 1962), eleven boats were built; all are still in existence and six or seven actively race every summer on St. Regis Lake in the Adirondacks, New York. They are gaff-rigged centerboarders 32 feet long. (For the benefit of those who have forgotten their Latin, *Idem* means *Same*.)

After 1900 one-design classes multiplied rapidly, most of them large boats by present one-design standards. Perhaps the best-known boats in these early one-design classes were the New York Thirties, like the Newport Thirties designed and built by Herreshoff. At the time the Thirties began racing they were the smallest yachts permitted to fly the burgee of the New York Yacht Club.

Smaller one-design classes soon spread like an epidemic and in 1911 the Star class came into being, to become perhaps the best known of all one-design classes, with fleets in many parts of the world. Some of these early one-design classes grew so fast that it took a while for the rules and regulations to catch up with their racing activities. The late Commodore George W. Elder, in his delightfully written *Forty Years among the Stars*,[*] gives an example of the irregularity of these regulations. The story was told by George ("Pop") Corry, an almost legendary character in the early days of the Star class. The event occurred before 1907, when the Bug one-design class, predecessor of the Stars, made its appearance.

[*] Published in 1955 by Schanen and Jacque, Port Washington, Wisconsin.

A race was arranged for Swampscott dories and other small centerboard boats; they were to sail from Cow Bay (now called Manhasset Bay) to Hempstead Harbor, the next bay to the east.

"This was a free for all," as George Elder describes it, based on Pop Corry's story. "No rules, other than right-of-way, were to apply. That meant that you didn't have to round any given buoys, but cut corners as pleased. The first in was to be the winner. Since there were no power boats, the question of a tow was not considered. Immediately after crossing the starting line, one of the entries sailed back to the club and beached the boat.

"The crew went overboard and carried the boat to a farm wagon which was waiting. Passing through the village of Port Washington, they picked up a little German band that was playing in front of a saloon. It was only a short distance overland to Hempstead Harbor. When they reached there they launched the boat, stepped the mast, and as there was no crew limit, crowded the four-piece German band aboard. It almost sank the boat, but the weather was light and they only had a short distance to go. With the band playing 'There'll Be a Hot Time in the Old Town Tonight,' they crossed the finish line.

"Having complied with all the conditions of the race, the triumphal procession started home with the cup before the first sail was sighted in the mouth of Hempstead Harbor."

Modern rule-beaters might study this episode with profit. George Elder ends his yarn by saying that George Corry was always known to be a pious, temperate, and truthful yachtsman. However, the first of these characteristics must have been sorely tried when Pop heaved an anchor off Larchmont while his foot was in the center of a coiled anchor cable. Pop went overboard after the anchor and must have been somewhat disconcerted when laughter delayed the rescue operations.

Examples such as the decline of yacht-racing entries described by the Boston *Globe* and the lack of adequate racing rules described by Pop Corry, convinced many of the doubters that there was a need for one-design classes racing under proper regulation.

There were many reasons for one-design classes: such as putting sailing skill on an equal competitive basis; much lower costs per boat, since a number could be built at once; lower obsolescence costs—one-design boats often last for many years; a large enough group under one class to make practical a class association to promote and regulate the competition among boat owners in a class; a great enlargement in the number and geographical distribution of the competitors; no handicapping problems; making rule-beating more difficult.

There are also some obvious disadvantages to one-design classes, the most important being a lessening of the stimulus toward the development of new and improved designs. Some of the great creative steps forward by yacht designers have come from their efforts to create boats that are different from their predecessors and faster. This, however, has sometimes resulted in freak rule-beaters, such as W. Starling Burgess's *Outlook* with its tremendous overhangs which made waterline length ridiculous as a basis of competition. Thus, creative design efforts had to be brought under control and new sets of rules came into being which would *restrict* the area within which designers would be allowed free scope for their imagination. Hence, we now have *restricted* or *development* classes such as the International 14s and the Moths, which allow scope for creative effort but attempt to keep it within practical limitations.

Sometimes the line between one-design and development classes is closely drawn. For instance, some one-design classes such as the Stars, while keeping to the same hulls, have allowed much latitude in the improving of equipment. Other classes have been rigid and when a change is permitted, such as a shift from wooden to fiber-glass hulls, it affects all members of the same class simultaneously. There is little doubt that *both* one-design and development classes are desirable for the good of yachting.

Fessenden S. Blanchard, 1963

INTRODUCTION TO THE REVISED EDITION

The sailing world has changed considerably in the short time since the late Fessenden S. Blanchard published the first edition of this book. There are many more classes and many thousand more people sailing. Existing classes have grown, and there are several that number more than ten thousand, whereas only the Snipes exceeded that mark in 1963. Growth has been most pronounced in the cruising classes, with fiber-glass construction accounting for all but one of the new classes in the supplement to this book.

In spite of this tremendous growth, Mr. Blanchard's original writing is still valid. He had unusual insight, and with rare exceptions the comments he made remain astute judgments of the characteristics and future developments of the classes. Granted, class secretaries have changed or moved away, prices have risen (the 1963 prices are retained in these pages for comparison value), a few companies have gone out of business, but all the classes now listed are in existence and race actively. Up-to-date addresses, prices, and numbers of boats extant can be found in the *One-Design & Offshore Yachtsman* catalog issue usually published in January of each year or *Boat Owner's & Buyer's Guide* published each spring by Yachting Publishing Corporation.

Theodore A. Jones, 1968

PART ONE
RACING CLASSES: *Single Hull*

INTRODUCTION

This part of the book is an attempt to include a description and some interesting facts in the history of each of the principal *racing* classes of sailboats in the United States. Consequently, we are devoting more space to the classes with a history, such as the Comets, Stars, and Snipes, than we are to some of the smaller and more recently organized classes.

While some classes seem to go on forever, such as the Star class (for which more boats were built in 1961 than in any previous year), many classes, like old generals, just fade away and are replaced by new ones on the racing circuits. Every year, especially since the recent sailing boom, new classes come into being; some will undoubtedly take to the water while this book is on the press. We hope, however, that we have "caught" the important classes and even some which only seem destined to become important—in prestige, like the Shields class, if not in numbers. As William H. ("Bill") Taylor of *Yachting* said, after being kind enough to go over my list:

"I found a lot of class names I never heard of, naturally. Probably there are some missing which I should have remembered. And I am sure there are a lot neither of us have thought of that ought to be included, and their admirers will raise hell. But it's a good list."

Explanation of Class Descriptions and Terms. While most of the following will be obvious to experienced yachtsmen, it seemed best to insert here a few explanations.

1. *Addresses of Associations and Class Secretaries.* Many of these change from time to time, though some of the larger associations with paid Secretaries continue at the same address year after year. Communications to the Secretaries noted here will in most cases be forwarded to a succeeding Secretary. The *Boat Owners Buyers Guide*, published annually at one dollar by *Yachting* (205 East 42nd St., New York 17, N.Y.) includes a list, "One-Design and Class Boats," in which addresses of Secretaries and builders are brought up to date yearly.

2. *Builders.* Where there are no more than several builders for a class, I am including here their names and addresses. If there is a long list I refer

the reader to the class Secretary for information, or suggest looking in the *Boat Owners Buyers Guide* mentioned above.

3. *Crew.* Where specified or limited, we have included the racing crew (or in some cases the crew weight) allowed in each class. This includes skipper plus crew; that is, the total in each boat.

4. *Mainsails* are always considered to be *Marconi* (jib-headed, or Bermudian) unless otherwise noted. We use "Marconi," despite the preferences of some yachtsmen, because we have found that this is the most commonly used term.

5. *Meter.* Though often spelled *metre* by others, in this book we have tried to be consistent and have used the first spelling regardless of the way it may be spelled in class literature or letters.

6. *Number in Class:* At time of writing—spring, 1962.

7. *Prices* are those given us as being in effect at the time of writing. They are, of course, "subject to change without notice," but they were all obtained early in 1962 and at approximately the same time for all classes. They should, therefore, provide a good basis of comparison. Prices for used boats are, of course, approximate and vary widely.

8. *Vital Statistics.* These include basic measurements in feet and inches, weights in pounds, and other items listed and explained below, though most of them are obvious to experienced yachtsmen.

L.O.A.—Length over-all

Waterline—Length on waterline

Beam—Width

Draft—Without centerboard (board up)
  With C.B. (centerboard) or D.B. (daggerboard) down fully, or of boat with keel

Sail area—Square feet in regular sail or sails
  Rated sail area is given where it applies.
  Spinnakers, if permitted, are not included.

Weights—Approximate, including spars, rig, etc. (or at least that is what we asked for and I think usually got)

Trailable—Means trailable on a standard trailer, unless a special trailer for the class is mentioned.

ALBACORE. *Courtesy Fairey Engineering, Ltd.*

ALBACORE

The Albacore is an English 15-foot sloop-rigged dinghy designed by the famous English racing authority Uffa Fox. The idea was to "provide a very stable planing dinghy for family sailing suitable for experts and novices, *not a desperate dinghy,* but with the feel and characteristics similar to International 14." Perhaps the fact that the mast is only 20′6″ above the gunwale helps to make the dinghy less "desperate" than some others. There are buoyancy tanks and bags giving six hundred pounds of flotation, enough to make it fairly easy to right a capsized boat. The foredeck extends to the mast. As you may have gathered, the Albacore is safer to sail and more suitable for family use than the common extreme type of light planing dinghy.

There are nearly thirteen hundred of these boats in the world, of which a large proportion are in England. Some are in Toronto, Canada, some in Cyprus, and about 250 are used by the armed forces of the United Kingdom. About 150 are in the United States, including some on Long Island Sound.

Fairey Marine, Ltd. (Hamble, Hampshire, England), is the exclusive builder of the hulls, though others may complete a hull within the rules. Construction material is molded mahogany plywood on an approved class mold. Write Fairey for the names of dealers in the United States or write for information on the class to O. B. Sayer, Albacore Association (The Coach House Cottage, St. Mary's Road, Long Ditton, Surbiton, Surrey, England). Prices are reported as follows (in England—pounds converted to dollars): new $784, used $616, kit $532.

VITAL STATISTICS: L.O.A. 15′; waterline 14′9″; beam 5′5″; draft without centerboard 8″, with C.B. down 4′5″; sail area 125 sq. ft. (spinnakers not allowed); weight 330 lbs.; trailable. Racing crew allowed is not less than two.

ARROW

The 18-foot Arrow round-bottomed centerboard sloop had its origin on Lake Michigan in 1935 when Albert Britain, of Wilmette, then Commodore of the Sheridan Shore Yacht Club, commissioned A. M. Deering, Chicago naval architect, as designer. Most of the early boats were built by Jen Christensen, who came to Chicago from Denmark at an early age. Christensen went out of business during World War II and others took over. The Arrow is light enough to be trailable and is said to be "very lively in light weather, goes to weather as a Universal, also is as wet; it can also take a blow."

The aim was to have a decked-over boat with a large enough cockpit for six and for family sailing, but also to have a good racing boat. There is a fifty-three-boat racing fleet at Wilmette, another fleet at a suburb of Chicago, and another at Montrose Harbor. With 110 altogether, it is said to be one of the largest one-design classes on the Great Lakes.

Construction materials are mahogany or fiber glass. Nimphius Boat Com-

ARROW. *Courtesy Stamm Boat Co.*

pany (Route 2, Neshkoro, Wis.) uses the former material; Stamm Boat
Company (P. O. Box 5, Delafield, Wis.) builds them of fiber glass, using
Styrofoam to make them unsinkable. Aluma Craft Boat Division (Hupp
Corp., 1515 Central Ave. N.E., Minneapolis, Minn.) is now said to be working on nationwide distribution. At the time of writing the class Secretary
is Ernest Heineman (337 Essex Rd., Kenilworth, Wis.). Price is about
$2300 new, $1000 used.

VITAL STATISTICS: L.O.A. 18′; waterline 16′; beam 5′4″; draft without centerboard 1′2⅛″, with C.B. down 4½′; sail area 195 sq. ft. (spinnakers not allowed); weight 1100 lbs. minimum; trailable. Under average
conditions on Lake Michigan three or four people are considered about
right for a racing crew; in light weather two can handle an Arrow.

ATLANTIC

The Atlantic is a good example of a class that is being revitalized by fiber glass with flotation tanks added. Originally made of wood in Germany in 1929 by Abeking and Rasmussen, it is now built of fiber glass by the Cape Cod Shipbuilding Company (Wareham, Mass.). Designed by the late W. Starling Burgess, Atlantics have been a familiar and beautiful sight on Long Island Sound for many years; some of them are also to be seen on Blue Hill Bay, Maine. To quote the class Secretary: "The class has been decreased to about seventy active boats with the loss of about twenty-five boats to storms and hurricanes through the years. The class has been opened up again with the allocation of number 101 to be used when the first new Atlantic is built."

"The Atlantic," to quote an enthusiast, "combines the ideal sailing of a

ATLANTIC. *Courtesy Atlantic Class Association.*

deep-keeled boat for family use with the ease of handling of a racing machine. Most boats are raced with the principals of the family, and the national championships are a combination of fierce competition during the day and the warm friendship of old friends in the evenings."

The Atlantic Class Association was founded in 1929; its rules were adopted in 1933 and amended on June 1, 1956. Among the interesting provisions in recognition of the era of outboards is one which allows outboards to be carried provided they are detached before the preparatory signal of a race and not moved or reshipped until after the race. Some noted yachtsmen own Atlantics, among them Briggs S. Cunningham, the successful skipper of the *Columbia* in the America's Cup Races in 1958. The class Secretary is R. W. Ray, Jr. (118 Long Lots Rd., Westport, Conn.). Price of a new boat $5000, used $1000 to $2000.

VITAL STATISTICS: L.O.A. 30′6″; waterline 21′6″; beam 6′6″; draft (keel) 4′9″; sail area 385 sq. ft.; displacement 4559 lbs.; not trailable.

BARNEGAT BAY SNEAKBOX.
Courtesy Allan R. Chadwick.

BARNEGAT BAY SNEAKBOX

The Sneakboxes began as gunning skiffs for use on the shallow waters of Barnegat Bay. Howard I. Chapelle[*] points out that the name "box" was probably taken from a "sink box" which was used as a floating duckblind,

---

[*] *American Small Sailing Craft,* by Howard I. Chapelle, W. W. Norton Co., Inc.

anchored with its deck almost awash and covered with marsh grass or reeds. When used as a skiff to "sneak up" on the ducks, it became known as a sneakbox. Sometimes described as looking like a deep spoon covered by a shallow spoon, larger boats of the same general design began to appear in the early part of the nineteenth century.

Authorities differ as to when the Sneakboxes began or when they first acquired sail. One version states that the first boat was built on Barnegat Bay, New Jersey, by Hazelton Seaman, in 1836. Despite its being called the "devil's coffin," other boats followed, in many ways like forerunners of the modern racing scows. While these boats were very fast under sail, when not properly equipped they had a tendency to bury the bow if the sail was too large or the mast was too far forward. By the late 1800s more than fifty Sneakboxes had been built, and they were racing at the turn of the century, some of them operating as sandbaggers on which shifted sandbags supplemented shifting people in helping the boats to carry sail.

In the early 1900s, when J. Howard Perrine of Barnegat designed and built his famous 15-foot gaff-rigged catboat, the Barnegat Bay Sneakboxes came into wide use. Over three thousand were sold. No national association was formed nor was there any insignia on the sails. The principal sailing areas are in Barnegat Bay and in New England camps.

VITAL STATISTICS for the 15-foot, gaff-rigged version are: L.O.A. 15′; waterline 13′; beam 5′9″; draft without centerboard 6″, with C.B. down 5′; sail area 156 sq. ft. (no spinnaker); weight 350 lbs.; trailable.

During 1960 Allan R. Chadwick of Barnegat, a former associate of the late Howard Perrine, redesigned the Sneakbox into a 14-footer with a sloop rig and called the new model the 8 Ball, with that as an insignia. There are also versions of the Sneakbox in a 12-foot sprit rig and in an 18-foot sloop rig, as well as the 15- and 14-footers, all built by Chadwick.

Mr. Chadwick writes: "Could you possibly incorporate in your book something about the durability, seaworthiness, and safety of the Sneakboxes? Although we ask this as lovers of Sneakboxes, we are backed up by most of the experts. There are Sneakboxes over forty and fifty years old that are still being sailed. When all other boats their size have had to head for port in a blow, the hardy Sneakbox is in its glory. And it is generally agreed that the Sneakbox is the safest small sailboat for training youngsters."

The 8 Ball Sneakbox class President at the time of writing is Earl Beard (Beach Haven, N.J.); the Secretary-Treasurer Rev. A. David Seeland (Barnegat, N.J.). About thirty boats of this class have been built.

VITAL STATISTICS for the new 14-footer: L.O.A. 14′; waterline 11′6″; beam 5′10″; draft without centerboard 3½″, with C.B. 4′; sail area 105 sq. ft. (spinnaker allowed); approximate weight 275 lbs.; trailable.

B.B. 11 sailing at Cannes, France. *Courtesy Getz Brothers and Co.*

B.B. 11

This is an attractive 20-foot keel sloop, designed and built by Borge Bringsvaerd of Dröbak, Norway, and sold by Getz Brothers & Company (Nils Juelsgt 33, Oslo, Norway). It is a one-design "racer-cruiser." Conceived in 1956 and started in 1958, there are now fleets in at least ten countries and it is said to be one of the fastest-growing classes in Europe. With 520 boats altogether, including 42 in the United States, the class seems to have moved fast.

The principal areas of sailing activity in the United States are on San Francisco Bay, the vicinity of Seattle, Florida, and New York. In Europe there are a number on the Mediterranean (France and Italy), in Norway, Sweden, Denmark, etc. The boat is said to be dry and unsinkable, due to its watertight compartments. The United States class Secretary is A. D. Hurd (582 Silverado Drive, Lafayette, Calif.). Price of a new boat (cost and freight, as offered by Getz for the U. S. East Coast) is $1364 with Dacron sails. In San Francisco it costs $214 more.

VITAL STATISTICS: L.O.A. 20′3″; waterline 13′8″; beam 5′10″; draft (keel) 3′; sail area 121 sq. ft. (spinnaker used); approximate weight 1430 lbs.; trailable.

BEETLE CAT

Though some of the boats carry a beetle insignia on their sail, this class is named not for a bug but for a man, or rather a family: the Beetle family, for many generations resident on Clark's Point, New Bedford, Massachusetts. Those who belong to the author's generation and have many pleasant memories of wooden boats and gaff rigs can prepare for an attack of nostalgia when they watch a fleet of Beetle Cats racing on Buzzards or Narragansett bays. For the Beetles still swarm in those waters, over two thousand strong, from Cohasset, Massachusetts, to Babylon, Long Island.

It all began in 1921, when the Beetle family designed and built the "Original Beetle Cats." Until 1946 the Beetles continued to manufacture these cats, but during that year the company became engaged in the manufacture of fiber-glass boats with Marconi rigs. It then transferred all rights concerning the "Original Beetle Cats" to the Concordia Company, Inc., of South Dartmouth, Massachusetts, builders of the famous Concordia yawls. Thus the tradition of gaff-rigged, wooden catboats has been carried on to this day, with no essential changes in boat or rig.

The New England Beetle Cat Boat Association, organized in 1937, and at last account with a membership of over thirty clubs, has had a great deal to do with the continued success of the class, as has the Concordia Company. But the boat itself is primarily responsible. It takes a good small boat to behave well in the choppy waters and smoky sou'westers of Buzzards Bay and Nantucket Sound. The Beetle Cats (not to be confused with a catamaran) are seaworthy for their size, safe, and comfortable. Extremely pop-

BEETLE CAT. *Photo by Norman Fortier.*

ular among the children of southern New England, and the largest one-design racing class in that area, the Beetles are also used by the Peppy Pappies, Dashing Daddies, Tired Fathers, and Wet Hens of Narragansett Bay in efforts to prove to their progeny that some parents at least can practice what they preach. Leo J. Telesmanick (124 Frederick St., New Bedford, Mass.) is Secretary of the class. He served his apprenticeship in 1930 with the Beetle family and has been in charge of Beetle production with Concordia.

At the time of writing, the price for a new boat is $865; used ones can be bought for about $550. Construction is cedar planking with oak frames.

VITAL STATISTICS: L.O.A. 12'4"; waterline 11'8"; beam 6'; draft without centerboard 6", with C.B. 2'; sail area 100 sq. ft. (no spinnaker); racing crew two or three; weight 450 lbs.; trailable.

BEVERLY DINGHY. *Courtesy Cape Cod Shipbuilding Co.*

BEVERLY DINGHY

Doubling as a sailing dinghy and yacht tender, this class was designed for the Cape Cod Shipbuilding Company of Wareham, Massachusetts, by A. Sidney De W. Herreshoff. Since 1951 the dinghies have been actively racing under the auspices of the Beverly Yacht Club of Marion, Massachusetts. Made of fiber glass, the boat is light in weight with a simple, easily detachable Marconi cat rig. Brown University, after trying a number of fiber-glass dinghies, selected the Beverlys for their fleet. About three hundred have been built. Prices are $645 new; about $500 used.

VITAL STATISTICS: L.O.A. 11′6″; beam 4′6″; draft with centerboard 1′7″; weight about 200 lbs.; trailable.

BLUE JAY

Called "kid sister" to the Lightning and designed by Sparkman and Stephens, the 13½-foot Blue Jay centerboard sloops came on the yachting scene about 1950, starting at the Larchmont and Manhasset Bay Yacht Clubs. With a hard chine adding to the stiffness and ease of construction, this class has proved to be one of the most rapidly growing classes in the United States, with about five hundred a year being added to the three thousand or so already on the water.

Considered an ideal and relatively safe boat for children, the Blue Jays are raced largely by the younger generation, though parents are not averse to sailing them. While those who prefer the excitement of a more readily planing type of hull and rig may turn to lighter and faster types, the popularity of the Blue Jay is due to the combination of safety and stability with ease of handling, and a good turn of speed. At Larchmont Race Week in 1954 all but one of thirty-eight competing Blue Jays weathered a sudden squall which capsized many of the larger Lightnings.

The list of Blue Jay manufacturers and dealers is too long to include here; the latest *Boat Owners Buyers Guide,* published by *Yachting,* lists forty-two of them. Check over the list for their names and addresses, or ask Robert J. Sparkman, Secretary of the International Blue Jay Class Association (11 E. 44th St., New York 17, N.Y.). A leading manufacturer in the vicinity of New York, whom the writer has visited, is McKean Boats (Mamaroneck, N.Y.). But there are many others who also do a good job. This includes a good many amateurs. Some boys and girls at Mamaroneck High School formed the M.H.S. Sailing Club and, under the direction of a faculty adviser, built their own Blue Jay, and painted it in the school colors of orange and black. Other group undertakings have helped to swell the fleet. Construction is of plywood and kits are available.

During Larchmont (N.Y.) Race Week in 1961, over two hundred Blue Jays came to the starting line, representing the largest number in any class.

BLUE JAY. *Courtesy McKean Boats.*

A widely available competition in many parts of the United States is one of the Blue Jay assets for those who like racing.

Over 90 per cent of the class is in the United States, with about five hundred on the Pacific Coast and a good many of the rest on Long Island

Sound. The price for a new boat is about $1200, used boats cost $500 up, kits $675.

VITAL STATISTICS: L.O.A. 13′6″; waterline 11′5″; beam 5′2″; draft without centerboard 5″, with C.B. 2′10″; sail area 90 sq. ft. (spinnakers allowed); weight 275 minimum; trailable; racing crew, three maximum.

BRUTAL BEAST. *Courtesy Herbert E. Harwood.*

BRUTAL BEAST

W. Starling Burgess, designer of three defenders of the America's Cup, once owned at his home in Marblehead, Massachusetts, a great Dane to whom the neighbors gave the nickname "Brutal Beast." While I am not sure whether it was Starling who suggested this as a name for his new class, with his sense of humor it would not have been out of character. He designed the boat in the early part of this century and built it in his Marblehead yacht yard. As an old friend of his put it, "he wanted a boat for his children and grandchildren which would be safe and yet have zip." The boats were 14-foot-long, hard-chine V-bottom cats, and became successful far beyond the needs of the Burgess family. During 1937 the class used to sail in Marblehead in four divisions, with twenty-five or thirty boats in each group.

Beginning with gaff rigs, they were later converted to Marconis and served as trainers for many men, such as Ted Hood and others, who later became expert racers. They also at one time demonstrated to one of the country's great skippers that success in racing a J boat does not necessarily assure success in sailing a 14-footer—at least not a Brutal Beast.

On August 29, 1937, a pretty fifteen-year-old girl, "Janny" Harwood, the proud owner of a new Brutal Beast, the *Rip Tide*, brought her boat to the dock of the Eastern Yacht Club at Marblehead and waited. She was one of five skippers of these wicked-sounding boats who had been asked to meet at the dock with their craft. The America's Cup had been successfully defended at Newport by Harold Vanderbilt and he and the other J-boat skippers were in Marblehead for a series of races in their great 135-foot (or so) racers. Besides Vanderbilt, Thomas O. M. Sopwith, the unsuccessful English challenger, was there with his *Endeavour I* and *Endeavour II*, together with his skipper, Sigrist. Chandler Hovey was in Marblehead with *Rainbow* and Gerard Lambert with *Yankee*. As an interesting diversion, a Brutal Beast Challenge Cup had been offered for a series of two races in Brutal Beasts by the J-boat skippers.

Janny waited at the dock with *Rip Tide*. A tall figure approached and explained that he had drawn *Rip Tide* for the first race.

"How close will she point?" Mike Vanderbilt inquired of Janny. "About five points, I'd imagine?"

Janny didn't quite know where five points would be but she took a chance and said that she guessed that was about right. But she failed to remind the new skipper that in Brutal Beasts it was important to keep a proper balance of weight between bow and stern. Vanderbilt hadn't worried much about this when he was on the *Ranger*, at least so far as the distribution of his own weight was concerned. He sat too near the stern, I am told, and came in last in the first race of Brutal Beasts. Tom Sopwith was first in a boat belonging to Barbara Connolly.

For the second race Sopwith had drawn *Rip Tide* and asked Janny for instructions. Again he won. Obviously there had been nothing wrong with the boat in the first race. Vanderbilt, in another boat, was again last. The final results were in this order: Sopwith, Hovey, Sigrist, Lambert and Vanderbilt. The winner was so pleased with his success that he invited the owners of the two Brutal Beasts on which he had raced to be his guests on *Endeavour II.*

"Did you and Barbara accept the invitation?" I asked Janny (now Mrs. John C. White, Jr.), as she reminisced about Brutal Beast days.

"You bet" was her answer.

The Brutal Beast class is dwindling in numbers. Though a few are still sailed in Marblehead, and some have scattered to Blue Hill Bay in Maine, Orleans on Cape Cod, and other waters, none have been built since World War II. The reason is the high cost of their construction due to the materials from which they were made and the high price of skilled labor. The Brutal Beasts are important to those interested in sailboat classes, not for their present and future, but for their past.

VITAL STATISTICS: L.O.A. 14'; beam 6'2"; sail area 127 sq. ft.

BULL'S EYE and HERRESHOFF "TWELVES"

The Bull's Eye 15'8½" sloop is the modern version of the Herreshoff "Twelve," well known from the days when boats were described by their waterline length. In 1914, the great Nathanael G. Herreshoff, who came to be known as the "Wizard of Bristol" (Rhode Island), designed a gaff-rigged keel sloop which became extremely popular in southern Massachusetts and Rhode Island. This boat, which was known as the "Twelve," proved well suited to Buzzards Bay waters, where, as in Kipling's Baltic, "the seas are steep and short," piled up by the perennial sou'wester which blows almost daily during the yachting season. Her over-all length was about 15½ feet; her waterline about 12'5"; her beam 5'10", and the draft 2'5"; with a sail area of about 140 square feet. Hundreds of the Twelves were built and many are still seen on Buzzards Bay—together with the Beetles they constitute one of the few active classes still carrying a gaff rig. The writer and his wife and daughters used to sail a good deal in these boats, out of Marion, Massachusetts and acquired a great deal of respect for their seagoing abilities, as we have for the fiber-glass version.

The Bull's Eye is the Twelve "gone modern," with all of its seaworthy qualities remaining, but with a fiber-glass hull, a cuddy forward, adequate flotation, a Marconi rig, aluminum spars, roller reefing, Dacron sails, etc. The writer thought it was the prettiest sailboat of its size at a recent New York Motor Boat Show, and that is saying a good deal.

BULL'S EYE. *Courtesy Cape Cod Shipbuilding Co.*

In 1948 the well-known Cape Cod Shipbuilding Company of Wareham, Massachusetts, purchased the exclusive rights to manufacture the Bull's Eye and selected this as the first keel-model boat to mold with fiber glass. Sidney De W. Herreshoff, son of Nathanael, designed the new rig.

The Bull's Eye is obviously a displacement boat, not a planing type, but it is a good sailer in almost any kind of weather, particularly in rough water. About 475 of the Bull's Eyes are reported to have been built at the time of writing, of which 400 are in the United States. The principal areas of activity are Buzzards Bay, Massachusetts; Narragansett Bay, Rhode Island; the Mount Desert region in Maine; Long Island Sound, including the Fishers Island waters; Marblehead, Massachusetts; the South Shore of Cape Cod, Massachusetts; New Jersey, and Miami. At the time of writing, Dr. Gordon W. Douglas (Pelham, N.Y.) is Secretary of the recently organized Bull's-Eye Class Association, which had sixty-three members. Prices are $2000 to $2150, depending upon the equipment and delivery location. Used boats cost $1500 to $1800.

VITAL STATISTICS: L.O.A. 15′8½″; waterline 12′6¾″; beam 5′10″; draft (keel) 2′5″; sail area 140 sq. ft. (spinnaker allowed); weight 1350 lbs.; trailable with special equipment.

BUTTERBALL

In the summer of 1958 Captain Richard T. Miller, of the Ship Design Division, Bureau of Ships, U.S.N., who lives in Annapolis, Maryland, designed the 9′6″ Butterball pram dinghy as a junior training boat. The most distinctive feature of the class is said to be a thick (1¾″) daggerboard with a symmetrical airfoil section. This is said to give the boat a good lift, so that she sails close to the wind and balances nicely. The designer reports that Bob Bavier (*Yachting*) sailed Number 1 boat in the spring of 1959 and appeared pleased with its handling qualities. Of the thirty boats so far built, most of them are located in the vicinity of Charleston, South Carolina; some are at Tacoma, Washington; others are in Texas, Michigan, Missouri, Australia, and New Zealand. Material is mahogany plywood. Captain R. T. Miller (R.F.D. 3, Box 392, Melvin Rd., Annapolis, Md.) is the source of information on the class. The principal builder is Bill Dodds Boats (Route 1, Box 156A, Johns Island, S.C.). The price is about $400 new, one of the least expensive sailing dinghies of which we have heard.

VITAL STATISTICS: L.O.A. 9′6″; waterline 7′9″; beam 5′4″; draft without centerboard 5″, with C.B. 2′5½″; sail area 49 sq. ft.; weight 150 lbs.; trailable or cartop.

BUTTERBALL. *Courtesy of Captain Richard T. Miller.*

CADET.
*Courtesy The Bell
Woodworking Co., Ltd.*

CADET

This 10½-foot decked-over centerboard sloop looks like a big boat in the distance until you notice the relative size of the crew. Known in England and elsewhere as the International Cadet, it was designed there by Jack Holt for *Yachting World*. As in many other boats of this size, the purpose was to produce a boat suitable for youngsters. In England the boat may be raced only by juniors up to eighteen years old. The Cadet has a hard chine and is easy to construct. Over three thousand have been built and they are sailed in twenty-six countries. Material is mahogany plywood.

So far, relatively few of these boats are sailing in the United States; the principal areas are reported to be near Boston, on Long Island Sound, and on the Severn River, near Annapolis, Maryland. For information on the International Cadet Class, write *Yachting World* (Dorset House, Stamford St., London S.E. 1, England). Another source of information is The Bell Woodworking Company, Ltd., of Leicester, England, and, in this country, John Wright, Jr. (308 W. Queen Lane, Philadelphia 44, Pa.), who sells the complete boat or kits. Price for the former with Dacron sails is about $650. Kit prices depend on how much is to be done by the purchaser.

VITAL STATISTICS: L.O.A. 10′6¾″; waterline 9′3″; beam 4′1⅜″; draft 6½″ without centerboard, with C.B. 2′6″; sail area 44½ sq. ft.; weight about 150 lbs.; trailable.

CAPE COD BABY KNOCKABOUT—
also EIGHTEEN-FOOT KNOCKABOUT

Soon after World War I, Charles Gurney, founder of the Cape Cod Shipbuilding Company, designed and built an inexpensive centerboard sloop which became the well-known, 18-foot, Cape Cod Baby Knockabout. Thousands of these boats have been built over the years; at one time, it is said, they sold at $175, including a "sail-a-way" lunch. Nothing was fancy; this was before the days of fiber glass, chrome, genoas, and Dacron. The sails were either a high leg-o-mutton or a "modified Marconi." The jib was small and the boats had a heavy-weather helm. The sails were cut in vertical strips and were innocent of battens. Nevertheless, the boats proved to be good sailers and safe family boats which would come up into the wind and spill the sails with a strong puff of wind or at the slightest inattention on the part of the helmsman. The writer once owned one of these boats and can vouch for what is said above.

Among about sixteen thousand boats of all types built by the Cape Cod Shipbuilding Company, the Baby Knockabout was for many years the best known. Their production in numbers began in about 1921. By 1925 they were being raced. An authority on the class and its modernized successor gives some interesting comments gleaned from some old ship carpenters who worked on the original Knockabouts.

"The hull was framed in white oak and planked in white cedar. The boats were known for their ability to take the dusty sou'westers of Buzzards Bay. More were purchased around the southern shores of Cape Cod for teaching children to sail. The rudders and jibs were so small that puffs over

A race between two types: CAPE COD BABY KNOCKABOUT (CC 27) and
EIGHTEEN-FOOT KNOCKABOUT (K 302). *Courtesy Robert O. Bigelow.*

12 knots would send the boat head to wind. With such a weather helm the
boats were thought safe for children. However, the knockabouts were purchased by some retired captains who had been racing spritsails with the
summer people. And this is where the fun started.

"About 1930 the class had gathered some 'hot shots.' Three or four of
them were retired yacht captains who had a tradition of yachting in the
grand manner. These men began enlarging rudders and jibs to reduce the

weather helms. The summer people were being beaten so they went out to win by imitating. Soon the standard rudders and jibs were of a wide variety of shapes and sizes. Eventually a class association was set up to regulate the boats. A crude set of specifications was adopted, but as racing became keener even these were discarded for a more rigid set in 1937. This was the year of the first SOUTHERN MASSACHUSETTS YACHT RACING ASSOCIATION for 18' Knockabouts Class Championships.

"During the winter months the boats were still being 'doctored' for speed, and a spy system was used for trying to discover what was going on in the various garages. Rudders changed shape as did centerboards, cockpit arrangements, height of mainmast, etc. By 1946, the year following World War II, the first honest attempt was made to keep the class 'one-design.' Today the Specifications Committee is still the most active and abused, but the boats do race evenly and no class has as much fun trying to out-gadget the other. The specifications have never been able to agree on one standard shape for a rudder, but they did agree on one standard over-all area for a rudder. So racing today are perhaps ten different types of rudder designs. This is also true of centerboards. The rule reads that '. . . if the centerboard is of proper thickness ($\frac{3}{4}''$) and of wood and fits the centerboard box when housed, it is legal.' There again, perhaps one might find no two centerboards absolutely alike in weight and shape. Some are of heavy oak, some of light plywood.

"To go on in this manner is perhaps not necessary. Yet the untold stories of some of the characters who sail these boats would fill a book. Before major regattas poems may be stuck to masts announcing a hazard, or light-weather sails may be mysteriously shifted to the heavy-weather bag by the same person who invites you to dinner and PROVIDES the baby sitter. I suppose this goes on to some degree in all classes.

"The future of the class is uncertain. Fiberglass boats are the only new boats being built. The young sailers have been tending toward fast light displacement hulls with parachutes. However, along Vineyard Sound and Buzzards Bay where a good sou'wester keeps the average 18' boat at its mooring, knockabouts continue to race. Some family-type sailors who have not done much sailing as youngsters are beginning to adopt the boat for day sailing. The older wooden boats are a very bad risk for a novice because of the care needed to keep them seaworthy. The people who are coming into the yachting market are not knowledgeable enough to recognize the fine sea-keeping qualities of these boats, consequently the market for new boats is primarily with the established sailors. Six new boats have been sold this year."

Eventually innovations began to make their way into the class, at first unwelcome among some of the old-timers. Crosscut sails, tracks on mast and boom, overlapping jibs, spinnakers, "barn-door" rudders, longer tillers all came in. The boats became better balanced, faster, easier to handle, if not safer. Jam cleats, snatch blocks, even wire halyards with winches helped to complete the modernization. But this was not enough. Hurricane Carol had wiped out several fleets in 1954; many boats were beyond repair. Then the Cape Cod Shipbuilding Company stopped making the boats and turned to other classes. Something had to be done if such a well-liked class were to be kept alive. A committee of the Southern Massachusetts Yacht Racing Association commissioned Robert S. Fox to make a set of drawings for a new, uniform, fiber-glass class based on the measurements of one of the Cape Cod Knockabout Class.*

The revitalized, fiber-glass class is now known as "The 18-Foot Knock-about Class," which has an association of that name of which Webster A. Collins (5 Wilder Rd., Shrewsbury, Mass.) is the Secretary. The Frost Boat Company of Falmouth, Massachusetts, makes the fiber-glass boats. A new K insignia was adopted.

The racing class as it exists today is thus not limited to Cape Cod Baby Knockabouts but also includes fiber-glass knockabouts built by Frost. In 1962 over one hundred knockabouts were registered with the association, most of them located along the South Shore of Cape Cod, Massachusetts. Price of the new boats is $2300; used wooden hulls are from $300 to $1000.

VITAL STATISTICS of 18-Foot Knockabout (fiber-glass) Class: L.O.A. 18'; waterline 15'9"; beam 6'; draft with board up 14", with C.B. down 4'2"; sail area 187½ sq. ft. (spinnaker allowed); construction materials wood and fiber glass; weight 1200 lbs. with ballast (weights of wooden boats vary).

---

* Data in this paragraph from "Cape Cod's Baby Knockabout Grows Up," Winthrop P. Munro in *Motor Boating*, July 1961.

CAPRI 14. *Photo by Beckner Photo Service, courtesy W. D. Schock Co.*

CAPRI 14

Built by W. D. Schock Company (3502 S. Greenville St., Santa Ana, Calif.) this is one of the many classes of attractive fiber-glass sloops which have recently been coming on the market. The cockpit is relatively large and the boat looks like a good sailer with flotation added to enhance safety. She has a keel and is said to be self-righting. Mainly used on the Pacific Coast, she is priced there at about $1462.

VITAL STATISTICS: L.O.A. 14'; beam 6'; draft 2' (keel); sail area 105 sq. ft.; weight 575 lbs.

CELEBRITY.
Courtesy P. Evanson Boat Co.

CELEBRITY

The 20-foot Celebrity sloop (now available with centerboard or keel) made its appearance on Chesapeake Bay about 1953 or 1954 and has grown rapidly since that time until now there are over five hundred in the class. It is reported that the Celebrities at the Annapolis Fall Series in 1961 had the largest single fleet of the fifteen classes entered. Originally built of strip planking, the molded mahogany hull was introduced in 1959. The Celebrity is said to be a good family boat as well as a racer, and it is possible for those not seeking too much comfort to go cruising. In the summer of 1960 one Celebrity owner, Helmuth Braendel, and his two young sons took a seven hundred-mile trip on a two weeks' cruise in his Celebrity. The athwartships cockpit seats may be removed and with the aid of the cuddy and a cover she can be made into a cruiser.

The mast is stepped in a tabernacle, making stepping or tilting the mast to go under bridges a not-difficult performance. The principal areas of sailing are in the vicinities of Chicago and Springfield, Illinois; Atlanta, Georgia; Edgewater Park and Riverton, New Jersey; Great South Bay, Long Island, New York; Hessel, Michigan; Elk River and Annapolis, Maryland; Indian River, Delaware. Fleets are starting in other New Jersey ports and on Long Island Sound; also in Madison, Wisconsin.

CHECKMATE.
*Courtesy Commodore
Corporation.*

P. Evanson Boat Company (4110 Freeland Ave., Philadelphia 28, Pa.) is the builder, and the Secretary of the International Celebrity Class Racing Association is Oliver D. Goldman (104 Parkview Rd., Melrose, Pa.). Evanson designed the boat as an adaptation of the Six Meter. Price for new boats is $1875, for used $1200 to $1650.

VITAL STATISTICS: L.O.A. 19′9″; waterline 15′9″; beam 6′4″; draft without centerboard 6″, with C.B. down 3′3″; draft of keel (K) model 2′5″; sail area 172 sq. ft. (genoa allowed, not spinnaker); weight 820 lbs.

CHECKMATE

The Checkmate is a 13′4″, lightweight, fiber-glass centerboard sloop which planes. There are about 165 of them in the United States and four in Europe. Kingdon Watt, Jr., was the designer, and the Commodore Corporation (1649 Washington St., Holliston, Mass.) is the builder. They have been sold rather widely in the United States, though New England and Long Island are their principal areas of use.

Arnold Mills (32 Fearing Rd., Hingham, Mass.) is Secretary of the Checkmate class at the time of writing. The cost is $1195 new, $1000 to $1100 used.

VITAL STATISTICS: L.O.A. 13′4″; beam 4′11″; draft without centerboard 6″, with C.B. down 3′2″; sail area 120 sq. ft. (spinnaker allowed); weight 275 lbs.; trailable; racing crew, two.

CHESAPEAKE 20

The Chesapeake 20, a centerboard boat, was designed and built by Ernest H. Hartge of Galesville, Maryland, in 1937. About thirty were built and did their sailing on Chesapeake Bay. Costs following World War II skyrocketed and Hartge gave up making them. They were of wooden construction and the competition of new fiber-glass boats and planing hulls got too much for them, though twenty or so are still active on the Bay. Price new would be $3000; old $900 to $2000. The boats race under the auspices of the West River Sailing Club. They will not plane, but are said to be good sailers.

VITAL STATISTICS: L.O.A. 20′; waterline 15′; beam 6′7″; draft without centerboard 5″, with C.B. 4′; sail area 250 max.; weight 900 lbs.

COAST 13

The Coast 13 was developed by members of the Lake Merced Sailing Club of San Francisco in 1952. It is a 13′5″ centerboard sloop made of plywood and has raced successfully since 1953 on the often turbulent waters of San Francisco Bay. It can plane on reaches and runs and has reached thirty in number. Plans are available for amateur builders and the construction has been kept simple. Jack Kimberly, Jr. (57 Montclair Ave., Daly City, Calif.), is the class Secretary and furnishes plans without charge to those interested in building. For a boat of this size the price seems unusually low: $500 for new boats, about $400 for used.

VITAL STATISTICS: L.O.A. 13′5″; beam 4′11″; draft without centerboard about 3″, with C.B. 3′4″; sail area 104 sq. ft.; weight 104 lbs.

COMET

When I began my explorations for *A Cruising Guide to the Chesapeake* I was told to be sure to look up C. Lowndes Johnson, who knew more about Chesapeake cruising than anyone. He didn't say anything about Comets when I saw him, and it wasn't until later that I learned that he had

CHESAPEAKE 20. *Courtesy Ernest H. Hartge.*

COAST 13. *Courtesy Jack Kimberly, Jr.*

COMET. *Booz Photos.*

designed one of the most popular one-design racing classes in American yachting history.

When in 1932 he was asked to design a small centerboard boat for Mrs. Elliott Wheeler of Easton, Maryland, his own home town, he had no idea that he was about to start something important. Mrs. Wheeler wanted a boat for her sons which would be inexpensive to build, easy to handle, and a good enough sailer to compete in the handicap races then being held at Oxford, Maryland. Having crewed for his brother in winning the World's Championship of the Star Class at New Orleans in 1929, and admiring the Star lines, Johnson designed a boat somewhat similar to a Star, but smaller and with a centerboard instead of a keel.*

Ralph Wiley built the first Comet and, as I remember it, told me that it cost him about $120 and he made $10 on the deal. Later he built another for Jonathan S. Wilford of Oxford. The boats were first known as Crabs. When *Yachting* published the plans in its design section in March 1932, requests for copies of the plans began coming in from various parts of the country. The first real breakthrough came when Dr. John Eiman of Philadelphia, Pennsylvania, and Stone Harbor, New Jersey, saw the boats sailing at Oxford while he was on a cruise. He liked what he saw. At Stone Harbor they had a variety of small-sailboat racing on a handicap basis to the satisfaction of nobody. Deciding to get an inexpensive one-design class in those depression days of 1933, Dr. Eiman and Dr. Wilbur H. Haines went to the New York Motor Boat Show and began looking around. There, in the *Yachting* booth they saw a model of the "Star Junior," as it had come to be called. Eiman remembered having seen the boats sailing at Oxford and he and Dr. Haines decided that this was *it,* so far as Stone Harbor was concerned.

Things began to move fast. Realizing from the experience of the Star class the desirability of having a strong class organization, the growing group of owners held a meeting in February 1933 at the *Yachting* office, adopted preliminary rules, changed the name again—this time from Star Junior to Comet—elected Dr. Eiman President, and the Comets were on their way. By 1935 there were twenty-one at Stone Harbor. Since then the Comet growth has been steady and widespread. There are now over thirty-six hundred registered owners in the eastern United States and as far west as Michigan, Colorado, and the Pacific Coast; also in Canada. The first national championships were held at the Raritan Yacht Club, Perth Amboy, New Jersey.

* Historical material from "A 20th Birthday" by Charles E. Lucke, Jr., *Yachting*, February 1952.

Like the Stars, the Comet has a hard-chine hull and was among the earliest of the sailboats which would plane. The Comet has fared very well in the intense competition among small-sailboat racing classes for public attention and has ranked high in several recent feature articles about the most popular sailing classes in the United States. That this popularity will continue seems likely in view of the strong organization behind the Comets —the Comet Class Yacht Racing Association, with fifteen regional branches, including those in the Pacific Northwest, Puerto Rico, Ohio, and many on the East Coast. Miss Mary C. Swaine (Pleasant Points Farm, Royal Oak, Md.) is Corresponding Secretary at the time of writing.

The hull may be of wood or fiber glass. While all the basic features of a one-design class have been adhered to, there have been modernizations of equipment and material from time to time, including approval of fiber-glass hulls with flotation material.

There are many builders, the names of whom can be obtained in *Yachting's Boat Owners Buyers Guide* or from the Corresponding Secretary, who also sells plans at fifteen dollars.

Some famous yachtsmen have raced Comets: Roger and Warner Wilcox (Comet Class National Champions in 1935 and 1937, respectively), Bob Lippincott (International Star Class Champion in 1950), "Bus" Mosbacher (famed skipper of *Weatherly* in the 1962 America's Cup races), Bob Mosbacher (winner of the 1958 Men's North America Sailing Championship), Andy Schoettle and Harry Sindle (members of U. S. Olympic Sailing Teams). Price of new boats is about $1400 in fiber glass.

VITAL STATISTICS: L.O.A. 16'; waterline 14'6"; beam 5'; draft with centerboard down 3'; sail area 130 sq. ft.; weight not less than 300 lbs.

COTTONTAIL

Designed and sold by Holiday Yachts (Centerport, Long Island, N.Y.), the Cottontail is a 16-foot lightweight planing fiber-glass sloop (or catboat) which is said to be very fast. The builders claim that she has been clocked at 20 knots when planing. There are now sixty in the United States and five more outside. Robert F. Matteson (Box 756, Center Moriches, N.Y.) is the class Secretary. The Cottontail Association was formed by the Babylon Yacht Club during the fall of 1959. Since then the Cottontail has become popular in various parts of Long Island, New York, and recently a new organization was formed at the Cleveland Yacht Club, Cleveland, Ohio.

COTTONTAILS. *Courtesy Holiday Yachts, Inc.*

Two special features of Cottontail are the inboard rudder and modified skeg which, it is claimed, help to give the boat good stability at high planing speeds. The mast is footed on a track so it is possible to sail as a sloop or cat by changing the position of the mast. Price is $1244 for new boats.

VITAL STATISTICS: L.O.A. 15′10″; beam 5′1″; draft with centerboard down 3′; sail area 120 sq. ft. (standard), 140 sq. ft. (racing); weight 286 lbs.; trailable.

DABCHICK

DABCHICK

South African Jack Köper designed the Dabchick as a junior trainer to teach children the handling of both a mainsail and jib. The first boats were built in 1960 and the class was introduced to North America in 1963. In this relatively short time, more than 2100 Dabchicks have been built throughout the world, with about 130 in the United States, principally in the lake regions from Kentucky to Oklahoma.

The Dabchick is a development of the "boardboat" idea. She has a flat—slightly V'd—bottom, is exciting to sail, and will plane readily. The normal crew is one, but she will easily take two adults and still handle well. Class rules require her to be raced singlehanded by skippers over age fifteen.

Construction of either plywood or fiber glass is allowed. The simple plywood hull is easily built by amateurs. Minimum hull weight is 85 lbs. Spars may be either wood or aluminum.

An interesting feature the Dabchick shares with several recent small boat classes is her ability to accept either a cat or a sloop rig. For teaching very young sailors, the mast may be stepped forward to rig the boat as a cat. When a child learns the basics of sailing, he can graduate to the more sophisticated sloop rig without having to switch to a different boat. David B. Blue, Jr., P. O. Box 1090, Tulsa, Oklahoma 74101, is the U.S. class secretary.

VITAL STATISTICS: L.O.A. 12′0″; waterline 9′2″; beam 3′10″; draft (centerboard) 2′6″; sail area 60 sq. ft. (sloop), 40 sq. ft. (cat); weight 85 lbs.; racing crew, one; can be trailed or car-topped.

DAY SAILER

The 17-foot Day Sailer, a centerboard sloop, was conceived by George D. O'Day in the summer of 1957 and the design worked out during the 1958 London Boat Show with Uffa Fox, who calls it "one of the most pleasing boats that I have yet designed." The combination of these two outstanding sailers, an Olympic winner for the United States and one of the most creative designers in England, ought to make for a very successful boat. It has, for there are already 1075 Day Sailers in the world, most of them in the United States. The earliest American fleets are as widely scattered as Annapolis, Maryland; Marblehead, Massachusetts; Palm Beach, Florida; Palo Alto, California; Belleville, Ontario, Canada; and Canandaigua, New York—formed in the above order. A Day Sailer Association has been formed, of which the Secretary is Hans Gottschalk (Genesco, N.Y.), and the publication *Day Sailer* is issued from time to time, telling of doings in this fast-growing class. The so-called California Day Sailer is the same boat.

The O'Day Corporation (9 Newbury St., Boston, Mass.) is the builder and states that the Day Sailer "goes to windward exceptionally well, will move in the lightest airs, stand up in the heaviest, and even plane under proper conditions." The boat has an almost straight stem, a small cuddy, and is constructed of single-mold fiber glass. Being fairly heavy (580 pounds) compared to some planing boats, we should expect it to take more favorable conditions to get it planing than would be the case with smaller and lighter craft. The cockpit is large and it seems to be a good all-around, versatile boat, easy to handle. The boom is stepped high enough

DAY SAILER. *Courtesy O'Day Corporation.*

so that it is easy to escape a knockout. Price new is $1890, secondhand about $1600. Kits are not available.

VITAL STATISTICS: L.O.A. 16′9″; waterline 16′; beam 6′3″; draft without centerboard 7″, with C.B. down 3′9″; sail area 145 sq. ft. (spinnaker allowed); weight 580 lbs.; trailable.

DRAGON

After slow going in North America for a number of years, two circumstances have combined to put Dragons on the map in America: first, the fact that in 1948 Dragons became an Olympic class; second, the publicity arising from the fact that Queen Elizabeth's husband, Prince Philip, became an enthusiastic Dragon racer. The Dragon is a long, narrow, rakish-looking 29-foot keel sloop, with a high and narrow Marconi rig leaving considerable deck room beyond the sails at each end. Slow in light winds under working sails, she is at her best in strong winds and rough, choppy waters, though not a dry boat under such circumstances. With a genoa or spinnaker she is said to "come alive" even in light winds.

In 1928 Johan Anker, the great Norwegian designer and builder, designed the Dragon as an inexpensive boat for the Twenty Square Meter Class, suitable for the turbulent North Sea waters. She became a one-design class and spread to Denmark, Sweden, Germany, the Low Countries, England, France, and Italy. Early efforts to import several into the United States did not meet with much success, and in the Olympic Games of 1948, the American crew, selected without Dragon experience, came in eleventh out of twelve.*

* Information from "The International Dragon in America," by Garrett Horder, *Yachting,* January 1956.

DRAGON. *Courtesy International Yacht Sales, Inc.*

In 1950 about nine Dragons were imported from Norway and Holland for Woods Hole and Long Island Sound owners, but did poorly, especially in the light airs of the Sound. During that year the Pacific International Yachting Association gave a tryout to a Dragon in competition with seven other boats, from which they hoped to select a good weatherly sailer which wouldn't cost over $3000 without sails, and which could be fitted out for cruising. The Dragon was selected by the committee but the decision was reversed by the general membership. Despite this unfavorable decision the Dragon class gradually developed in widely separated places, including New Orleans, Louisiana; San Francisco Bay; the Los Angeles area; Puget Sound, Washington; Annapolis, Maryland; Detroit, Michigan; Wisconsin, etc. There is a large fleet in Canada, and Dragons have made good headway in Argentina and Uruguay.

The organization of the American International Dragon Association has helped considerably in American Dragon development. Garrett Horder (1030 Washington Bldg., Seattle 1, Wash.) is Secretary. The International Dragon Association, of which Sir Gordon Smith is President (44 Walton St., London S.W. 3, England), is the over-all international class association.

In the 1960 Olympics at Naples, Italy, the winner in the Dragon class was Crown Prince Constantine of Greece, another bit of evidence that royalty is interested in Dragons. King Baudouin of Belgium also sails a Dragon. Eugene Walet, the United States representative, who is a fine sailor but with little experience in Dragons, came in tenth. Perhaps with all the glamour attached to the Dragon class, they will spread sufficiently in the United States to provide a wider basis of experience among our sailors. This is most likely, however, in areas where the breezes are strong and the waters rough.

Importers or builders of Dragons in the United States can be located through class officials or yacht brokers, as can the names of foreign builders. Construction is of wood; fiber glass is not permitted. The American price with sails is $6300 for new boats; old ones can be bought for $1000 up. In Finland and possibly elsewhere in Europe, Dragons can be bought, it is reported, at considerably less.

VITAL STATISTICS: L.O.A. 29'2½"; waterline 18'8"; beam 6'5"; draft (keel) 3'11"; sail area 235 sq. ft. (spinnaker allowed); weight 3800 lbs.; racing crew permitted, three.

DUSTER

This is a 14-foot centerboard, cat-rigged pram, first built in 1935, designed primarily for racing in sheltered inland waters, such as lakes, bays, and rivers. The designer is Owen P. Merrill, and about 250 have been built, chiefly for use in New Jersey, Pennsylvania, and various places on the Atlantic Coast. Some also are used in the Midwest and Far West. Among the leading builders are Roberts Industries (105 Post Rd., Branford, Conn.), J. D. Person (Box 86, Pocono Pines, Pa.), and Andrew McCulloch (3 Russell Terrace, Wayne, N.J.). Dusters were organized as a class in 1946. Write the Secretary, Duster Class Yacht Racing Association (Riverton, N.J.) for further information about the class or the names of other builders. Construction is plywood on a wood frame. Price new is $800 to $900, used about $350, kits $250.

VITAL STATISTICS: L.O.A. 13′9″; waterline 9′8″; beam 4′6″; draft without centerboard 3″, with C.B. down 2′4″; sail area 117 sq. ft. (no spinnaker); weight 250 lbs.; trailable.

DUSTER. *Courtesy Joseph Geyer.*

DUXBURY DUCK. *Photo by Ralph Lawson, Jr.*

DUXBURY DUCK

The Duxbury Ducks, a class of sloops, were designed by John G. Alden in 1925 for the shoal waters of Duxbury Bay, Massachusetts. Twenty-four boats were built in that year. By the late thirties about sixty boats made up the fleet, with forty racing regularly. Nearby Plymouth, where the harbor is also shoal, had a fleet of fifteen. Today a small fleet of eight or ten races at Duxbury, as do some on Crystal Lake at Wakefield, Massachusetts. There are said to be seventy still in existence, but none have been built for ten years or more.

"There never was a better 18-foot boat," writes one of the owners nostalgically, "for use in a shallow bay, which combined a comfortable family sailboat with a good racing boat. Obviously, today, people want a tall modern rig, parachute spinnaker, planing hull, and hence the class faded."

The Chairman of the class at the Duxbury Yacht Club is Howard P. Chandler (79 Ledgeways, Wellesley Hills, Mass.).

Its heavy weight (750 pounds) makes the Duck difficult to trail and it is obviously not a planing type. While the cost of a new boat would be about $1800, old boats can be bought at from $100 to $600, perhaps a real bargain if you want a good old-fashioned family boat.

VITAL STATISTICS: L.O.A. 18'; waterline 15'1"; beam 6'4"; draft without centerboard 7", with C.B. down 2'6"; sail area 342 sq. ft. (spinnakers allowed); weight 750 lbs.; racing crews, two or three.

DYER DHOW

The 9-foot Dyer Dhow with cat rig is one of the more recent dinghies designed and produced by the man who is generally regarded as the foremost manufacturer of sailing dinghies in the United States: William J. H. Dyer, of The Anchorage, Inc. (Warren, R.I.). Dyer developed the Dhow for the Bureau of Ships (U. S. Navy) during World War II for use on P.T. boats and Aircraft Rescues. The idea was to obtain maximum carrying capacity and stability when loaded and minimum resistance when light and towing. Because many of these Dhows were supplied with sailing rigs and created considerable interest, they were continued after the war for civilian activities, particularly for teaching youngsters how to sail.

One of the earliest classes was formed at Mystic seaport, location of the famous Museum. Prominent yacht clubs, including the Cruising Club of America, New York Yacht Club, Off Soundings Club, Seawanhaka Corinthian Yacht Club, Indian Harbor Yacht Club, and Edgartown Yacht Club were among the original donors of boats to the seaport for this purpose. It

DYER DHOWS racing at Mamaroneck, N.Y. *Courtesy The Anchorage, Inc.*

is reported that over seventy-five hundred youngsters have been taught sailing in Dyer Dhows over the last thirteen years.

Hundreds of Dhows are raced during the winter Frostbite seasons, including a fleet of over seventy-five at Mamaroneck, New York. Since they can be rowed, towed, sailed, or used with an outboard, they are versatile boats. Their lightness of weight (120 pounds) makes them easy to carry on top of a car. The class Secretary at the time of writing is Richard B. Nye (Georgeson & Co., 52 Wall St., New York, N.Y.).

The Dhows are built by The Anchorage in Warren, Rhode Island, and over 1950 are now in use. Principal sailing areas are New England, New

DYER DHOW MIDGET. *Courtesy The Anchorage, Inc.*

York, and California. Price new is $495 to $595 depending on requirements, sails, etc. There are no kits and Bill Dyer won't guess at the secondhand price.

VITAL STATISTICS: L.O.A. 9'; beam 4'5"; sail area 45 sq. ft. (no spinnakers); weight 120 lbs.; trailable or cartop; racing crew, two.

DYER DHOW MIDGET

This class of Sailing Midgets, built by The Anchorage, Inc. (Warren, R.I.), was developed by William J. H. Dyer to provide a combination sailing and rowing dinghy which could be easily carried by ocean-going yachts. The fact that for a number of years these dinghies have been carried by Bermuda Race winners as well as by many others in that race would seem to indicate that Bill achieved his purpose. A list of well-known yachtsmen carrying these dinghies as tenders, or for scooting around in port when the hook is down, would be a long one. About thirteen hundred of the Midgets have been built to date, most of them for the purposes described, though here and there they are raced actively. They are very appealing little fiber-glass boats with their red or blue sails.

The Midgets come in two models: a *regular* 7'9" model at $440, f.o.b. Warren, Rhode Island, and a slightly larger 7'11" high sheer model at $450. Both prices include the sail, oars, rowlocks—the complete boat.

VITAL STATISTICS: L.O.A. 7'9" and 7'11"; beam 4'; draft, several inches without daggerboard; sail area 35 sq. ft.; weight (regular) 78 lbs., (high sheer) 80 lbs.; cartop carried.

DYERSIN (Class D) DINK

The original 10-foot one-design Class D Dinks, cat rigged, were designed by Philip L. Rhodes and introduced in 1934 at the New York Motor Boat Show, where Bill Dyer has been introducing dinghies and other boats ever since. Like the more recent Dyer Dhows, they are made at The Anchorage (Warren, R.I.). At the beginning of World War II this was the largest class of one-design Frostbite (winter-racing) dinghies in the United States. Fleets raced at many points along the Atlantic Coast, on the Great Lakes, and on the Pacific Coast. The first Inter-collegiate Frostbite Dinghy Race was held in Class D Dyer Dinks at Bristol, Rhode Island, and several colleges adopted them for racing.

Some of the original Class D Dinks are still racing, but the class has now turned to fiber-glass construction and the two most active fleets are at the Riverside Yacht Club, Riverside, Connecticut, and the Huntington Yacht Club, Huntington, Long Island. The Long Island Sound Frostbite Championships were held in these Class D (now called Dyersin) Dinks at the Riverside Yacht Club in the spring of 1961.

John P. Hansel (191 Riverside Ave., Riverside, Conn.) is the class Secretary. Price is $666 new, no kits. There are about 970 now in use—making the total of Dyer Dhows, Sailing Midgets, and Dyer D Dinks over forty-two hundred.

VITAL STATISTICS: L.O.A. 10'; beam 4'3"; sail area 66 sq. ft. (no spinnaker); weight 135 lbs.

DYERSIN CLASS D. DINKS. *Courtesy The Anchorage, Inc.*

ENSIGN

The popular Ensign, designed by Carl A. Alberg and built by the Pearson Corporation (Bristol, R.I.), is a modified version of the Electra cruising-racing class (see Part II—Cruising Classes). The day-sailing and class-racing version has the same hull as the other Electra, but a tiny cuddy with two bunks instead of a cabin, and a very large 9-foot cockpit instead of a small self-bailing cockpit. Though not equipped for cruising, a toilet can be put in if desired, cushions bought for the bunks and air mattresses for extra sleeping space in the cockpit under a boom tent.

ENSIGN. *Photo by Morris Rosenfeld, courtesy One-Design & Offshore Yachtsman.*

Like its cruising and ocean-racing sister, the Pearson Ensign is a very good-looking boat and is a fast sailer. A strong class organization has been formed. With fleets throughout the United States, Ensigns are now one of the biggest classes racing on Long Island Sound, and the boats have been used for several district and national women's, men's, and junior championships. The boats are made of fiber glass with built-in flotation. They have a lockable cabin with provisions for sleeping two. A toilet may also be installed, making the Ensign a reasonably comfortable overnight cruiser.

The National Secretary of the Ensign Class is Jerome Freedman, 114 East 32nd St., New York, New York 10016.

VITAL STATISTICS: L.O.A. 22'6"; waterline 16'9"; beam 7'0"; draft 3' (keel); sail area 219 sq. ft.; weight 3000 lbs.

EL TORO

The idea behind the El Toro 8-foot cat-rigged pram dinghy was to get a boat which would serve as a child's trainer and which adults could also enjoy occasionally; also which would be as cheap as possible. The Florida

EL TORO. *Photo by Beckner Photo Service, courtesy W. D. Schock Co.*

Optimist Pram is light and cheap but its flat bottom and sprit rig is said to make it very slow in carrying adults to windward. Other boats cost too much or are too heavy. The New England Clamshell pram was considered not buoyant enough to take care of a load of over 120 pounds. Designed by McGregor for the Richmond Yacht Club and San Francisco Bay, El Toro has engaged in comparative test races with a typical Clamshell (East Coast) pram and has done better, carrying successfully forty more pounds than a Clamshell of the same length and weight because of its slightly greater width, deeper sides, and fatter girth.*

El Toro has now been in use for about twenty years and there are said to be about fifteen hundred boats, chiefly in California waters. Construction materials are fiber-glass reinforced plastic, with flotation tanks. Hull shape is similar to that of the Naples Sabot and has a hard chine, with a V cross-section. Price is about $400. Write for information on builders, etc., to the El Toro Association (2820 Telegraph Ave., Berkeley 5, Calif.). The *Boat Owners Buyers Guide* (published by *Yachting*) has a long list of builders and dealers. Our information came from W. D. Schock Company, a leading builder (501 29th St., Newport Beach, Calif.).

Whether an adult can be comfortable in an 7′10″ or 8-foot sailing dinghy depends a good deal upon how small and agile he is or on his standards of comfort. For instance, as William A. Smith puts it (see note below): "In the El Toro [a grown man] must sit either a bit too far forward on the raised center thwart, or aft of it on the bottom where a wet stern piece soon results."

VITAL STATISTICS: L.O.A. 7′10″; beam 3′10″; draft without board down 3½″, with daggerboard down 1′6″; sail area 37½ sq. ft.; weight 85 lbs.

ELVSTROM JR.

Designed by the man whom *Yachting* has called the "Amazing Paul Elvstrom," Danish winner of four straight Olympic championships, three in the Finn Monotype Class, the 11-foot cat-rigged Elvstrom Jr. was first introduced in Denmark in 1960. It was developed for boys and girls who have graduated from 8-foot dinghies but are not quite heavy or strong enough for the larger boats, such as the Finn. Here is a boat aimed particularly at one target, though adults would certainly find it more comfortable than an 8-foot pram such as El Toro. Sailing qualities, in some respects, are said to resemble those of the larger Finn. The boat has a planing hull, an un-

* See "El Toro vs. Clamshell," by William Allen Smith, *Motor Boating*, February 1960.

ELVSTROM JR. *Courtesy International Marine Sales.*

stayed flexible mast, flotation tanks on the outside which serve the multiple purposes of providing good seating when reaching over the side and added stability in a sudden puff, besides aiding flotation. If the boat is handled right, the outside tanks don't get into the water; being outside they don't take up valuable space inside.

The boats are made of mahogany marine plywood and are imported by International Marine Sales (6445 Via de Anzar, San Pedro, Calif.). Write Paul Elvstrom (Hellerup, Denmark) for information about the class, or consult Captain Arne N. Nielsen of International Marine Sales.

Although the boats were very recently brought to America, there are already twenty in the United States, two hundred in the world. Backed by a man with the reputation of Elvstrom, this boat seems likely to do well. The price in the United States is $595 for the complete boat, $425 for a kit.

VITAL STATISTICS: L.O.A. 11′2″; beam at waterline 3′9″, maximum 5′4″; sail area 70 sq. ft. (spinnaker allowed); weight 152 lbs.; a one-man dinghy for racing purposes, but will hold three or four.

ENTERPRISE. *Courtesy The Bell Woodworking Co., Ltd.*

ENTERPRISE

This 13-foot centerboard sloop, designed in England by Jack Holt at the request of the *News Chronicle,* has had a spectacular history. The spectacular part began with a trip across the English Channel by Numbers 1 and 2 of the class on January 7, 1956. Starting from Dover at 3 A.M., they sighted the French Coast in two and a half hours. In the six years since that audacious beginning, numbers for over eight thousand boats have been given out, a large proportion of them in England. It now vies with the Lightning class as the second largest one-design class in the world, with only Snipes in the lead. As far as we know, no other class has ever grown so fast. Of eight thousand boats, about eight hundred are in the United States.

According to a possibly prejudiced importer: "She is very fast. This author (who sells other boats also) knows of *no* boat her size or under that can beat her. She will easily take the measure of many larger boats of prominent racing classes. She is a planing boat. With all this she has amazing stability."

The Enterprise is said to fill the gap between the G.P. 14 and the 11′3″ Heron, both designed also by Holt. Several American companies are reported to be handling the boat, including the P. Evanson Boat Company (4110 Freeland Ave., Philadelphia 28, Pa.), John Wright, Jr. (308 W. Queen Lane, Philadelphia 44, Pa.), Hugh Doherty's King Harbor Boats (901 Pier Ave., Hermosa Beach, Calif.); and the Gallant Distributing Company, Inc. (Newmarket, N.H.). Write one of them or A. R. Lanning (12–22 Bouverie St., London, England). Price, new, is about $880 complete with Dacron main and jib. Used boats are sold at from $650 to $750.

VITAL STATISTICS: L.O.A. 13′3½″; beam 5′3″; draft without centerboard 7″, with C.B. down 3′3″; sail area 113 sq. ft. (no spinnaker); weight 200 to 230 lbs.; trailable.

EXPLORER

The 17-foot centerboard sloop Explorer was designed by Robert Baker and has had its principal development in New England, though some boat owners are scattered along the Atlantic Coast. Some are in the Midwest and even in Texas. While reports vary as to the number of boats now in existence, it seems probable that there are about 350 at the time of writing. The boat has a planing hull, a self-bailing cockpit (if desired), a cuddy which can double as a cabin with some help from the cockpit, roller reefing, and a "Kickerpit" motor-well for an outboard. For those who want to use

EXPLORER. *Photo by Norman Fortier, courtesy Henry S. Parker, Jr.*

the Explorer for cruising, an almost rectangular tent called a "cockpit cabin" is provided nearly boom-high at the sides. The centerboard and rudder will "kick up" if grounded.

This appears to be a comfortable boat with room for six or even more in the cockpit. One owner said he got his boat planing with four aboard.

In January 1961 the International Explorer Class Association was formed in New York. Alexander R. Fowler (6 Morse St., Freeport, Me.) is the present Secretary. The builder is Sailstar Boats, a division of the Talman Corporation (770 Main St., West Warwick, R.I.). Construction is of fiber glass. The price, new, is $2045, with used boats selling at $1700. Kits are not available.

A similar Robert Baker-designed boat, but with a steel centerboard or keel and a 160-square-foot sail area, is being marketed by Sailstar under the class name Pioneer, at a slightly higher price than the Explorer.

The first National Championship was held at Marblehead, Massachusetts, in 1961.

VITAL STATISTICS: L.O.A. 17′; beam 6′4″; draft without centerboard 9″, with C.B. down 4′6″; sail area 155 sq. ft. (spinnaker allowed); weight 520 lbs.; trailable.

FINN

The 15-foot cat-rigged Finn centerboarder is one of the five recognized Olympic types. She is the single-hander in which Paul Elvstrom, four-time Olympic winner, made his reputation as "unquestionably the finest single-hander the world has ever seen." The Finn was designed by Richard Sarby of Sweden to be used in the Olympics at Helsinki in 1952. Since then it has been the choice as the Olympic single-hander at Melbourne, Australia (1956), and Naples, Italy (1960), and will be in Japan in 1964.

There is a story, quoted by Fred Miller, Jr., in *One Design Yachtsman,* about how the Finn came to be "designed" by Sarby:

"The Helsinki Olympic Yachting Committee organized the famous 1951 international design competition to come up with a permanent Olympic singlehander starting with the '52 Games. Sarby had some definite ideas, but then (as today) Sarby has been incapable of making a drawing any builder, other than himself, could understand and build to.

"So, the story goes, Sarby set to building a duplicate hull of his fastest (before or since) boat of the open-design class E sailing canoe class. After doing so, making a few minor alterations here and there, he sawed off the last four feet and nailed on a transom. After making sails and putting the rest of the boat together, he went sailing, coming right back in to telephone a naval architect to come up and make a drawing as quickly as possible.

"The Finnish authorities chose 'Sarby's sawed-off canoe' over hundreds of other fine design entries. It touched off a new trend in yacht design in what was to become the world's largest singlehander class."

There are said to be about three thousand now in the world, including about a thousand in Russia and three hundred in the United States. There are National Finn Associations in Africa, Australia, New Zealand, various countries in Europe, and in the United States. Leading builders or importers in the United States are the O'Day Corporation (168 Stevens St., Fall River, Mass. 02722), Newport Boats (Gloucester, Va. 23061), John C. Conrad (4939 N. 16th St., Philadelphia, Pa.); the Nautica Corporation (P. O. Box 26, Paramus, N.J.). Construction may be of wood, molded plywood, or fiber glass. Henry H. Anderson, Jr. (50 E. 89th St., New York, N.Y.) is Secretary of the U. S. A. Finn Association, Inc.

The Finn is a very sporty, planing boat, with an unstayed mast. It is capable of great speeds and it is reported that a Finn was officially clocked for a measured kilometer at a rate of 24 miles per hour. She has a rounded cross-section and is decked over. As one man describes her: "Hot Olympic singlehander, planing hull, athletic workouts."

An unusual feature of the Finn is the way the boom passes through a slot in the mast. It is reported that in spite of the large single sail, the Finn is surprisingly seaworthy in the hands of a skilled helmsman. Among the reasons given for her great speed are the ample sail area, the light total crew weight (only one instead of the usual two), and the absence of rigging windage. To quote the English *Yachts and Yachting:* "The mast is hollow, 3.9 inches at the deck, tapering to 1.6 inches at the top. When on the wind the main sheet is hauled taut, the mast bends. This improves the aerodynamic efficiency of the sail plan, which is unusually high, due to the small gap between the hull and the boom and the absence of rigging." Another man explains that the efficiency of the above process is assisted by the behavior of the boom. "The main sheet is led to the center of the boom so that its pull tends to put a downward bend in the middle, thus pulling out the fullness in the foot of the sail." Price is about $1250 new, $750 to $1000 for used boats.

VITAL STATISTICS: L.O.A. 14'9"; waterline 14'6"; beam 5'1"; draft without centerboard 7", with C.B. down 2'6"; sail area 108 sq. ft. (no spinnaker); weight 320 lbs.; trailable; racing crew, one.

FINN. *Courtesy Newport Boats.*

FIREFLIES. *Courtesy Fairey Marine, Ltd.*

FIREFLY

This was the boat in which Paul Elvstrom sailed and won in the 1948 Olympics, before he continued his winning ways in the Finn Monotype, which replaced the Firefly in Olympic racing. The 12-foot Firefly, designed by Uffa Fox, had its origin in England and in 1946 was sponsored by the British Royal Yachting Association as a planing dinghy ideal for a crew of two with a total weight of 260 pounds. There are now about three thousand in the world with a fairly steady annual increase of about a hundred and fifty; four hundred is the number estimated to be in the United States. Their principal sailing areas are the United Kingdom; British Service Garrisons throughout the world; the East Coast and the Great Lakes in the

United States; Toronto and Montreal, Canada. Fairey Marine, Ltd., are the sole builders (Hamble, Hampshire, England). Construction is molded mahogany on approved class molds.

B. Gadsby (21 Birchtree Drive, Emsworth, Hants, U.K.) is the class Secretary. The Secretary of the Firefly Association of North America is Allan E. Fearn (care of Regatta Point Community Boating, Lake Ave. N., Worcester 5, Mass.). Price delivered in the United States is $800 for new boats, $450 to $600 for used; kits are $600.

VITAL STATISTICS: L.O.A. 12'; waterline 11'9"; beam 4'8"; draft without centerboard 10", with C.B. 4'3", sail area 90 sq. ft. (no spinnaker); weight 260 lbs.; trailable or cartop; racing crew, two.

FIVE POINT FIVE METER

Since this is an Olympic class (the largest) and international, the letters *U.S.* appear under 5.5 on the sails of American boats. There are over four hundred in the world, of which about forty are in the United States. This is not strictly a one-design class but is a "development" or open class, and the rules under which the boats are designed allow some leeway. Thus the

5.5 METER boats. *Photo by Jane Jones.*

dimensions (such as the 33-foot over-all length) given here are approximate. For information about the rules and other matters consult Victor Sheronas, class Secretary (1600 Hamilton St., Philadelphia 30, Pa.).

The 5.5 Meter class, with its tall and narrow mainsail, is designed to a rule very different from the International Rule used for the 6, 8, 10, and 12 Meter classes. While the 5.5 rule is too involved to be quoted here, it includes length, girth, sail area, and displacement, which can be varied so long as the result does not exceed 5.5 meters. Despite the apparent metrical closeness, the 5.5s are much smaller and lighter than the 6 Meters and carry much less sail. Genoas are not used, because the total sail area is measured.

The 5.5 is a high-quality day racer with long overhangs and a short keel. Standards of construction and equipment are high. "The class came into being," says the English *Yachts and Yachting*, "because the 6 Meter Class was producing a yacht that was too heavy and expensive. The Skerry cruisers or Square Meter Classes were considered too light and long, so that the late C. E. Nicholson and Major Maldon Heckstall-Smith adopted the 1912 Boat Racing Association Formula with modified constants to evolve a new class."

Up to now the 5.5s in the United States have been so widely scattered that there has been little regular racing on a regional basis, and large fleets of 5.5s have raced only on such occasions as the U. S. Championships. Despite this, the Olympic record of the class is exceptionally good.

The first time the 5.5s were in the Olympics was at Helsinki in 1952. That year the Gold Medal was won by *Complex II* (U.S. 1) owned and sailed by Dr. Britton Chance of Philadelphia. In the next Olympics, at Melbourne in 1956, the U.S. entry was *Rush IV* (U.S. 3), owned by Victor Sheronas of Philadelphia and sailed by Andrew Schoettle. She placed fourth out of ten, handicapped in one race by a jammed spinnaker halyard. In 1960 at Naples, Italy, the United States won again, our only Olympic sailing victory that year. The *Minotaur* (U.S. 26), owned and sailed by George O'Day of Marblehead, took the Gold Medal. C. Raymond Hunt was the designer. The 5.5s were selected for the Seawanhaka Cup Races in 1962.

Principal sailing activities are in Italy, Sweden, Switzerland, Finland, Norway, Denmark, Canada, England, and the United States. The designers are various, including, in the United States, Luders, Hunt, Sparkman and Stephens, and others. Many of the boats owned in the United States were built in Scandinavian countries, but conversely, many of the boats racing abroad were built to U.S. designs. A number of 5.5s built by Bjarne Aas in Norway from designs by Herman F. Whiton are used by the Sailboat Training Facility (Suite 2714, 551 Fifth Ave., New York 17, N.Y.), which is sponsored by Mr. Whiton. They will be used for advanced, pre-Olympic training. The rest are scattered along the East Coast with others at Houston, Texas, and Rochester, New York.

VITAL STATISTICS (approximate): L.O.A. 32′ to 33′; waterline 22′ to 23′; beam (minimum) 6.23′; draft (maximum) 4.43′; sail area maximum 312 sq. ft., minimum 285 sq. ft. (spinnaker allowed); weight maximum about 4520 lbs., minimum about 3857 lbs.; crew of three.

5-0-5 CLASS

Some people confuse this class with the 5.5 Meter sloop. They are very different. "The 5-0-5," as Bill Taylor has described it, "is a very light open boat, 16′6″ long (or 5.05 meters, hence her name); a centerboarder; open except for a foredeck and side flotation tanks; molded plywood built in England, carrying some 150 feet of sail. She is an extremely fast planing boat, which takes some acrobatics to sail—she depends on the crew hiking out on a 'trapeze' from the mast for stability in strong winds. It was one of these 5-0-5s that won *Yachting's* One-of-a-Kind series in 1954."

The 5-0-5 is an out-and-out racing machine, not a boat for the inexperienced. Unlike the 5.5 Meter, she is a one-design boat.* She is very light for her size and is trailed easily from race to race. Between races, like many others, she is kept out of the water.

The affairs of the class are taken care of by the International 5-0-5 Class Yacht Racing Association. At the time of writing, John Isbister (91 Chatsworth Ave., Larchmont, N.Y.) is Secretary-Treasurer of the American Section. There are over thirteen hundred boats in the world, of which about a hundred are in the United States. Principal areas of sailing activity are the United States, Mexico, Canada, England, Ireland, France, Switzerland, Australia, Denmark, South America. Construction may be fiber glass and/or wood. Fourteen builders are listed in the American Section Handbook, most of them in England. Fairey Marine, Ltd. (Hamble, England), is one of them. Lucian Laverre (Bordeaux Bastide, France) is another. His boats are imported by the Nautica Corporation (P. O. Box 26, Paramus, N.J.).

---

* Some latitude is allowed in choice of rudder shape, centerboard shape (provided it fits in the standard trunk), and the staying arrangements on the mast.

5-0-5. Courtesy Fairey Marine, Ltd.

THE SAILBOAT CLASSES OF NORTH AMERICA

Eric Olsen (Essex, Conn.) is another listed American importer, as is Joseph Cressy (Manchester, Mass.).

The 5-0-5 had its real beginning in 1953 when John Westell of England designed an 18-foot boat, the *Coronet,* to take part in trials to determine the world's best two-man centerboard boat. The *Coronet* took first place easily and proved clearly superior to all other boats entered, including the Flying Dutchmen, Thistles, and others. The trials were sponsored by the International Yacht Racing Union. Later, at the request of the French Caneton Racing Association, the design was modified by Westell, the bow overhang being shortened six inches and the stern overhang a foot, giving a length of 5.05 meters. Otherwise there were no changes. The present name was then adopted. One of the characteristics of the hull is a pronounced topside flare, giving added hiking leverage to the crew without increasing the waterline width and preventing solid water from coming aboard under most conditions. This feature, plus the trapeze, means the 5-0-5 can be sailed harder in stronger winds than other light centerboarders.

While the 5-0-5 is usually kept out of the water ("dry sailed") between races, it is often left at a mooring for weekends, sometimes longer, and it is said, seldom capsizes there. Being very light, it swings quickly to meet puffs of wind.

While the trials mentioned above would make it appear that the 5-0-5 was faster than the Flying Dutchman, *Yachts and Yachting* pointed out in their issue of March 1, 1957, that there is little to choose between the two boats so far as speed under average conditions is concerned. This comment is based on the Portsmouth Harbor (England) list of speed figures, assembled with great statistical care from the results of a large number of races. As it turned out, the Flying Dutchman was picked out for the Olympic Games as the two-man centerboarder. Price new is $1200 to $1800, used from $600 up.

VITAL STATISTICS: L.O.A. 16½ feet (5.05 meters); waterline 15'; beam 6'2" (at waterline 4'1"); draft with centerboard up 6", with C.B. down 3'9"; sail area 150 sq. ft. (spinnaker allowed); weight 280 lbs. complete; trailable.

FLYING DUTCHMAN

Chosen as one of the five Olympic classes in 1960 and again for 1964, the 19'10" (6.05 meter) Flying Dutchman, like the 5-0-5, is a very exciting boat to sail and extremely fast when planing. It is no boat for children or neophytes. After World War II a group of prominent Dutch yachtsmen aided by some internationally known helmsmen, with the help of designer U. Van Essen, worked out the prototype of the Flying Dutchman. In a series of races in the Netherlands in 1952, against competitors from seven different countries, the new boat came out on top. The International Yacht Racing Union officially recognized the class first for inland waters and later without that restriction.

There are now about two thousand Flying Dutchmen in thirty-five countries, including five hundred in the United States. An International Flying Dutchman Class Association has been organized, of which the United States Honorary Secretary-Treasurer is Oliver P. Alford III (St. Michaels, Md.). Principal sailing areas are Australia, South Africa, South America, Mexico, Canada, Germany, Holland, Belgium, England, Italy and elsewhere on the Mediterranean, Norway, New Zealand. Also there are boats on the East and West Coasts of the United States, in Ohio, Michigan, Missouri, Texas, the Great Lakes region, and Florida. The World Championships in 1962 were held at St. Petersburg, Florida.

Builders are found in various parts of the world, including the United States, where there are also importers. Since there are too many to list here, it is suggested that those interested communicate with the Secretary-Treasurer (above) or consult *Yachting's Boat Owners Buyers Guide*. Construction materials have no restrictions, but are generally plywood or fiber glass.

Mr. Alford points out that "the tremendous shoulder and long easy run allows the Flying Dutchman to 'get on top of the bow wave' rather than trying to push it. Use of the trapeze enables the crew to place their weight advantageously." The official publication of the U. S. Flying Dutchman Association is called *The Trapeze*. We are told that it is possible to get the Flying Dutchman planing to windward.

The enthusiastic Mr. Alford disagrees with those who consider the Flying Dutchman suited mainly for the experts, and writes: "It will respond to the expert and give to him the ultimate in speed, but fundamentally it is a big flat-bottomed boat that is very easy to sail, and one that does not have any tricks. The big genoa jib is very difficult to handle in a high wind, but I turn the kids loose with a small working jib with excellent results. Advance Sailboat Corporation, Parkville, Missouri, is building a Fly-

FLYING DUTCHMAN at the world championships, St. Petersburg, Florida, March 1962. *Courtesy O. P. Alford III.*

ing Dutchman for the family trade. In Europe many families trail these boats to the coast and cruise in them. You and I would probably not take to it, but they apparently have great sport.

"My boat is 'fully recoverable,' which means that if you can take it out you can bring it back by itself. This, in my opinion, is the greatest advance in sailboat construction that I have ever seen. I can turn my boat over, all the way over or 360 degrees, and sail it away dry."

In an article in the English magazine *Yachts and Yachting*, comparing the Flying Dutchman with the 5-0-5, it was pointed out that the stability of the Flying Dutchman permits her to lie afloat at a mooring with the mast up, whereas this cannot be done with some other kinds of light planing boats.

In the 1960 Olympics the winners were eighteen-year-old Peder Lunde and young Bjorn Bergvall of Norway. Harry Sindle, the U.S. skipper and a topnotch racing man, had never been in it, and wound up twentieth. The competition was terrific and Sindle had a few bad breaks. Prices of new boats run from $1200 to $2000, old $800 to $1000.

VITAL STATISTICS: L.O.A. 19'10"; waterline 18'; beam 5'11"; draft without centerboard 6", with C.B. 3'8"; sail area 200 sq. ft. (spinnaker allowed); weight 276 lbs. minimum; trailable, also cartop; racing crew, two.

FLYING FIFTEEN

Designed in the late forties by Uffa Fox, the idea behind the Flying Fifteen (20 feet over-all) was to create a fast planing boat which wouldn't capsize. It is claimed that she is capable of 16 knots and is the "only true planing keel boat," combining the exhilaration of a fast centerboarder with the safety of a keel yacht.

There are over five hundred boats in the class throughout the world, including between twenty-five and fifty in the United States. Foreign boats are located in England, Ireland, France, Africa, the Bahamas, New Zealand, Mexico, Guatemala, and Venezuela. In the United States fleets are being organized in Sorrento, Maine; California; Marblehead and Martha's Vineyard, Massachusetts; and on Narragansett Bay, Rhode Island.

Narrow for her over-all length, shallow considering her keel, she is an attractive, sporty boat which has the appearance of being fast, wet, and exciting.

Principal importers or builders are Geonautics (23 Arrow St., Cambridge 38, Mass.) and Wayne Wilson (San Clemente, Calif.). W. H. Wainwright (61 Highland St., Cambridge 38, Mass.) is Secretary of the association in

FLYING FIFTEEN. *Photo by Beken & Son, courtesy Geonautics, Inc.*

the United States. Boats are registered with the Royal Yachting Association Flying Fifteen Owner Association. Price is about $2000 for new boats, $1000 for used.

VITAL STATISTICS: L.O.A. 20′; waterline 15′; beam 5′; draft 2′6″; sail area 150 sq. ft. (spinnaker allowed); weight 750 lbs.; trailable; racing crew, two or three.

FLYING JUNIOR

Designed by U. Van Essen of Holland, who also designed the famous Flying Dutchman, this class started out as the Flying Dutchman Junior and now has become the Flying Junior. Not only the name but the design has been modified slightly in the hope of arriving at the best boat possible as a basis for one-design class rules in 1963. This is a fast fiber-glass boat with a very light planing hull, great fun to sail but by no means foolproof for the inexperienced, though the boat has full flotation.

Like all boats, you can't have one asset without incurring a liability somewhere else. Although the use of aluminum instead of wood has reduced the mast weight (according to the American builders) from as much as 22 pounds to the 17½ pounds minimum allowed, the Flying Junior is not a boat to be left at a mooring in a good-sized harbor. My son-in-law, John P. Ware, and I owned one of the original Flying Dutchman Juniors with the heavier wooden mast, but sold it and bought a fast planing but more stable Flying Tern after the former boat had capsized several times at her mooring in Milton Harbor, Rye, New York. This was during breezes which failed to upset any other boats of her size, such as Blue Jays and others. I have been told that another of the early owners of the Flying Junior had the same experience.

In response to an inquiry about this to the Advance Sailboat Corporation (108 E. 3rd St., Parkville 1, Mo.), which builds Flying Juniors, I received the following explanation from E. K. Huschka:

"First, the boat is not well suited for mooring because of its very light weight and relatively narrow hull design which incorporates a fair amount of keel in the forward portion, preventing it from swinging freely in the wind shifts. In the matter of mooring it shares the same problems with the 5-0-5 and the International 14, the Thistle, the Windmill, the Mobjack, and in short, most of the newer light planing designs. Conversely, these very factors make it an ideal trailer or cartop boat and this is the manner in which almost all FJ's are stored. In my wanderings thru Europe, where I came in contact with several hundred FJ's, I did not see one that was kept at mooring, while it was not at all unusual to see one on top of a Volkswagen or Renault. Accordingly, we strongly suggest that the FJ be dry sailed; a point which is very advantageous here in the Midwest, at least."

Mr. Huschka lives in an area where there is considerable lake sailing and good-sized lakes have launching ramps or beaches with adjacent parking space for empty trailers. This "dry sailing" isn't so practical along many parts of the Atlantic Coast, particularly in areas like western Long Island Sound, where waterfront land is generally too expensive for such facilities

FLYING JUNIOR. *Copyright photo courtesy G. L. W. Oppenheim.*

and launching ramps with adequate parking are rare or nonexistent. Also many people don't want to go to the trouble of putting their boat in and out of the water every time they go for a sail or, as an alternative, hoisting the mast and later lowering it each time, as we had to do on our Flying Junior. They like to have a boat as nearly ready to sail as possible. Purchasers of the Flying Junior should have this in mind. However, if they are young, interested primarily in class racing rather than day sailing, and don't mind the extra trouble, they can have a great deal of fun in a boat which the builder says is intended for "dry sailing."

A good many sailors apparently do come in this last category, for about 1050 Flying Juniors have been built, of which 550 are in the United States. Holland has about 250 of the European boats, Italy 200. Ovingsteel, Inc. (30 Church St., New York 7, N.Y.), which imports Flying Juniors, expressed the belief that the lighter mast of the improved model makes the boat now satisfactory for mooring purposes and explained that they (who succeeded Van Breems as importers) had had no complaints on that score.

The International Secretary of the Flying Junior Organization is C. Th. Gulcher (Gr. W. de Oudelaan 69, Naarden, Holland). The United States Secretary is Sam Dawkins, Jr. (1201 Fidelity Union Tower, Dallas 1, Tex.). The association is aggressive and publishes an interesting *Flying Junior Bulletin*. Prices of the boat range from $900 to $1200; used boats cost $500, as do kits.

VITAL STATISTICS (approximate): L.O.A. 13'2"; waterline 12'2" to 12'6"; beam 4'11½" (5'3" including wide gunwale); draft without centerboard 6", with C.B. 2'7" to 3'; sail area 100 sq. ft. (no spinnaker, but under consideration); weight 200 lbs.; trailable; racing crew, two.

FLYING SCOT

Designed by Gordon K. ("Sandy") Douglass of Oakland, Maryland (who also designed the Thistle and Highlander), the Flying Scot 19-foot centerboard sloop was completed in July 1957. At the time of writing there are 358 in the United States, with the greatest concentration to date in the Midwest. Mr. Douglass writes: "I was convinced that the time had come to introduce a new boat in the field of the family-racing boat, the center of which field had for so long been held by the Lightning. The first requirement for such a boat would be stability and roominess so that she would be a boat anyone could sail with comfort, a boat the entire family could enjoy severally and together. She should have a good performance

FLYING SCOT. *Photo by Jack Beierwaltes, courtesy Gordon Douglass Boat Co., Inc.*

but would not try to be the world's fastest boat . . . a good all-around boat for all sorts of conditions and uses."

Having been reading about several other classes whose sponsors claimed or implied that they had the "world's fastest boat," it was a pleasure to find someone who did not make such a claim. However, the boat planes well and from all accounts seems to be a good compromise between the boats requiring acrobats for crews and the displacement boats of earlier vintage.

The principal builders are the Gordon Douglass Boat Company (Oakland, Md.) and Customflex (Toledo, Ohio). Construction is of fiber glass. There is a Flying Scot Sailing Association, aimed at maintaining rigidly the one-design features of the class. Joseph S. Stout is Secretary (Room 1904, 14 Wall St., New York, N.Y.). It is interesting to note in the name of the association emphasis on *sailing* rather than racing, implying that the members expect more than just a racing boat. The price new, with Dacron sails, is $2435.

VITAL STATISTICS: L.O.A. 19′; waterline 18′4″; beam 7′; draft without centerboard 8″, with C.B. 4′; sail area 190 sq. ft. (spinnaker allowed); total weight 850 lbs.; trailable; racing crew, two to four.

FLYING TERN

I'll have to begin by admitting a prejudice in favor of the 14-foot Flying Tern. My son-in-law, John P. Ware, and I own one and like it immensely. Also, it doesn't easily capsize at its moorings as our previous boat did. I know and have a high regard for the Dutch designer and builder, whom I have visited: E. G. Van de Stadt of Zaandam, Holland. His firm, which imports these boats into the United States, is E. G. Van de Stadt Scheepswerf N.V. (P. O. Box 113, Zaandam, Holland). Dealers at present are Don's Marine Center (P. O. Box 387, Islamorada, Fla.), Annapolis Boat Rentals (Box 1669, Annapolis, Md.), Clifford Marine Sales (2120 Lake Ave., Ashtabula, Ohio), and Sunnapee Company (1136 W. Montana Drive, St. Paul 13, Minn.). The boat is built under license in Canada by Grampian Marine (P. O. Box 413, Oakville, Ontario, Canada).

About one thousand Flying Terns have been built since the boat was first designed in 1956. Of these about 150 are in the United States, 45 in Mexico, 45 in Germany, 100 in Canada, and 100 in France. Saudi Arabia even has 20. It is a National Racing Class in Holland with over 400 competitors.

The Flying Tern has a round section and is a good planing boat. In a very light wind one day I was surprised to see her sail through the lee of a modern 26-foot displacement racer without planing. When planing she has gone by various displacement boats twice her size, as planing boats will. Besides being fast, she is an extremely pretty and well-built boat, comfortable and fun to sail.

There is now in the United States an active North American Flying

FLYING TERN. *Courtesy Lansing Reynolds.*

Tern Class Association aimed at maintaining the one-design features, encouraging racing, and promoting the affairs of the class. I was glad to read in the bylaws that the official language "shall be English." The Secretary is Lansing Reynolds (2 Sunnywood Drive, Westfield, N.J.). There is an active fleet at Shoreham, New York, on the north shore of Long Island, where boats are hauled up on the beach, as there is no harbor. Races are also held on Candlewood Lake, Connecticut, to which boats are hauled on trailers.

Construction is of fiber glass with flotation tank. Price is about $1100.

VITAL STATISTICS: L.O.A. 14'; beam 5'1"; draft with centerboard down 3'2"; sail area 120 sq. ft. (spinnaker allowed); weight 250 lbs.; trailable; racing crew, two.

GANNET

The Gannet is a 14-foot centerboard sloop based on the Mark VII International 14 hull which was designed by Uffa Fox and modified in 1957 by George D. O'Day, who improvised a new deck and more moderate sail plan. The first thirty-one boats were sold to the U. S. Naval Academy at Annapolis, which led to the class growing to over one hundred boats. The boat has been adopted by the Severn River (Md.) Yacht Racing Association as its official junior-training-program boat and also is being used for intercollegiate sailing not only at the Naval Academy, but at Yale and Tulane universities. About 110 Gannets have been built to date.

The boat has a good planing hull but is considered wide and stable enough to be suitable for children as well as college men. For instance, it is five inches wider than several other planing boats of its length.

The boat is sold by the O'Day Corporation (168 Stevens St., Fall River, Mass. 02722). She is made of fiber glass. Price is $1248 for new boats; used cost about $950.

VITAL STATISTICS: L.O.A. 14'; waterline 14'; beam 5'5"; draft without centerboard 6", with C.B. down 4'; sail area 125 sq. ft. (spinnaker allowed); weight 300 lbs., trailable.

GEARY 18 (Formerly Flattie)

In February 1928 the arrival of the centerboard sloop Flattie (now Geary 18) was announced as follows in a Seattle, Washington, paper: "Unsinkable Sailboat Provided for Junior Yachtsmen." The boat was designed by L. E. ("Ted") Geary and is 18 feet long; hence the new name. She is a flat-bottomed adaptation of a Great Lakes racing scow and up to now eleven hundred numbers have been issued in the United States (chiefly on the Pacific and Gulf coasts) and in Canada.

GANNET. *Courtesy O'Day Corporation.*

GEARY 18. *Courtesy Geary 18 International Yacht Racing Association.*

With a V bottom and hard chine she is stiff and easy to build. While not a typical planing boat, she will plane on a reach when conditions are right. Her principal attribute is a very low cost for a boat of her size. Another attribute is a live, active association—the International Geary 18 Yacht Racing Association. The Secretary is Larry K. Shorett (P. O. Box 116, Main Post Office, Seattle 11, Wash.). Leading builders include Varalyay Boat Works (1868 W. 166th, Gardena, Calif.), fiber-glass hulls; Sullivan Hardwood Lumber Company (703 W. F St., San Diego 1, Calif.). Delta International (14th and Franklin Sts., Oakland, Calif.) imports boats. Construction is cedar plank, plywood, or fiber glass. Price is $1000 to $1500 new, $300 to $500 used; kits are $500 to $600.

VITAL STATISTICS: L.O.A. 18'; waterline approx. 15'6"; beam 5'2"; draft without centerboard 6", with C.B. 3'9"; sail area 157½ sq. ft. (no spinnaker); weight 525 lbs. minimum; trailable; racing crew, two.

GEMINI. *Photo by C. Alan Merry, courtesy Cape Cod Shipbuilding Co.*

GEMINI

The 16'1" sloop Gemini, designed by Sidney De W. Herreshoff, came on the market early in 1962 when it was shown at the New York Motor Boat Show. Built by the Cape Cod Shipbuilding Company (Wareham, Mass.), with a modern round-bottom planing hull and rig, its unusual feature is twin boards instead of one centerboard. While this has been a feature of the Inland Lake Scows, it is seldom seen on other single-hulled craft. The builder calls attention to the following points:

"In our testing, the boat with two boards was much faster than the same model with one centerboard. The experts will surely agree that a board kept perpendicular, when heeling, offers more efficient lateral resistance, consequently, a much smaller board is used with less wetted surface, resulting in a faster boat. Thus our reasoning for installing the boards at the angle of average heel rather than vertical. The Gem does have a board for each tack where it is most efficient. She sails best with leeboard down and weatherboard up. However, she will sail well with both boards down and, of course, downwind with both up. She is easy to sail. Neither skipper nor crew need any particular training to handle her twin boards."

The centerboard box is completely enclosed. There is an outboard-motor well molded as an integral part of the deck and draining through the transom. This looks like a most interesting boat and should go fast. Construction is of fiber glass. Price is $1500.

VITAL STATISTICS: L.O.A. 16'1"; waterline 14'9"; beam 5'7"; draft without centerboard 7", with C.B. 3'4"; sail area 140 sq. ft. (spinnaker allowed); weight 440 lbs.; trailable.

G.P. 14

This is a 14-foot, hard-chine sloop-rigged dinghy designed for the *Yachting World* in England by Jack Holt. There are now about four thousand in the world, chiefly in England. The class Secretary in America is W. D. M. Mitchell (Box 1043, Cornwall, Ontario, Canada).

Builders or importers are John Wright, Jr. (328 W. Queen Lane, Philadelphia 44, Pa.), and the J. N. T. Marine Company (17 Gray Terrace, Bedford, Mass.). Construction is mahogany plywood. The boat is consid-

G.P. 14s. *Courtesy The Bell Woodworking Co., Ltd.*

ered easy for an amateur to make. Stability is very good and the price is inexpensive. It will plane under some conditions and is considered in England as a good general-purpose boat. Price is about $1000 with Dacron sails. Kits are $328.

VITAL STATISTICS: L.O.A. 14'; waterline 13'6"; beam 5'; draft without centerboard 7", with C.B. 3'; sail area 102 sq. ft.; weight 285 lbs.; trailable.

HAMPTON

The Hampton 18-foot centerboard sloop was designed by Vincent J. Serio in 1934 for a group of yachtsmen in the Hampton Yacht Club, Hampton, Virginia. The group was seeking a fast, light, able, shoal-draft boat for a one-design racing class in local waters. There are now over five hundred Hamptons, raced principally on Chesapeake Bay, where there are fleets at Hampton, Norfolk, Portsmouth, the Potomac River, Annapolis, South River, Chester River, Choptank River, and Langley Field, Virginia. There is also a large fleet on Kerr Lake, North Carolina.

HAMPTONS. *Courtesy Serio Boat Yard.*

The boat has a V bottom, making it easy for amateurs to build. While most of them are of cedar, recent boats have been constructed of plywood or fiber glass, or have been fiber-glass-covered. There is an active Hampton One Design Racing Class Association, of which Bev Bryan is Secretary-Treasurer (Box 43, McDaniel, Md.). National Championships are held in August. Builders include Serio Boat Yard (16 House St., Hampton, Va.); Riverside Boat Works (Dorr Willey) (Elizabeth City, N.C.); David W. Brown (32 Adriatic Ave., Hampton, Va.).

While the boat is not one of the late planing models (though some owners are "having fun with the trapeze idea"), it sails well and is fairly inexpensive: about $1600 new and from $300 up, old. Serio sells kits.

VITAL STATISTICS: L.O.A. 18′; waterline 14′; beam 5′9½″; draft without centerboard 7″, with C.B. 3′6″; sail area 160 sq. ft. (no spinnaker); weight 500 lbs.; trailable; racing crew, two.

HERRESHOFF "TWELVE" (See Bull's Eye)

HIGHLANDER

The 20-foot centerboard sloop Highlander, like the Flying Scot and Thistle, was designed by Gordon K. Douglass, the first one being launched in
1951. There are now reported to be 325 registered owners, including 40 in
France and the rest in the United States. The class Secretary is Donald

HIGHLANDER. *Booz Photos.*

C. Southam (3904 Glenwood Rd., Cleveland Heights 21, Ohio). The boats, and plans are sold by Douglass and McLeod (Box 311, Painesville, Ohio).

The Highlander is roomy and a good all-around boat for family use and racing. The cockpit is fairly large. Construction is of mahogany or fiber glass. Price new is about $2300, kits $1620.

VITAL STATISTICS: L.O.A. 20′; beam 6′8″; draft without centerboard 8″, with C.B. 4′10″; sail area 225 sq. ft. (spinnaker allowed); weight 590 lbs.; trailable; crew, three or four for racing.

HORNPIPER

The 9-foot Hornpiper cat-rigged dinghy hit the water of Raritan Bay, New Jersey, late in 1960. She was designed by Navesink Laminating, Ltd. (75–77 Bay Ave., Highlands, N.J.), which also builds them. Miss Mary E. Huntsman is Secretary of the Hornpiper Association (22 Pine Drive, Little Silver, N.J.). The class has just started and has twenty members. Constructed of fiber glass, the boat has a foam-filled bilge area. Price is $495.

VITAL STATISTICS: L.O.A. 9′4″; waterline 8′10″; beam 4′10″; draft without centerboard 5″, with C.B. 2′4″; sail area 56 sq. ft. (no spinnaker); weight 140 lbs.; trailable; crew, two, minimum total 200 lbs.

HORNPIPER. *Courtesy Mary E. Huntsman.*

INDIAN. *Courtesy John MacDonald.*

INDIAN

The 21-foot Indian-class centerboard sloop was designed by the late John G. Alden and took the water in 1924 at the Squantum Yacht Club. About one hundred were built, of which about fifty are still sailing, chiefly on Massachusetts and Narragansett bays. Former Secretary John MacDonald writes that eighteen to twenty-four are still being raced actively on Massachusetts Bay and "we are, at the present time, trying to develop interest in this type of boat, rather than the planing type, and I think we have been having some success. Interest is on the upswing because of the boat's ability to sail well under all conditions."

Ford Dame (35 Coolidge St., Weymouth, Mass.) is now Secretary of the class. Construction is of wood. This is one of the old-time classes and seems destined eventually to give way to the swarming group of new ones. It is comforting, however, to old-timers to know that efforts to keep a fine old class going are meeting with some success. We have no price on new ones.

VITAL STATISTICS: L.O.A. 21′2″; waterline 16′9″; beam 6′4″; draft without centerboard 18″, with C.B. down 3′6″; sail area 230 sq. ft. (spinnaker); weight 1200 lbs.; racing crew, two.

INLAND CAT. *Courtesy G. G. Gray, Inland Cat Class Sailing Association.*

INLAND CAT

The 14'6" Inland Cat is a Marconi catboat, *not* a catamaran. There are about 160 of them, designed in 1956 by Norman Bell and John Larimore and built by Maritime Plastics (1131 Goshen Ave., Fort Wayne, Ind.). The most active fleet is located on Lake George, on the Indiana-Michigan border, eleven miles north of Angola, Indiana. Others sail in the Middle West and Southeast sections of the United States. Three principal aims, we are told, inspired the designers: (1) To reduce maintenance costs by using fiber glass; (2) To have a boat large enough to carry four to five adults; (3) To have the sail, draft, and maneuverability desired for inland waters.

Production started in 1957 and with no great sales effort the class continues to grow. As no used boats have yet come on the market, it would seem a reasonable deduction that the boat is well liked. It is called a family racing boat and not a racing machine. Nothing was said about trapezes in the correspondence I received, though the boat planes and looks as though she would move fast. Price, new, is $1195, kits $795.

G. Gourley Gray is Secretary of the Inland Cat Class Sailing Association (618 Miami Ave., Box 98, Terrace Park, Ohio).

VITAL STATISTICS: L.O.A. 14′6″; waterline 11′4″; beam 5′4″; draft without centerboard 5″, with C.B. 3′3″; sail area 115 sq. ft. (no spinnaker); weight 385 lbs.; trailable.

INLAND LAKE SCOW

Long before the present rage about planing hulls and catamarans, the Inland Lake Scows were planing at phenomenal speeds on the lakes of Wisconsin, Michigan, Minnesota, Illinois, Indiana, and points eastward. Speeds of 20 to 25 knots are reliably reported for these scows and we have heard a "rumor" that a Class A Scow has been timed at 28 knots.

In the One-of-a-Kind Series conducted by *Yachting* magazine, the scows have done extremely well boat for boat, though sometimes losing out on corrected time. In the 1952 regatta a Class C Scow (20 feet over-all) was first on corrected time (fourth, boat for boat), while a Class E Scow (28 feet) was first, boat for boat. In 1954, while the 5-0-5 won on corrected time, the Class E Scow was again first, boat for boat. In the 1959 regatta, in which catamarans (led by the Tiger Cat) excelled, the Class A Scow came in first, boat for boat, in a fleet of forty, and sixth on corrected time.

There are several classes of Inland Lake Scows, of which Classes A, E, C, and M are said now to be the most active. Their lengths run from 38 feet (A) to 16 feet (M and X).

The scows have an early history.* In 1896 Nathanael Herreshoff of Bristol, Rhode Island, built one of the earliest scows for Milton Griggs of Minneapolis, Minnesota; this was the *Alfreda,* which was sailed on Lake Minnetonka. Lucius Ordway, active in making the arrangements for this boat, was one of the early promoters and sailors. By the end of the century more of the scows began to appear. Some were fizzles. In fact, Kimberly reports that he made better progress in a "deep-bellied" boat by moving the mast toward the stern and sailing her backward. However, this wasn't typical and the scows grew fast in number, on inland lakes, rivers, or sheltered bays, where the seas are unlikely to build up to more than a sharp chop.

* "The Inland Lake Scows," by James H. Kimberly, *Yachting,* March 1947. (I owe much of the historical material on the scows to Mr. Kimberly.)

INLAND LAKE SCOW. *Photo by Morris Rosenfeld.*

Besides their almost rectangular, long narrow shape and their very shallow hulls, the scows, which must sail heeled 15 degrees to attain maximum speed, are equipped with twin "bilge boards" run through the hull at either side of the cockpit at an angle of about 15 degrees to the vertical. Twin rudders, as on the Class A and E Scows, enable good control despite a pronounced heel. In disagreement with Bob Bavier, Jr. (see below), a leading scow racer says that "scows excel to weather more so than on free legs in comparison with other boats of size and sail area." As will be imagined, the excitement of sailing a scow can be intense. A Class C Scow owner told the writer that he had been timed at 23 miles per hour in his 20-foot boat.

Bob Bavier, Jr.,[*] points out that an Inland Lake Scow is great sport planing but has some drawbacks. She is only fair to windward and is not fast running in light air. "She is also wet and unseaworthy, tending to submarine in heavy seas. Yet for all their limitations, scows are the most popular type on a number of inland lakes and semi-protected bodies of salt water. In fact, few scow sailors are happy sailing any other boat and, under proper conditions, I can understand why."

While Inland Lake Scow designers are various, they include Harry Melges, Sr., and J. O. Johnson. Melges Boat Works (Zenda, Wis.) makes boats for most of the classes of scows and is considered the leader in this field. Other builders covering one or more classes are Johnson Boat Works (323 South Lake, White Bear Lake 10, Minn.), Bay Boats (120 North St., Sharon, Wis.), Aluma Craft (1515 Central Ave. N.E., Minneapolis, Minn.), and Stamm Boat Company (P. O. Box 5, Delafield, Wis.). The Inland Lake Yachting Association Inc., Ernst C. Schmidt, Secretary (212 N. Main St., Walworth, Wis.), represents twenty-six clubs, and sponsors an active racing program. Estimates received as to the number of boats in each class vary considerably. However, one source of information giving the numbers in each class reports the following: A (40), E (600), C (1000), M (150), D (30), and X (500). They are, of course, scattered among many lakes. Material varies. Prices reported are: A ($6000 to $8500 new, used $500 up), E ($3300 new, used $300 up), C ($2200 new, used $150 up), M ($1395 new, used $500 up), D ($2500 new), X ($1195 new, used $150).

[*] "The Planing Sailboat," by Robert N. Bavier, Jr., *Yachting*, January 1949.

VITAL STATISTICS (Approximate):

	A	E	C	M	D	X
Length over-all	38'	28'	20'	16'	20'	16'
Length waterline	34'	24'	16'	13'	16'	14'
Beam	8'6"	6'9"	6'9"	5'6"	6'9"	6'6"
Draft, bilge boards up	6"	4"	4"	4"	4"	6"
Draft, bilge boards down	5'	3'8"	3'3"	3'	3'3"	2'6"
Sail area, sq. ft.	550	320	216	150	251	110
Spinnaker	Yes	Yes	No	No	Yes	No
Weight lbs.	2000	965	600	450	650	500
Trailable	Yes	Yes	Yes	Yes	Yes	Yes
Rig	Sloop	Sloop	Cat	Sloop	Sloop	Sloop

Note: One authority does not consider that Class X belongs in the scow group, as it is not properly a scow, being "more on the order of a Lightning."

INTERCLUB

The 11½-foot Interclub cat-rigged dinghy was designed by Sparkman and Stephens to the specifications of a group of Frostbite dinghy racers at the Larchmont Yacht Club, on Long Island Sound, New York. The first boats were molded in mahogany veneer and about one hundred were built

INTERCLUB. *Courtesy O'Day Corporation.*

between 1939 and 1953. Another hundred were molded in fiber glass from 1953 to 1959, when the O'Day Corporation took over the rights to build the boat.

The original boat is still being raced by many of the "hottest" sailors on Long Island Sound, at the Larchmont Yacht Club. As a Frostbite racer, the class is beginning to spread, with fleets now at Marblehead, Duxbury, Scituate, and Harvard University in Massachusetts; Manhasset Bay, City Island, and Kingspoint on Long Island Sound; Rochester and Cornell University in upper New York State. The class has no central organization and is primarily used for winter Frostbite or intercollegiate racing. There are about 295 now in the class. Price is $875 for new boats, $750 for used; kits are not available.

VITAL STATISTICS: L.O.A. 11'6"; waterline 11'6"; beam 4'8"; draft without centerboard 6", with C.B. 3'6"; sail area 72 sq. ft. (no spinnaker); weight 200 lbs.; trailable; racing crew, two.

INTERLAKE. *Courtesy Customflex.*

INTERLAKE

The 18-foot Interlake sloop, designed by Francis Swiesguth in 1932, came before the planing-class era but has survived. Since being converted from wood to fiber glass in 1955, she has become one of the fast-growing classes. With a hard chine and no "freak characteristics," as someone has described her, she has good stability and is a good all-around boat. There are now about 450 of the Interlakes, sailed on the Great Lakes, on the East Coast, and in the Southwest.

Jack Harshberger is Secretary of the Interlake Sailing Class Association (care of Customflex, Inc., 1817 Palmwood Ave., Toledo 7, Ohio). Customflex is the sole builder. Price is $1695 new, about $1500 for used boats.

VITAL STATISTICS: L.O.A. 18'; waterline 15'3"; beam 6'3"; draft without centerboard 8", with C.B. down 4'8"; sail area 175 sq. ft. (no spinnaker); weight 650 lbs.; trailable; racing crew, two or three.

INTERNATIONAL DECKED SAILING CANOE

Many years ago Charles P. ("Chippy") Burgess, brother of W. Starling Burgess, the great designer, introduced me to one of these narrow sleek sailing canoes with the sliding seats. The month was March; even in summer the waters of Marblehead Harbor are very cold. Came a sudden puff of wind as we were tacking back and forth. In approved style each of us slid out to the windward end of our hiking seats. Unfortunately, one of us, aiming to keep warm, had on a long overcoat. When the puff suddenly ended, the unlucky skipper, trying to slide back inboard, caught the tail of his coat on the windward end of the seat, which was a bit slow in sliding back. The water was very cold, but we righted the boat; as the tiny cockpit was watertight and the canoe was decked over, there was no bailing to be done, only considerable shivering.

These decked sailing canoes are exciting sailers, as you may have gathered, and very fast. "Imagine, if you can, a 17 foot boat that will sail at 16 knots—and one that you can watch from a distance of five feet when you sail

INTERNATIONAL DECKED
SAILING CANOE. *Courtesy
George Wascheck.*

her. Imagine yourself taking a full capsize, getting your boat up again and
under full way in just 30 seconds without a drop of water in her bilge. And,
if you are interested in design, imagine a boat of 450 [today 400 or less]
pounds displacement putting a 900-pound stress on her weather shroud—a
boat whose center of gravity may sometimes be a good two feet outboard
of her weather rail."[*]

Prior to the 1890s all sailing canoes looked like paddling canoes except for
the sails and leeboards. In the early nineties a man named Paul Butler
developed four "gimmicks" that are now characteristic of the modern racing
canoe: (1) a thwartship sliding seat for hiking (Butler weighed only 110
pounds and had to make his weight count), (2) a crosshead tiller which
could be reached at the windward end of the hiking seat, (3) an automatic
cleat, and (4) a self-bailing cockpit and bulkheads. The value of this combination, says Tyson, "can be gauged by the fact that our conservative
British cousins have adopted all but the crosshead tiller in less than 60

[*] "The Modern Sailing Canoe," by Irwin W. Tyson, *Yachting*, July 1949.

years. Which would be a much better joke if they hadn't walked off with the International Cup the first time they tried the hiking seat. That was in 1933 and it marked the beginning of the sailing canoeist's 'modern era.'"

The American Canoe Association, founded in 1880 and one of the oldest boat clubs in the country, is the governing body of the class in the United States. It adopted the decked sailing canoe from the beginning and for many years has actively promoted class affairs, including international as well as national races. George Wascheck is Sailing Chairman (care of the American Canoe Association, 400 Eastern St., New Haven 13, Conn.). Principal designers are Louis Whitman in the United States, Ian Proctor, Uffa Fox, and Peter Nethercot in England. Leading builders are Max Andersson (Vasteras, Sweden), W. Kempner (London, England). Raymond Dodge (Niles, Mich.) is an importer. While there have been numerous match races between countries, the first World's Championship was held in England in 1961. This was won by Great Britain, with the United States, Sweden, and West Germany also participating.

The International Decked Sailing Canoe, now sloop-rigged, is a *development* class, though limitations are, of course, prescribed. There are about one hundred in the world, of which about twenty are in the United States. Principal sailing waters are off City Island, New York; in the Chicago area; at Hayling Island, England; Stockholm, Sweden; and in West Germany and France. There are no restrictions on construction material: molded plywood is usual. Hiking seat may not extend more than five feet outboard.

In *Yachting's* One-of-a-Kind Regatta in 1959 the Sailing Canoe ranked third out of forty boats on corrected time, being beaten only by two catamarans. Boat for boat, she was fifteenth, beating many larger and redoubtable competitors. The canoes are at their best in sheltered waters, though they can live in rough seas. Under many conditions they are faster than most of the displacement-class boats, and in winds above 10 or 12 miles an hour it is reported that the canoes will usually pass leading planing boats on a close reach, the reason being that they can begin to plane at a higher point of the wind. The decked canoe is not a family sailer. It is an exciting one-man racing machine which requires acrobatic agility and a sensitive understanding of a type of sailing somewhat different from any other. Prices range from $1200 to $1800 new, from $600 to $1000 for used boats.

VITAL STATISTICS (approximate): L.O.A. 16' to 17'; waterline about 6" less than over-all; beam 3'1⅜" to 3'7¼"; draft without centerboard 4", with C.B. 3'7.3" maximum; sail area 107.64 sq. ft. (maximum) or 10 square meters (no spinnaker); weight 128–145 lbs. stripped-hull minimum, depending on dimensions; trailable or cartop.

INTERNATIONAL 14

Considered the "daddy" of modern planing sailboats, the International 14 with its straight up-and-down bow and sloop rig is still one of the most popular and sporty planing boats in the world. There are now about two thousand of these "overgrown dinghies" with the large sail area, including seven hundred in the United States. Planing sailboats developed since World War II, such as the Thistle, the Jollyboat, the Raven, the Flying Dutchman, the 5-0-5, and many others are all based upon principals initially evolved in the International 14 class. This is a *development* class, and, within certain restrictions, improved designs continue to appear. Thus, dimensions given herein are approximate; designers are various and include Uffa Fox, Austin Farrar, Ian Proctor, Charles Bourke, and Bruce Kirby.

In the early 1900s a multiplicity of similar classes began to appear in England and Canada, calling for efforts to agree on a class which would concentrate racing talent and competitive activities. Matters were brought to a head in 1923 when the British Yacht Racing Association called a meeting and formed a committee composed of representatives from the various areas of 14-foot sailing. Under Chairman Sir John Field Beale, this committee laid the foundation for the present International 14. There were still "growing pains"; cat rigs gave way to sloops, gaff rigs to Marconis; the built-in buoyancy tank arrived.

Three breakthroughs came in 1927: the Prince of Wales donated his famous cup to the Fourteens; Uffa Fox sailed his *Avenger* one hundred miles across the English Channel and back; and the International Yacht Racing Union granted the class international status. Placing restrictions only on such factors as sail area, mast height, weight, length, etc., the rules were intended to perpetuate an entirely undecked boat of the greatest speed and sail area which two skilled people could manage. The International 14 attracted some of the best designers of the era and had great influence in changing the face of small-boat racing by showing the speed possibilities of the planing hull.

By 1935, under the leadership of George Ford, the class began to develop rapidly in the United States. Gordon ("Sandy") Douglass, a leader in racing-class development, produced a U. S. One-Design International 14, hundreds of which were built and raced in North America during the 1940s and 1950s. At present the principal North American areas in which the boats are sailed are Boston, Massachusetts; Essex, Connecticut; Barnegat Bay, New Jersey; Chesapeake Bay; the St. Lawrence River Valley; Michigan; Seattle, Washington; Los Angeles and San Francisco, California.

Among the present North American builders are Grampian Marine (P. O.

INTERNATIONAL 14. *Photo by Beckner Photo Service, courtesy W. D. Schock Co.*

Box 413, Oakville, Ontario, Canada), W. D. Schock Company (3502 S. Greenville St., Santa Ana, Calif.), Hugh Doherty's King Harbor Boats (901 Pier Ave., Hermosa Beach, Calif.), and Mobjack Manufacturing Company (Gloucester, Va.). For information as to other builders or importers or data about the class, write Dr. Stuart H. Walker, United States International 14 Association (Mercy Hospital, Calvert and Saratoga Sts., Baltimore 2, Md.).

Construction may be of any material of uniform thickness which meets the weight and other requirements. Despite the fact that deep-water voyages have been made, this is not a boat for family sailing but a very sporty, fast racing machine, capable of speeds of 14 knots or more. Prices are $1200 to $1700 for new boats, $450 to $1500 for used; kits are $300 and up.

VITAL STATISTICS: L.O.A. 14'; waterline 14'; beam 5'6"; draft without centerboard 10", with C.B. 5'; sail area 165 sq. ft. (spinnakers allowed); weight 225 lbs.; trailable.

INTERNATIONAL ONE DESIGN

In his extremely interesting "History of the International One Design Class," included in an attractive booklet brought out on the occasion of the twenty-fifth anniversary of the class, the senior Cornelius Shields tells of how this well-known class first came into being and attracted the cream of the Long Island racing skippers.

"In 1935 a splendid situation existed in our Sound Interclub Class wherein we had mustered about the best talent available in this area. There were 28 boats. Excellent racing prevailed and the Class spirit was high. Even though the set-up was an extremely happy one, I was considerably concerned because the boats were not of the best design nor the most beautiful in appearance. I constantly made a most earnest effort to persuade other Class champions and top skippers to join us in the Interclubs, as it was my feeling that when I was beaten I wanted it to be by the best. I was fearful that a new competing class might appeal to the members, which could conceivably deteriorate the Interclubs. I had in mind that this wonderful crowd of competitors could be moved over in a body to a new boat of better design, and that a strong and somewhat permanent class could be established."

In 1935, while racing in Bermuda, Mr. Shields saw the prettiest 6-meter boat he had ever seen. She was designed and built by Bjarne Aas of Fredrikstad, Norway. "My immediate reaction," he writes, "was how wonderful it would be to have a One-Design Class similar in appearance, but, of course, smaller, with slightly less displacement than is necessary for the Six Meter rule, with relatively wider beam for the comfort it would provide."

Working quietly so as not to alarm Interclub-class members, Mr. Shields got Bjarne Aas to submit a design for the 33-foot sloop he had in mind. Eventually, with the help of his partner, Egbert Moxham, all of the details were worked out with the designer. Mr. Shields and a small group underwrote the purchase of twenty-five of the newly designed boats. All of the

INTERNATIONAL ONE DESIGN boats. *Bermuda News Bureau photo by Len Mocklow, courtesy Albert A. Young.*

Interclubs were sold at a good price, agreed to in advance by the owners. Delivery of the new boats began in December 1936. Enthusiasm for the class, called the International One Design, ran high, and the new boats began racing in the summer of 1937, owned and skippered by some of the ablest racing men in the country—a standard which has been maintained ever since.

Starting with the first fleet of twenty-five which came to Long Island Sound, the International One Designs now have fleets as follows: Long Island Sound, thirty-two (including eight boats belonging to the Sailboat Training Facility, recently organized and sponsored by Herman F. Whiton); Marblehead, Massachusetts, nine; Northeast Harbor, Maine, fifteen; San

INTERNATIONAL 12s. *Courtesy The Anchorage, Inc.*

Francisco, California, seventeen—totaling seventy-three in the United States. Elsewhere in organized fleets, Norway has thirty-two; Cowes, England, twenty-two; Bermuda, thirteen; Marseilles, France, five—totaling seventy-two abroad. Thus 145 are organized in fleets. In addition it is estimated that there are about one hundred in various parts of the world not so organized. While efforts have been made to get the International to convert to fiber glass, up to the present these efforts have not been successful, due to the desire to maintain the one-design feature. The price of new boats, which had been $2670 in 1936, delivered in New York, for the first boats, is now from $12,500 to $13,000. Since 1959 there has been a World Championship every year, with one representative from each fleet participating.

The Chairman of the International One-Design Class committee, at the time of writing, is William E. John, Jr. (5 Hunter Lane, Rye, N.Y.).

VITAL STATISTICS: L.O.A. 33′5″; waterline 21′5″; beam 6′9″; draft (keel) 5′4″; sail area 461 sq. ft. (spinnakers used); weight 7120 lbs.

INTERNATIONAL 12

Designed by H. C. Hall and built at The Anchorage, Inc. (Warren, R.I.), this 12-foot cat-rigged dinghy was introduced by Bill Dyer at the New York Motor Boat Show in 1941 and a class of over thirty boats was purchased by the U. S. Coast Guard Academy at New London, Connecticut, for racing in the Intercollegiate Dingy Racing Association. Other classes were formed at Tufts and the University of Maine, and some boats were bought for family sailing, including one by the writer. At first of plywood, they were later constructed of fiber glass. There are now about 120 in the United States. Price of new boats is about $925.

VITAL STATISTICS: L.O.A. 12′; waterline 12′; beam 4′8″; draft with centerboard down 4′; sail area 72 sq. ft. (no spinnaker); weight 130 lbs.; trailable.

JAVELIN

The 14-foot Javelin centerboard sloop was designed by Uffa Fox for George D. O'Day in order to fill what was felt to be a need for a good all-around safe trainer for juniors. A self-bailing cockpit, a bow designed to minimize spray, flotation tanks, nonskid cockpit floors, and a beam greater than many boats of her length emphasize the safety features. The elimination of the conventional protruding centerboard case would also seem to be a good feature and add to cockpit comfort. The boat is said to be a good sailer. Construction is of fiber glass and the boat is built in the United States by the O'Day Corporation (9 Newbury St., Boston, Mass.).

The Javelin was introduced in the United States by the O'Day Corporation at the January 1962 New York Motor Boat Show. There are said to be ninety-four in the world at the time of writing. Price is $1370 for a new boat.

VITAL STATISTICS: L.O.A. 14′; waterline 13′2″; beam 5′8″; draft without centerboard 6″, with C.B. 3′10″; sail area 125 sq. ft. (spinnaker allowed); weight 450 lbs.; trailable.

JAVELIN.
Courtesy O'Day Corporation.

JET 14

The Jet 14 was designed by Howard Siddons (Island Heights, N.J.) soon after World War II. The hull design is similar to that of the International 14 but the rig is like that of a Snipe, with a much smaller sail area than the International. The Jet 14 started as a sloop, but a catboat rig has recently been approved in order to make the boat eligible for single-handed racing. The purpose was to get a low-cost boat which would plane. The popularity of boat and price are attested by the fact that there are now about seven hundred boats and thirty-three chartered fleets in the United States with an active Jet 14 Class Association, organized in 1955. Mrs. William Olsen is Secretary (66 Alexander Drive, Red Bank, N.J.). *Jet Blasts* is the official publication.

Fleets are located in the Middle West, Southwest, and on the East Coast,

JET 14.
Courtesy Jet 14
Class Association.

in thirty states, and judging by the association yearbook a great deal is going on. There are a number of builders, of which Siddons (the designer) and Sindle (Central Ave., Island Heights, N.J.) are among the leaders. Consult the Secretary for the others or refer to *Yachting's Boat Owners Buyers Guide.*

The Jet 14 was selected for the Midget Championship eliminations in 1956 and for several of the Mallory Cup eliminations in 1957. Prices range from about $1000 to $1100 in plywood or fiber glass respectively.

VITAL STATISTICS: L.O.A. 14'; waterline 14'; beam 4'8"; draft 4'2" with centerboard down; sail area 113 sq. ft.; weight 165 lbs. minimum; trailable.

JOLLYBOAT

Again the name of Uffa Fox comes up as the designer of a fast small sailboat. The Jollyboat is an 18-foot sloop and one of the largest of the modern, fast planing dinghies, "frozen," it is said, "into a true one-design class." Molded plywood, only, is allowed as the material. Ratsey is the sole sailmaker and Fairey Marine, Ltd. (Hamble, England), the sole builder. The Chesapeake Jollyboat Sales and Service Company (Richmond, Va.) is the importer. The Secretary of the U. S. Jollyboat Association is Ralph C. Lynn (P. O. Box 6643, Richmond, Va.).

Even if one discounts somewhat the enthusiasm of President Clinton R. McKim of the association (25 Flint St., Marblehead, Mass.), this is a very fast boat, certainly one of "the fastest single hull class(es) for its size except for the sailing canoe." It is especially fast to windward and was second to a catamaran in the Channel Race from England to France several years ago. In *Yachting's* One-of-a-Kind Regatta in 1959 the Jollyboat entry was eighth on corrected time, being beaten only by catamarans or scows except for the 5-0-5, which finished fifth on corrected time but was behind the Jolly-boat, boat for boat—thirteenth to the Jollyboat's eleventh. As the class has now approved a trapeze, this will add to the speed.

Mr. McKim ends an interesting and helpful message by stating: "I honestly know of no weakness except that some people still do not know the Jollyboat. I'm sure your book will help." I doubt, however, if she would be considered ideal for a family boat or for teaching children how to sail. As another enthusiast points out: "She is first and foremost an efficient racer. It is not a compromise attempt to be all things in one. She does not have any of the built-in handicaps to maximum performance that the beamy 'bathtub' family boats have, nor is she carrying any excess weight that

JOLLYBOATS. *Courtesy Fairey Marine, Ltd.*

would slow her up on climbing onto a plane. She can be made docile enough by rolling down some main or by taking a few extra people aboard in a blow—any fast boat can be slowed down, but a slow boat cannot be speeded up—so she is only incidentally a day sailer."

The Jollyboat's principal sailing areas, besides the United Kingdom, are Marblehead, Massachusetts; Long Island Sound; Chesapeake Bay; Augusta, Georgia; Rochester, New York; Ohio; the U. S. West Coast; Montreal, Canada; and Naramata, British Columbia, Canada. There are between three hundred and four hundred in the world, including about one hundred in the United States. The price is about $1950 in the United States for new boats, $1200 for used.

VITAL STATISTICS: L.O.A. 18′; waterline 17′6″; beam 5′2″; draft without centerboard 9″, with C.B. down 4′9″; sail area 160 sq. ft. (spinnaker allowed); weight 375 lbs.; trailable; crew, two or more.

KNARRS. *Photo by Glenn Austin, courtesy H. Robb Holt.*

KNARR

This one-design, 30-foot, keel racing-cruising sloop was designed by Erling Kristoffersen of Norway in 1946, for use on the North Sea. Knarr (the *K* is pronounced in Norway) was a special name for Viking ships used in coastal trading; many coastal town names in Norway begin with Knarr. About forty had been built by 1949 and were successfully racing on the windy waters of the North Sea. The first export to the United

States was to Long Island Sound in 1948. Since then the American fleet has grown to about sixty, located principally on the Great Lakes; Lake Pontchartrain, New Orleans; and San Francisco Bay. Others are scattered.

In 1958 the North American Knarr Association was organized. William H. Devonshire is Secretary-Treasurer (48 Mt. Hope Ave., Rochester 20, N.Y.). Boats are obtainable through E. Lund-Baltzersen (Lokkevein 11, Oslo, Norway). The builders are all in Norway. While the Knarr is primarily a racing boat, it has a cabin with limited cruising accommodations. Price in Norway is about $3800.

VITAL STATISTICS: L.O.A. 30'4"; waterline 20'4"; beam 7'; draft 4'3"; sail area 297 sq. ft.

KNICKERBOCKER

This is a new Sparkman and Stephens design of a 26-foot fiber-glass keel sloop primarily for racing but with a cabin having two berths and a "head." The American Boatbuilding Company (Warwick, R.I.) at the time of writing is completing the first eighteen boats in this class. A rapid class growth on the East Coast is expected by the designers, particularly on Long Island Sound. It is believed that "her generous sized cockpit and below deck accommodations combine to make this an ideal one-design class for day sailing and over-night races." Price is now $6950 plus sails.

VITAL STATISTICS: L.O.A. 26'4"; waterline 19'; beam 6'6"; draft 4'6"; sail area 339 sq. ft. (spinnaker allowed); weight 4000 lbs.; not trailable.

LARK

There are about 150 of these 11-foot cat-rigged decked dinghies in California and Mexico, about 100 in the United States. It was designed by S. Paul and is sold by the John C. Beery Company (Aquatic Park, Berkeley 10, Calif.). Price is $698, used about $575.

VITAL STATISTICS: L.O.A. 11'3"; waterline 10'; beam 4'6"; draft without centerboard 2", with C.B. 2'6"; sail area 72 sq. ft. (no spinnaker); weight 135 lbs.; trailable or cartop.

LEHMAN INTERCLUB and LEHMAN 12

These two Pacific Coast cat-rigged dinghies, the 10- and 12-footers, both of molded fiber glass, are built by W. D. Schock Company (3502 S. Greenville St., Santa Ana, Calif.), for use in interclub and intercollegiate racing.

KNICKERBOCKER. *Courtesy Sparkman and Stephens.*

LARK. *Courtesy John C. Beery Co.*

LEHMAN INTERCLUB. *Photo by Beckner Photo Service, courtesy W. D. Schock Co.*

LEHMAN 12. *Photo by Beckner Photo Service, courtesy W. D. Schock Co.*

The former is also used as a yacht tender. Both have hollow aluminum masts; boom, daggerboard, and rudder are also of aluminum. The boats have buoyancy tanks. A striking feature is their light weight for their respective sizes. Stainless shrouds are plastic-covered to keep the sails clean and reduce chafing. Prices with Dacron sails are, respectively, $562 and $755.

VITAL STATISTICS: *Interclub:* L.O.A. 10′3″; beam 4′5″; draft without daggerboard 4″, with board down 3′; sail area 67 sq. ft.; weight 105 lbs. *Lehman 12:* L.O.A. 12′; beam 4′6″; draft 4½″, with board 3′; sail 81 sq. ft.; weight 126 lbs.

LIDO 14. *Photo by Beckner Photo Service, courtesy W. D. Schock Co.*

LIDO 14

This is another Pacific Coast sailing dinghy, used both for day sailing and class racing, a larger edition of the Lehman Interclub and 12, made by W. D. Schock Company (Santa Ana, Calif.). The boats are also built by Hugh Doherty's King Harbor Boats (901 Pier Ave., Hermosa Beach, Calif.). The cockpit with contoured seats accommodates six persons and provides 640 pounds of flotation. Construction is of fiber glass. An anodized aluminum hinged mast, tilt-up mahogany rudder, tiller with extension handle, plastic-covered stainless shrouds, Dacron running rigging, white neoprene gunwall guards are among the design features.

The first Lido 14 was launched in 1958. There are now eleven hundred boats in various parts of the United States, including Hawaii. The waters of Mexico and Canada also see the Lido 14s. There is now a Lido 14 Class Association, Inc., "to promote Lido 14 Class racing under uniform rules and regulations to maintain rigidly and without deviation the one-design features of the Lido 14 Class Sloop." Price is $1322 with Dacron sails.

VITAL STATISTICS: L.O.A. 14'; beam 6'; draft with centerboard up 5", with C.B. down 4'3"; sail area 111 sq. ft.; weight 325 lbs.

LIGHTNING

In these days of "molded hot rods," to use an expression of a Lightning Class Association President, it is a pleasure to find a well-balanced all-around boat which isn't a racing machine for acrobats or the nautical equivalent of an ice wagon. The 19-foot Lightning is a splendid family boat, with good initial stability, easy to handle and fast enough to provide fine racing under a wide variety of conditions. Good-looking, efficient, and, with her arc bottom and hard chine, easy to construct, she has appealed to so many middle-of-the-road yachtsmen that she has become the largest one-design class of 16 feet or more in the world. Only the 15½-foot Snipe class with over 13,500 registered boats is ahead of the Lightning class among *all* one-design classes of *any* size, though the surprising 13-foot Enterprise class is about on a par. At the time of writing there are more than eighty-one hundred registered Lightnings in the world, including about six thousand in the United States.

In 1938 John Barnes of Skaneateles Boats (New York, N.Y.) and several other Skaneateles friends decided to do something about an idea they had. They wanted a boat which would be large enough to hold a half-dozen people comfortably on a day's sail, stiff enough to enable some of them to move around without heeling the boat too much, small enough for a low cost, simple enough to be made easily by amateurs, easy for all ages to handle and enjoy, fast enough for good racing. Quite an assignment! But Sparkman and Stephens took it on. They also expressed a willingness, if a responsible class organization were formed, to turn the plans over to that organization so that they could be made available to amateur and professional builders alike at a moderate fee.

The first Lightning took to the water in October 1938, and the public introduction to the class came at the New York Motor Boat Show in January 1939. By that time nine builders had acquired the plans and twenty boats had been sold. The Lightning Class Association was then formed by a group of owners who met at the Show. A significant feature of the association's constitution is the provision:

"To keep the Lightning class within the financial reach of a man of moderate means without handicapping ability or encouraging neglect in conditioning yachts" . . . and "to rigidly maintain a strictly one-design class, in order to positively insure that all Lightning class races held under the auspices of this Association be to determine the skill of the skipper and to eliminate all variations in the constructions of the yachts."

While the great success of the Lightning class has more than justified the hopes of its promoters and designers, the tremendous vogue and growing popularity of the light planing racers, as well as the catamarans, pose a problem for the future. As the President of the class recently warned: "Things are good—but complacency will ruin us. The Lightning class has passed its period of greatest growth which took place in 1946 through 1950. Since then we have been losing per cent of industry at an alarming rate.

"The molded hot rods are taking the play away from us. These boats are not as seaworthy as ours—not as safe—and a considerable degree of expertness is necessary to obtain enjoyment and relaxation in them. But, they are selling because of inherent advantages in construction, ease of maintenance and transportation." The President might have added that the excitement and speed of a modern light displacement hull appeals greatly to many, especially the young and athletic.

The racing waters of Lightnings are in too many parts of North and South America to catalogue here. They are also in several European countries, in Australia, Japan, and the Hawaiian Islands. There are over three hundred chartered fleets. Boats are now built of wood, plywood, or fiber glass. Builders are many. For information on this or other class affairs, con-

LIGHTNINGS. *Photo by Morris Rosenfeld.*

sult either Miss Margaret Teske, Executive Secretary of the Association (308 Center St., South Haven, Mich.) or Martin O'Meara, Jr., International Secretary (653 Connecticut Blvd., East Hartford, Conn.). World's Championships are held in "odd years" and there are many other regional and interfleet regattas. Hemisphere Championships are held annually. New boats cost about $2900; used ones from $500 up; kits cost $800 up.

VITAL STATISTICS: L.O.A. 19′; waterline 15′10″; beam 6′6″; draft without centerboard 3″, with C.B. down 4′11″; sail area 177 sq. ft. (spinnakers used); weight 700 lbs. minimum; trailable; racing crew, three.

LITTLE BEAR. *Courtesy Sailstar Boats.*

LITTLE BEAR

Designed by Robert Baker, the Little Bear is an 11½-foot "compact" sloop (which can be converted to a catboat) made by Sailstar Boats (Division of Talman Corporation, 770 Main St., West Warwick, R.I.). There are said to be about three hundred of them in various parts of the United States. Made of fiber glass, the boats are used for day sailing, racing (including Frostbiting), and training. Price is $875 new, $650 up for old boats.

VITAL STATISTICS: L.O.A. 11½'; beam 4'9"; draft without centerboard 5", with C.B. 3'; sail area 86 sq. ft.; weight 200 lbs.; trailable.

LUDERS 16s. *Bermuda News Bureau photo by Higgs, courtesy Luders Marine Construction Co.*

LUDERS 16

Although designed by the Luders Marine Construction Company (Stamford, Conn.) in 1933 and first built by Luders in 1934, this is a modern boat, despite the fact that it is described by its waterline length. The first fleet went to the Fishers Island Yacht Club (Fishers Island, N.Y.), which wanted a boat for their juniors. The A. E. Luderses, Sr. and Jr., had figured that it would be a good idea to get away from the "chunky little boats"* usually sailed by juniors and to give the young folks a grownup-looking yacht. Their idea proved sound and after a lag of ten years or so the boats began to develop interest elsewhere, not only among juniors but by grownups. There are now about two hundred of them, chiefly on Long Island Sound and at Chicago, New Orleans, and Bermuda. Clifford Cox is Secretary of the International L 16 Association (care of Pacific Flush Tank Corporation, 4241 Ravenswood Ave., Chicago, Ill.).

The Luders 16 (26'4" over-all) is a most attractive, rakish-looking craft with its long overhangs and tall narrow rig, sometimes looking like a much larger boat far off. Though not a fast boat by modern standards, it is at its best in a stiff breeze, though its short waterline gives it a tendency to "hobbyhorse." In light airs it is a bit heavy for the sail area. Construction is of molded plywood and more recently of fiber glass. Although primarily a racer or day sailer, the L 16, with its small cabin, can be fitted out for cruising, and some have been. Luders is no longer building the boat but has turned over that job in the East to the American Boatbuilding Company (Warwick, R.I.), which is using fiber glass. The South Coast Company (Newport Beach, Calif.) has also built some of the boats. Price for the new fiber-glass model will probably be close to $6000; old ones are reported available at from $2000 to $3000.

VITAL STATISTICS: L.O.A. 26'4"; waterline 16'4"; beam 5'9"; draft (keel) 4'; sail area 207 sq. ft. (spinnaker also); weight 3200 lbs.

MAVERICK

The 14-foot Maverick is a keel Gannet, which in turn is a decked-over International 14 with a more moderate sail plan. While Uffa Fox designed the International 14, the modifications were the work of George D. O'Day. The keel version of Gannet came about because in 1959 or so, the Texas Corinthian Yacht Club (Houston, Tex.) ordered a batch of Gannets without centerboards but fitted with fin keels and promptly named the boat officially "Maverick." The boats are marketed only by the O'Day Corporation (168 Stevens St., Fall River, Mass. 02722), which also builds the boat, though a firm in Costa Mesa, California,

* Quoted from "The Luders 16," by Robert N. Bavier, Jr., in *Yachting*.

has built some recently. The hull is of fiber glass, with Styrofoam flotation.

The principal sailing areas are at Houston and Corpus Christi, Texas. There are about forty Mavericks altogether. The skipper of one of them reports on their performance as follows:

"The boats are perfect as a training boat for clubs or organizations having to sail under heavier than average winds and considerably choppy seas. We have never had one capsize even though weekly they are subjected to dozens of opportunities. Their comparative narrow beam allows extremely good beating-to-windward characteristics but lesser initial stability. Final stability is tremendous. . . . It would be debatable whether this, a keel-boat, will honestly plane—but, to some sailors who say that Lightnings, Snipes, and so forth plane, they must allow the same ability to the Maverick as they would to the British Flying 15, International 110, and so forth. To those of us who have realistically planed on such as Scows, 5-0-5, Sunfish, Thistles, and Highlanders, the Mavericks do not plane. The growth of the class has been rather slow. I believe this difficulty to lie in its relative trailer-to-water usage and lack of national promotion and advertising."

There is no class association. Price, new, is $1248, used about $950.

VITAL STATISTICS: L.O.A. 14'; waterline 14'; beam 5'4"; draft (keel) 3'; sail area 125 sq. ft. (spinnakers used); weight 400 to 450 lbs.; trailable, but not as easily as the Gannet.

MELODY

The 10-foot cat-rigged Melody is a pram dinghy, designed by W. G. Ashcroft. The boats are built by the John C. Beery Company (Aquatic Park, Berkeley, Calif.) and also by the Basin Boatcraft Company (601 Embarcadero, Oakland 6, Calif.). Built of plywood, light, cartop carried, and economical, there are now 230 of them in the San Francisco Bay area. Price is $454 to $475. Kits are $235 to $255.

VITAL STATISTICS: L.O.A. 10'; beam 4'3"; sail area 55 sq. ft.; weight 128 lbs.; trailable.

MERCURY (15-Foot)

This is the East Coast Mercury, a 15-foot sloop designed by Sparkman and Stephens and built by the Cape Cod Shipbuilding Company (Wareham, Mass.), principal source of information about the boat. It should not

MELODY. *Courtesy John C. Beery Co.*

be confused with the 18-foot Mercury (described next) which is sailed on the Pacific Coast. There are now about eight hundred of the 15-foot Mercurys, with a heavy concentration on Massachusetts Bay. First built in 1940 of wood, a new sheer line was drawn by the designer in 1952, and the boat was built of fiber glass with flotation tanks, and is now available in both keel and centerboard models. The Mercury was designed as a boat small enough and safe enough for beginners but large enough for a grown instructor and two teen-aged boys. Price is $1262 new, about $975 used, no kits.

VITAL STATISTICS: L.O.A. 15'; waterline 13'10"; beam 5'5"; draft without centerboard 8", with C.B. 3'3" (keel model 2'4"); sail area 119 sq. ft. (spinnaker used); weight—C.B. model 470 lbs., keel model 730 lbs.

MERCURY (15-Foot). *Courtesy Cape Cod Shipbuilding Co.*

MERCURY (18-Foot). *Courtesy Raymond C. Johnson.*

MERCURY (18-Foot)

The 18-foot Mercury keel sloop sailed on the Pacific Coast was designed in 1937 by Ernest Nunes (315 Main St., Sausalito, Calif.), who is also one of the builders. Another is Shelter Point Yacht Service (Sewall Mill & Manufacturing Company, P. O. Box 227, San Pedro, Calif.). The idea was to have a trailable keelboat which could be sailed with safety on the rough waters of San Francisco Bay and to utilize the then new marine plywood. Later, fiber glass was used.

METCALF. *Photo by Beckner Photo Service, courtesy W. D. Schock Co.*

The boats took the rugged going on San Francisco Bay so well that the class spread to Southern California, where the boats raced in the Catalina Channel. Later, Mercurys went to several inland lakes, to Hawaii, and to the Canal Zone. There are now 440 of them, aided by an active association: the Mercury Class Yacht Racing Association. Raymond C. Johnson is the Secretary (4661 Wishon, Fresno, Calif.). The Mercury has a displacement, not a planing hull, and is a very stable boat.

VITAL STATISTICS: L.O.A. 18′; waterline 13′; beam 5′4″; draft (keel) 3′; sail area 156 sq. ft. (no spinnaker); weight 1150 lbs.; trailable with special equipment.

METCALF

This is a 13-foot cat-rigged fiber-glass dinghy of the planing-hull type, designed by C. William Lapworth. The mast, boom, daggerboard, and rudder are anodized aluminum, and the stainless-steel shrouds are plastic-covered. The boat is equipped with buoyancy tanks. Builders are W. D. Schock (3502 S. Greenville St., Santa Ana, Calif.) and Hugh Doherty's King Harbor Boats (901 Pier Ave., Hermosa Beach, Calif.). The Metcalf is used primarily on the Pacific Coast. Price is $820.

VITAL STATISTICS: L.O.A. 13'; beam 4'5½"; draft without daggerboard 6", with D.B. down 3'; sail area 93 sq. ft.; weight 130 lbs.; trailable.

MOBJACK

There is a story that before the Revolution a British ship put into a bay on the lower Western Shore of Chesapeake Bay. The sailors, or Jack Tars, as they were often called, amused themselves by yelling and in turn being mocked by an echo peculiar to the area. The bay was promptly christened Mock Jack Bay, which was later corrupted to Mobjack Bay, now a popular cruising area on the Chesapeake. So when a new boat was designed by Roger Moorman in 1954, and built on the shore of Mobjack Bay, she became the Mobjack and her insignia became a jolly Jack Tar in blue in front of a red M.

With the flood of fiber-glass planing sloops and catboats which have been pouring into the boating market, it is not easy for any one of them to be different. I think, however, that the Mobjack has achieved that difficult feat. For one thing, her flat floor-boards are integral with the hull shell and transom, thus killing two birds with one stone: first, giving her a sealed double bottom to provide buoyancy; and second, giving her a really watertight cockpit. The cockpit floor is above the waterline even with twelve hundred pounds loading aboard.

In the fall of 1959, a year after the class got into production, thirteen Mobjacks were on the last leg of a race at the Fishing Bay Yacht Club. A wicked white squall hit them all. The skipper of the leading boat saw those behind him disappear in the wind-driven spray and dropped his sails. He stayed upright and finished first without sails. One other boat dropped sails in time and stayed upright. The other eleven boats capsized. All but one of these righted themselves without assistance and finished the race under sail, free of water. A striking photograph which we have seen, employed to advertise the righting characteristics of Mobjacks, shows the fleet apparently dodging lightning flashes. Though the boats all escaped in the real squall, we were sorry to learn on reliable authority that the lightning flashes were "dubbed in." However, that does not lessen the validity

MOBJACK. *Courtesy East Coast Boats.*

of the facts noted above. When a Mobjack capsizes, you simply stand on the centerboard, the boat rights itself and the water flows out of the scupper holes with no necessity of bailing. Her mast, sealed with flotation material, has lain parallel with the water.

Another characteristic of the Mobjack is the so-called "Syncore" type of fiber glass, developed by the boats' sole builders, the Mobjack Manufacturing Company (Gloucester, Va.). This is said to be of such strength and inflexibility that a much lighter-weight hull can be safely used than would ordinarily be the case for a boat of that size, capable of holding six men. The Mobjack cockpit is carried all the way forward, though a decking along the side makes good seating for the crew on the windward rail. To avoid impeding movement, the top of the centerboard trunk is almost flush with the cockpit floor.

The Mobjack is a planing boat and an authority writes that it "has been clocked over a measured mile at a speed exceeding 16 knots." About 130 Mobjacks are now sailing in twenty-one states and two foreign countries. They are most active, however, on the Western Shore of Chesapeake Bay, on the Potomac River (Washington, D.C.), on Long Island Sound, and on Lake Penn in central Pennsylvania. While the Mobjack Manufacturing Company, as stated, is the sole builder, East Coast Boats (P. O. Box 117, Oyster Bay, N.Y.) is national distributor. The affairs of the class are handled by the International Mobjack Association, Charles B. Raynor, Secretary (505 S. Davis Ave., Richmond, Va.).

"You ask me the reason for the class," said a member of the Potomac River Sailing Association, which uses Mobjacks. "I think it is obvious. It was designed, and is built, by a man who likes sailing more than painting. He likes to sail any time of the year, anywhere, and he designed a boat that can do just that. For the truly adventuresome, the Mobjack can be turned into a camper. There is adequate sleeping space for four under a boom tent and two can luxuriate in space. The floor is flat, so that unlike other boats, Mobjack doesn't force you to sleep rolling into the centerboard trunk."

Price is $1850 with working sails; used boats are about $1450.

VITAL STATISTICS: L.O.A. 17'; waterline 16'9"; beam 6'6"; draft without centerboard 9", with C.B. 4'; sail area 180 sq. ft. (spinnaker used); weight 460 lbs.; trailable; racing crew usually three men, 400 lbs. minimum.

MOTH. *Photo by Francis H. Gardner, courtesy Challenger Marine.*

MOTH

The Moths are a development class. With a few restrictions almost any-thing goes. The boats must be not more than 11 feet over-all, can have only one rudder, one centerboard, one mast, one boom, and one sail; the spars must be straight; the mast must be not more than 16½ feet above the deck, the boom not more than 9 feet long, and the angle between them not more than 90 degrees. On the mast there are to be markings: the top of the lower marking 12 inches above the deck, the bottom of the upper marking 15 feet above this; between these markings is the sail, which can-not extend more than 9 feet along the boom. These are the principal limita-tions. Widths can be anything and have been—from 3 feet to 5. Hulls can be of any shape which the designer can conceive, made of any material and of any weight. According to Knowles Pittman, Editor-Publisher of *One Design Yachtsman*, Moth regattas have seen catamarans (but with only one mast), scows, dinghies, arc bottoms; flat, deep, and shallow, very wide and very narrow, hull designs, but no hydrofoils so far.

At one time hiking boards were used and some boats were narrowed to 3 feet; but a majority of Moth skippers felt that the hiking board would turn them all into acrobats, so the hiking board was ruled out. Some Moths have rotating masts. One fellow tried a rotating daggerboard which could be adjusted when sailing, allowing a boat to slip to windward or leeward without seeming to change course.

The sky is almost the limit, so when we give the "vital statistics" of a Moth, we'll stick to one of the more conventional, typical models.

While Moth designers are many, the original designer and founder of the class was Captain Joel Van Sant of Elizabeth City, North Carolina, on the Pasquotank River. The original Moth was a scow-like boat of 11 feet which was built of juniper wood, so he called her the *Jumping Jupiter*. Before she was tuned up, she seemed to flit back and forth, so he called her a Moth. This was in 1929 and the sporty little craft caught the attention of other builders along the Pasquotank. Later, various yacht clubs on the Atlantic Seaboard took up the boat and the Moths spread far and wide until it is now estimated that there are three thousand in the world, including eighteen hundred to twenty-five hundred in the United States. Principal areas of sailing are in New Jersey, Florida, Holland, France, Belgium, Italy, Germany, Portugal. Captain Van Sant's *Jumping Jupiter* started something.

The National Moth Boat Association, which became in 1935 the International Moth Class Association, was organized in 1932, with Joel Van Sant as President. The Secretary (United States) is Benjamin H. B. Koons, Jr. (854 Buck Lane, Haverford, Pa.). There are many professional builders or importers, and probably hundreds of amateurs. Consult the Secretary or *Yachting's Boat Owners Buyers Guide* for their names and addresses. Prices range from $550 to $890 new, from $100 to $400 used. No kits are sold but "you can build one yourself for about $500."

VITAL STATISTICS (typical only): L.O.A. 11' (this is definite); waterline 10½' to 11'; beam 3½' to 5'; draft without daggerboard or rudder 4" to 6", with D.B. 2'7" to 3'; sail area about 72 sq. ft.; weight 72 to 125 lbs.; trailable; crew usually one, except in hard blows.

NAPLES SABOT

This is a one-design 7'10" cat-rigged pram dinghy, originated in 1946 in Naples, California. Construction is of wood or fiber glass. Designed by Mc-

NAPLES SABOT. *Photo by Beckner Photo Service, courtesy W. D. Schock Co.*

Cullough, Violette and Campbell from a plan published in *Rudder,* and often called just the Sabot, there are now at least twenty-eight hundred in the United States. Plans have also been sent "all over the world," but no one knows how many boats were built from them. Southern California is the principal sailing area. It is said to be an excellent trainer. Builders are many, including hundreds of amateurs. Consult the Secretary of the Naples Sabot One-Design Association or *Yachting's Boat Owners Buyers Guide* for their names. The Association Secretary is Mrs. Lewis J. Bedford (4952 Ensign St., San Diego 17, Calif.). The boats use leeboards instead of centerboards.

This boat has several special virtues; it is light and it is cheap: about $320 new and $100 to $225 used; kits are $200.

VITAL STATISTICS: L.O.A. 7'10"; beam 3'10"; draft without leeboard 6", with L.B. down 1'4"; sail area 38 sq. ft.; weight 95 lbs.; trailable; crew, one.

NATIONAL ONE-DESIGN

In 1936, five years after he had designed the famous Snipe, William F. Crosby designed a slightly larger centerboard sloop (17 feet instead of 15½ feet) along similar lines—the National One-Design class. The newer boat has an inboard rudder and with her genoa jib and high "aspect ratio" of mast and sail area is especially good in light winds, though not nearly as fast as some of the modern planing types. The boat sold well at first, but since World War II the demand has slowed down—probably, we should expect, due to the competition of many new boats, including planing types. The boat is long and fairly low in freeboard, with a hard chine, and has many loyal supporters. There are now about 550 to 600 of them in the United States and about 80 outside. Principal sailing waters are the Great Lakes; the Pacific Coast; Quincy, Massachusetts; Zurich, Switzerland; and Plymouth, England.

Mrs. William W. Steel, Secretary-Treasurer of the National One-Design Racing Association (331 Linden St., Winnetka, Ill.), is a principal source of information about the class.

Fiber-glass boats are built by Merl Barger (Traverse City, Mich.) and the Olympic Plastics Company (3215 17th St., Seattle 99, Wash.); plywood or planked boats by Peter A. Geis (425 McKinsey Rd., Severna Park, Md.),

NATIONAL ONE-DESIGN.
Courtesy National One-Design Racing Association.

who also sells kits, and Emmons Boats (Route 1, Box 74, Central Square, N.Y.). They are also built by many amateurs. Price is $1275 to $1525 for new boats, $300 to $600 for used.

VITAL STATISTICS: L.O.A. 17′; waterline 10′6″; beam 5′8″; draft without centerboard 20″, with C.B. 3′6″; sail area 137 sq. ft.; weight 425 lbs. (minimum 400 lbs.); trailable; crew, two or more.

NIPPER. *Courtesy Ray Greene & Co., Inc.*

NIPPER

Designed by Ray Greene, the 12-foot cat-rigged Nipper hard-chine dinghy was made of plywood for twenty years but has recently joined the fast-growing fiber-glass contingent. The cockpit "may be made" self-bailing, so evidently that feature isn't standard. The boat has won wide acceptance, as the number sailing in the United States indicates: twenty-three hundred. Ray Greene & Company (508 South Byrne Rd., Toledo 9, Ohio) is the builder and principal source of information about the Nippers. Sailing activities are principally on the Great Lakes, the East Coast, and Florida. Price with fiber-glass hull and Dacron sail is $847.50, with plywood hull and cotton sail $529.

VITAL STATISTICS: L.O.A. 12'; beam 5'2"; draft with board up 6", with board down 2'8"; sail area 100 sq. ft.; weight 250 lbs.; trailable.

NORTH HAVEN DINGHY

On the waters of Fox Island Thorofare off North Haven, Maine, a class of ancient gaff-rigged, high-sided, 14½-foot dinghies still races during the summer months where Champlain sailed in 1605. They have been doing so

NORTH HAVEN DINGHIES, the oldest of all one-design classes. *Courtesy Samuel C. Slaughter.*

since 1887, for this is the oldest sailboat racing class in the United States.*
On August 27, 1957, a fleet of twenty-eight North Haven dinghies held
their seventieth-anniversary regatta, thus establishing a record matched
by no other sailing class in America.

Dr. C. G. Weld is said to have been the designer, and Henry Calderwood,
a local carpenter, built two dinghies with spritsails in 1884. More dinghies
were soon built and in 1887 the first formal Grand Dinghy Race was run
at North Haven. By that time the boats had acquired gaff rigs. In that
first race, according to "Age before Beauty" (*Yachting*, July 1952), the
T. D., owned by Tucker Deland and sailed by Dr. Weld, had a luffing
match with Charles K. Cobb's dinghy, which enabled *Guffin*, owned by
Alfred Bowditch and sailed by Miss Ellen Hayward, to win. In view of
the fact that it wasn't until years later that the female sex won recognition
as skippers on other waters, it is interesting to note that the first winner
of the first recorded race of an essentially one-design class was won by a
girl, later to become Mrs. Henry Wheeler and the winner of many other
dinghy races.

In about 1920 John G. Alden took off the lines of the North Haven dinghy *Kidozo* and made up a construction detail drawing from which all
future dinghies were built. Our "vital statistics" are based on these drawings. To quote an authority:

"One reason for the continued popularity of the class is the manner in
which it is kept strictly one-design. No one is permitted trick gadgets, no
revolving masts, no ballast shifting (6 lbs. of lead on the long oak centerboard and 350 lbs. of inside ballast) during the 24 hours preceding a race,
no pot-leading—in short, no finagling."

In 1948 "an experienced small-boat sailor 'gal' from Connecticut, while
on vacation in the islands, bought one of the North Haven dinghies and
brought her down to Greenwich, where she entered her in the annual
Greenwich Day free-for-all race. To everyone's surprise she finished ahead
of the fleet. Last year (1951) the same boat, sailed by the new owner,
again won the Greenwich Day Race, beating every entry boat for boat,
including Hurricanes, Thistles and an L-16. You just have to hand it to
those North Haven dinghies. They must have something."

I sailed in one of them belonging to Mrs. Wheeler, a redoubtable dinghy
racer, many years ago, and I agree.

---

* In the April 1959 issue of *Yachting,* in connection with an article by Samuel C. Slaughter
("Three Score and Ten"), there appears the following Editor's Note regarding the North
Haven Yacht Club dinghy class: "Months of research by the *Yachting* editorial staff substanti-
ate the fact that this is indeed the oldest sailboat racing class in America." My thanks to Sam
Slaughter for his help on this history.

How many dinghies are left and still racing is uncertain. One authority reports that the class has dwindled to fewer than a dozen; another guesses that thirty-five are still racing. Two of the original boats are said to be still in existence, a real tribute to their builders and owners. At the seventieth-anniversary race, one well-known and well-beloved member of the summer colony, dressed in gob's togs, wore a sign reading "I learned to sail in 1893." And sail she did in her fifty-year-old dinghy with an ex-commodore of the club who had been a consistent winner before the turn of the century.

VITAL STATISTICS: L.O.A. 14′5½″; beam 4′11″; draft 13½″ with centerboard up; sail area 118 sq. ft. with two sets of reef points which are used at the direction of the race committee. Genoas are not permitted, nor are sail battens.

O'DAY 17

Uffa Fox designed this sloop in collaboration with George D. O'Day specifically with junior training in mind. The boat is the basic Day Sailer hull with an open cockpit, a larger sail area (160 sq. ft. compared to 145), and a heavier weight (620 lbs. compared to 580). Otherwise the boats are similar. This is a new class, put on the market by the O'Day Corporation (168 Stevens St., Fall River, Mass. 02722). The boat is said to be fast and will plane in strong breezes. It would seem too heavy for light wind planing. Price is $2000 compared to $1890 for the Day Sailer.

VITAL STATISTICS: L.O.A. 16′9″; waterline 16′; beam 6′3″; draft without centerboard 7″, with C.B. down 3′9″; sail area 160 sq. ft. (spinnaker used); weight 620 lbs.; trailable.

O.K. DINGHY

Designed by Knud and Axel Olsen of Denmark, the 13′1″ O.K. Dinghy is a cat-rigged, lightweight, fast planing boat with an unstayed rotating mast, intended for single-handed racing. It is a one-purpose boat and would not do for fishing or as a dinghy for a larger boat. Nor is it a boat for training. There are about fourteen hundred of these boats altogether, including eighty-five in the United States, chiefly in Seattle and the Pacific Northwest. Fleets are also forming in Los Angeles and San Francisco, California, and in Miami, Florida. Construction is ¼″ plywood or fiber glass.

There is an International O.K. Dinghy Racing Association which should be consulted for information on the class, builders, etc. Albert J. Van De-

O'DAY 17. *Courtesy O'Day Corporation.*

venter is Secretary (care of the Corinthian Yacht Club, 2116 N. 167th St., Seattle 33, Wash.). Price new $700 (plywood), $850 (fiber glass); used boats $400 to $500.

VITAL STATISTICS: L.O.A. 13′1″; waterline 12′6″; beam 4′8″; draft without centerboard 6″, with C.B. 3′; sail area 90 sq. ft. (no spinnaker); weight 158½ lbs. minimum; trailable or cartop.

O.K. DINGHY. *Courtesy International O.K. Dinghy Racing Association.*

110 CLASS

"In seven years an unorthodox one-design has grown from a local curiosity to an international class." So wrote Florence Van Wyck in the February 1946 issue of *Yachting*. The 110 story began in 1939 when the search of a then little-known young designer, C. Raymond Hunt, for a fast and inexpensive racing boat led him to the yard of George Lawley and Sons at Neponset, Massachusetts. After some experimentation with a boat called the 225, the first 110, a smaller boat, arrived at Marblehead in time for Race Week. Some yachtsmen eyed with skepticism the sleek 24-foot cigar-shaped sloop, with its very narrow plywood hull and flat bottom. When it had beaten the times of every small class boat in the fleet up to and including the Stars, the skeptics had to sit up and take notice. When they learned the cost (then slightly under $500 complete with sails) some of them went into action.

Early in 1940 a 110 was taken to the New York Motor Boat Show. That put her on the yachting map and a National 110 Class Yacht Racing Association came into being. In August 1941 the first National 110 Class Championships were held on Lake St. Clair, Michigan, with five fleets represented: Marblehead, Boston, Long Island Sound, Chicago, and Detroit. Eventually the Association became "International" and the 110s went to the Philippines, Canada, Bermuda, Mexico, Argentina, and the Canal Zone. However, the 110 is primarily an American class with an estimated 545 in the United States (out of 557 in the world), and fleets on the East Coast, Great Lakes, and Pacific Coast.

With their easily driven hulls, narrow and pointed at both ends, the 110s slice through seas which would slow up many other boats, though their flat bottoms sometimes slap the waves in a steep chop. While the low-cut genoa used to blot out the view on the lee bow, this has been remedied by a transparent window. The cockpit is small for a boat of its length and the 110 cannot be considered a family day sailer in the usual sense. But as a relatively inexpensive and fast racing boat in the days before light planing hulls took over a considerable part of the new-boat market, the 110s had a great deal to offer. There is no mistaking them, even if they didn't have 110 on their sails, though their younger sisters, the more recently developed 210s, have points of resemblance. A 110-racer has this to say about them.

"The 110 was designed to exploit the possibilities of plywood construction, both in respects to sailing ability and ease of construction. We who sail in this class feel that Mr. Hunt outdid himself. With its three hundred-pound cast-iron fin keel the 110 will not capsize (can be swamped but will

110 CLASS. *Photo by Pacific Camera.*

not sink, even without additional flotation material aboard) and does not depend entirely on crew weight to maintain proper angle of heel while sailing. Due to its shape it is very easily driven, and will outsail classes that carry more sail on smaller hulls. The hull, even when sailed and raced to the extreme, does not go out of shape, and even the first boats built are still sailing even up with the newest boats. It is easily maintained, and any part may be replaced if necessary. Attempts to build faster hulls within this class are not successful, so that the 110 gives one-design sailing in its best form, in that it is not necessary to buy a new hull every few years to keep up with the competition."

Among the leading builders of 110s are the Graves Yacht Yard (89 Front St., Marblehead, Mass.), Jesiek Brothers Shipyard (Macatawa Bay, Holland, Mich.), and Driscoll Custom Boats (San Diego, Calif.). Albert P. Peloquin is Secretary of the International 110 Class Yacht Racing Association (505 S. Birney, Bay City, Mich.). Prices are now about $2000 for new boats, $600 to $1500 for used; kits are $500 to $1000. Compared to the prices of other boats her length, these are low; Stars, for example, cost almost twice as much.

VITAL STATISTICS: L.O.A. 24'; waterline 24'; beam 4'2"; draft (keel) 2'3"; sail area 180 sq. ft. (spinnakers used); weight about 1000 lbs.; trailable.

OPTIMIST PRAM.
*Photo by
Morris Rosenfeld.*

OPTIMIST PRAM

These sprit-rigged Optimist Prams are about as simple and inexpensive as it is possible for an 8-foot children's sailboat to be. I first saw them being raced at Clearwater, Florida, by some of the tiniest children I had ever seen sailing a boat; it gave me the feeling that here was the ultimate for very young children at low expense with safety.

Ernest Green, a member of the Clearwater (Florida) Optimist Club conceived the idea of a "water-borne soapbox, or as it simply had to be called—orange crate." He took the idea to Clark Mills, a Clearwater designer and boat builder, who came up with a pram which was easily built at a low cost. Green and others of the Optimist Club took the idea to local businessmen and got many of them to sponsor and pay for boats, thus taking care of the children whose parents might not feel they could afford one. I can remember my surprise and amusement to see the small children sailing prams on the sides of which were emblazoned in large letters the name of a local marine railway, insurance agency, department store, or what have you. A child to whom a pram is assigned is responsible for its care and upkeep. At fifteen he turns it over to a younger child. The Optimist Pram idea took hold and has spread to many parts of the world. No one seems to know how many there now are, but several years ago over sixteen hundred were reported. While Florida has by far the largest number of the prams, there are said to be fleets operating in many of the states and Canada and also in England, Germany, Switzerland, Brazil, Sweden, Australia, and New Zealand. An Optimist enthusiast writes:

"The Clearwater Optimist Club . . . got behind the project, canvassed the merchants for donations, spent many hours teaching, and developed it along the lines that any child, rich or poor, could sail as long as he or she shows the desire. This is the way it is still done today, although with competition getting keener, more and more of the families who can afford it, and some who can't, are buying their children their own boats. . . .

"My wife and I are interested in children, having a seven-year-old daughter of our own, and I assure you when she reaches the age of eight she will own a pram. In my opinion the Optimist Pram teaches the children a few things I want my daughter to know, such as the initial frustrations that come with making a boat do what the others are doing, the self-confidence and satisfaction that comes when she finally does, then how to sail, how to lose, and last but most important how to win."

The Optimist Class Pram International Association is open to all children from the ages of eight to fifteen, sailing in active competition being permitted at the age of nine. Clearwater, Florida, where the idea started, is still the leading Optimist Pram community, and the association is a nonprofit affiliate of the Optimist Club of Clearwater. The Secretary is Joseph Flaherty (472 E. Shore Drive, Clearwater Beach, Fla.). A recent regatta had eighty-five young skippers in competition from many fleets. Besides many amateurs, principal builders are Ellie's Boat Works (1300 N. Betty Lane, Clearwater, Fla.) and the Halifax Marina (912 Halifax Drive, Port Orange, Fla.). The boats are of $\frac{1}{4}''$ plywood and cost $140 new, $50 to $100 used; kits with sails are $95.

VITAL STATISTICS: L.O.A. 8'; waterline 7'3"; beam 3'8"; draft without centerboard 4", with C.B. 2'8"; sail area 35 sq. ft.; weight 50 to 75 lbs.; trailable.

OSPRAYS. *Courtesy O'Day Corporation.*

OSPRAY

This is a smaller edition of a Cape Cod Knockabout: a conservative, fairly wide, 15'8" sloop with a small cuddy and plenty of cockpit room for a good-sized family or group of children. While she isn't a planing boat, she sails well. Charles Gurney designed the Cape Cod Knockabout and the

PELICAN.
Courtesy Glander Boats.

O'Day Corporation (168 Stevens St., Fall River, Mass. 02722) made this adaptation and built these "safe and sane" boats of fiber glass. There are over three hundred boats, of which the largest fleet is at Martha's Vineyard, Massachusetts. Price is $1570 for a new boat, about $1350 for used—no kits.

VITAL STATISTICS: L.O.A. 15'8"; waterline 14'8"; beam 5'11"; draft without centerboard 6", with C.B. 3'8"; sail area 125 sq. ft. (spinnaker used); weight 480 lbs.; trailable.

PELICAN

This is an 11-foot cat-rigged pram dinghy designed by Harold S. ("Dooley") Glander, made and sold by Glander Boats (11320 S.W. 208th Drive, Miami 57, Fla.). Kathlene Glander is Secretary of the Pelican Sailing Dinghy Association (5960 S.W. 78th St., Miami 43, Fla.), which was started about 1955. Seventy-seven boats were reported three years later. While most of the boats sail on Biscayne Bay, Miami, there are prams on

Buckeye Lake, Ohio, and on other waters of the East and Middle West. Pelican kits have been sold to amateur boat builders as far east as Larchmont, New York, and as far west as California. Price of boats is $495, kits $185, plans $10.

VITAL STATISTICS: L.O.A. 11′2″; beam 4′7″; draft without centerboard 6″, with board 2′6″; sail area 62 sq. ft.; weight 140 lbs.; trailable; racing crew, two.

PENGUIN

This 11½-foot cat-rigged dinghy is one of the largest classes in the world, with sixty-six hundred altogether, all but two hundred of which are in the United States. The heaviest concentrations are on Chesapeake Bay, Barnegat Bay, Long Island Sound, in Southern California and in Chicago. Otherwise they are well scattered along the coasts of the United States and the Great Lakes. The principal overseas fleets are at Rio de Janeiro and São Paulo, Brazil. Penguins have sailed on the waters of Tokyo Bay, the Canal Zone, the Philippines, and England. One of the founders of the class attributes its success to the "smartness-cost ratio."[*]

It all started on the Potomac River in the fall of 1938 when William W. Heintz, a well-known Chesapeake Bay skipper decided that he'd find a boat for his son which was inexpensive, easy to make, and as safe as a small boat could be. Joining five others with similar thoughts, the group wrote to naval architects for ideas. They liked best a design submitted by Philip L. Rhodes, showing a plywood boat with a chine and arc bottom, and a smart sheer. Six plans were bought and six boats were built in Arlington, Virginia, and other basements during the winter of 1939, with seven more recruits joining in the racing that summer. A Penguin Class Dinghy Association was formed, which later had the prefix International.

Stephen Leacock once wrote a story about parents monopolizing the children's toys at Christmastime. Apparently that is what happened in the Penguin families, even though the season was different. Some of the parents

[*] "The Penguins Get Around," an article in *Yachting* (May 1947) by the late Malcolm Lamborne, Jr., has been most helpful.

PENGUIN. *Photo by Ted Leighton-Herrmann, courtesy I.P.C.D.A.*

enjoy particularly the "novelty races" in which "big-boat skippers" compete before the club membership with boats drawn by lot and with the participants in a night-before Calcutta pool egging them on. Or they may engage in races in which each boat carries a balloon and each skipper a stick with a pin on the end—the idea of each being to cross the finish line with his balloon still inflated.

An article in *Yachting* (May 1940) by Rufus G. Smith got the Penguins under way on a national scale. Ella B. Leighton-Herrmann (1217 Fourth Rd., Baltimore 20, Md.) is Secretary of the association and will furnish a list of the current builders—of which there are at least fourteen at the time of writing. The class publishes a most interesting yearbook as well as an association handbook and *Penguin Patter*. Hulls are of plywood or fiber glass.

The Penguin class does not publish tolerances in the rules, thus helping them to become as truly one-design as possible. One interesting departure in the Penguin rules is that four different penalties for infractions are established, depending upon how seriously an infraction affects other boats in a race. Besides being one of the largest classes in the world for summer sailing, the Penguins have become a leading Frostbite class on Long Island Sound and elsewhere. Prices, new, run from $550 to $650; used, from $150 to $450.

VITAL STATISTICS: L.O.A. 11'5⅛"; waterline 11'3"; beam 4'8"; draft without board 4", with board 4'; sail area 82 sq. ft. (no spinnaker); weight 130 to 150 lbs.; trailable; racing crew, two.

PIONEER

Similar to Explorer class, except for steel centerboard or keel and a slightly higher price. See Explorer.

PIONEER. *Courtesy Sailstar Boats.*

QUAD TRAINER.
Photo by Zoltan Henczel,
courtesy Connecticut
Boat Co., Inc.

QUAD TRAINER (Redesigned Tri Trainer)

This 11-foot combination sailing-rowing dinghy, which can be cat- or sloop-rigged, was especially developed to meet requirements outlined by a workshop Committee of the Conference for National Cooperation in Aquatics (twenty-one organizations including the Red Cross, U. S. Power Squadron, Coast Guard Auxiliary, American Camping Association, National Safety Council, etc.). The Committee wanted a boat which would be economical, light, and safe, for children to sail, row, and run by outboard.

Based on the Tri Trainer design of William Atkin, but redesigned and built by the Connecticut Boat Company (154 Prospect St., Greenwich, Conn.), she is reported to have enough flotation to support three people, and to be stiff, a good sailer, rowboat, or outboard boat. Being a new boat at the time of writing, only twenty-five have been built, but it would seem to the writer that with the backing of the organizations above, it can't help being a success. The boat is of marine plywood and costs $500 cat-rigged, $400 for kit with sail.

A public education program is a major aim of those sponsoring the Quads. The Saugatuck River Power Squadron in cooperation with the Town of Westport, Connecticut, has been energetic in obtaining the support of various organizations active locally. There is now a Quad Trainer Association. Tom Hutson is the class President (5 Chelsea Court, Westport,

RAINBOW. *Courtesy Tidewater Boats, Inc.*

Conn.) and also the U. S. Power Squadron delegate to the Conference for National Cooperation in Aquatics.

VITAL STATISTICS: L.O.A. 11'3"; waterline 9'11"; beam 4'7"; draft without centerboard 5", with C.B. 2'8"; sail area 65 sq. ft. (cat), 83 sq. ft. (sloop) (spinnaker allowed); weight 164 lbs.; trailable; racing crew, two.

RAINBOW

This 24-foot round-bilged, keel sloop is a new design by Sparkman and Stephens, aimed at producing a comfortable day sailer which could be raced as a one-design class or converted to fit Midget Ocean Racing Club requirements and equipped with a galley, two berths, and a "head." The boats are built of fiber glass by Tidewater Boats (Box 1571, Annapolis, Md.). First introduced in January 1962, thirty had been sold by April and the builders expect to produce over a hundred during the first year. F. J. Wood, President of Tidewater Boats, reports that fleets have been formed in Mobile, Alabama, and on Chesapeake Bay. "We intend to have a fleet on Long Island Sound," he says, "if I have to buy them myself." By the fall of 1962 it is expected that the class will be organized.

The following, which appeared recently in *Motor Boating*, gives some background on the Rainbow and indicates where the boat is likely to fit:

"Because his organization needed just such a boat for its hire service, Jerry Wood of Annapolis Boat Rentals of Annapolis, Md., may unwittingly have filled a blank spot in the yachting picture with Rainbow, a 24 foot over-all length, fin keel, fiber-glass sloop which he has worked out with Sparkman & Stephens' designing section.

"Do you realize that, on the East Coast at least, there is no widely distributed, high performance, low cost, low maintenance, combination racing and day sailing yacht in the 20- to 24-foot range? Other than the Star, which is an out-and-out racing machine, what is there between such relatively small fry as Thistles, Rhodes 19s, Highlanders, O'Day Sailers, Lightnings, etc., and the larger, more expensive 210s, Herreshoff S boats, Atlantics, International One-Designs and the like? Remember, we're not talking about classes which are basically local in nature; we're discussing those which have fleets in more than one area.

"What keel boat is there to which juniors can graduate after having cut their sailing teeth in Beetle Cats, Blue Jays, Lido 14s, Snowbirds and the innumerable dinghy classes—a boat which Dad will buy for Billy or Betty because, when it isn't being raced and enjoyed by the children, it can be used by the whole family for day sailing? . . . Rainbow, of course, may not be the answer but at least it is a step in the right direction and may stimulate other designs in the currently vacant bracket."

F. J. Wood of Tidewater Boats points out in a letter to us that so far the racing and private-use demand has exceeded by ten times the demand for Rainbows as a rental boat. The price is very reasonable, it would seem: $2798 including Dacron sails.

VITAL STATISTICS: L.O.A. 24′; waterline 17′3″; beam 6′3″; draft (keel) 3′6″; sail area 216 sq. ft. (spinnaker used).

RAVEN

Designed by Roger McAleer and starting as a 24-foot plywood, centerboard sloop, the boat is now made of fiber glass by the Cape Cod Shipbuilding Company (Wareham, Mass.). The boat proved fast and turned in very good performances in *Yachting's* One-of-a-Kind Regattas, finishing third, boat for boat, in 1954, eighth in 1959. There are now about three hundred Ravens, with their principal sailing areas at Miami, Detroit, Marblehead, and St. Louis. There is also a fleet on Long Island Sound. Robert Kerr, Jr. (6081 12th St., Detroit, Mich.) is Secretary of the Raven Class Association. Price is $3500 new, $2000 to $2500 old.

VITAL STATISTICS: L.O.A. 24'2"; waterline 21'7"; beam 7'; draft without centerboard 7", with C.B. 5'4"; sail area 300 sq. ft. (spinnaker used); weight 1000 lbs.; trailable; racing crew allowed, four.

REBEL

The 16-foot Rebel-class centerboard sloop was designed by Ray Greene and is built by his company (508 S. Byrne St., Toledo, Ohio). *Yachting's Boat Owners Buyers Guide* reports 368 registered owners in various parts of the country, but Ray Greene says there are sixteen hundred boats in the United States and three hundred more in the world. So it is one of the larger classes of its type. The American boats are principally on the Great Lakes, in Florida, and scattered along the East Coast. The Secretary-Treasurer of the National Rebel Class Association is Thomas F. Ehman (1205 Cascade Lane, Ypsilanti, Mich.). This would appear to be one of a number of similar boats, attractive, and a good sailer.

Her principal feature is foam flotation underneath a cockpit floor which is an integral part of the fiber-glass hull and self-bailing. To reduce maintenance costs, all wood has been eliminated from the cockpit and elsewhere. The Rebel also has foam flotation material inside the aluminum mast. All these features, of course, add to safety. The boats are raced actively and are also used for camp training and, extensively, for military recreation. Price is $1669.

VITAL STATISTICS: L.O.A. 16'; beam 5'6"; draft without centerboard 6", with C.B. 3'; sail area 166 sq. ft. (no spinnaker); weight 700 lbs. minimum; trailable.

RAVEN. *Courtesy Cape Cod Shipbuilding Co.*

REBEL. *Courtesy Ray Green & Co., Inc.*

RESOLUTE. *Courtesy A. J. Harris, Jr.*

RESOLUTE

This class of 27½-foot keel sloops was designed in 1956 by William H. Tripp, Jr. While they are frequently seen on western Long Island Sound, where thirteen of them constitute the Manhasset Bay fleet, these are the only active boats except for some in Canada. No new ones are being built. Construction is of wood. They are among the prettiest boats on the Sound. Secretary of the association is Howard Seymour (17 State St., New York 4, N.Y.). Price new would be about $6500.

VITAL STATISTICS: L.O.A. 27'7"; waterline 18'; beam 6'4"; draft 4'7"; sail area 329 sq. ft. (spinnaker allowed).

RHODES BANTAM

Designed by Philip L. Rhodes shortly after World War II, the 14-foot Rhodes Bantam sloop is without decking and thus is light for her size, with plenty of room. It is a good planer. There are now about seven hundred in the United States and three hundred elsewhere in the world, including fifty in Sweden. The New York lakes, the northern Midwest, Florida, and Canada are the principal sailing areas. She seems to be a boat which is small enough and stable enough for juniors and large enough for their parents. For extra speed in a breeze, there are hiking straps along the centerboard box with a hiking stick for tiller extension. Material is usually of plywood, though some boats use fiber glass. Builders include the Gibbs Boat Company (Erie, Mich.), Emmons Boats (Route 1, Box 74, Central Square, N.Y.), Wright-Built Boat Company (Dundee, N.Y.). Price is about $700 in plywood, $985 in fiber glass; used boats cost $400, kits $450.

L. E. Bailey (4 Sunset Way, Binghamton, N.Y.) is Secretary of the Rhodes Bantam Class Association. "Glowing as it may sound," he writes, "the Bantam is a great little boat."

VITAL STATISTICS: L.O.A. 14'; waterline 13'11"; beam 5'6¼"; draft without centerboard 5½", with C.B. 4'2"; sail area 125 sq. ft. (spinnaker used); weight 325 lbs.; trailable; racing crew, two.

RHODES 18

This 18-foot sloop was designed by Philip L. Rhodes and is built now in fiber glass by the Cape Cod Shipbuilding Company (Wareham, Mass.). There are five hundred to six hundred of them, chiefly on western Long Island Sound, in the Cape Cod area, in Maine, and in Caracas, Venezuela. Donald McDonald (32 Bramble Ave., Riverside, Conn.) is Secretary of the International Rhodes 18 Racing Association. The boat has been going for some time with a wooden hull and is a good all-around family boat. It is made either with a keel or centerboard. Price new is $2000 to $2200; used $600 to $1800.

RHODES BANTAM. *Lutz Photo, courtesy Leslie Bailey.*

VITAL STATISTICS: L.O.A. 18′; waterline 16′; beam 6′3″; draft without centerboard 7″, with C.B. 4′, with keel 2′8″; sail area 162 sq. ft. (spinnaker used); weight 800 lbs. with centerboard, 920 lbs. with keel; trailable; racing crew, three.

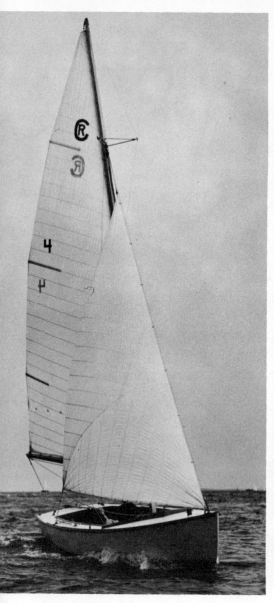

RHODES 18. *Courtesy Rhodes 18 Racing Association.*

RHODES 19. *Courtesy O'Day Corporation.*

RHODES 19

The Rhodes 19 sloop was originally designed with a centerboard by Philip L. Rhodes as the Hurricane class, of molded plywood. Later the Southern Massachusetts Yacht Racing Association asked Palmer Scott to design a keel version of the same hull with a cuddy. This was done in collaboration with Rhodes and the class became known as the Smyra. In 1959 the boats were molded in fiber glass and the class became the Rhodes 19. In 1960 a centerboard model of the boat was again established. In the various versions there are now reported to be seven hundred to eight hundred scattered among the major yachting centers of the United States—on the East Coast, Gulf Coast, West Coast, and the Great Lakes, about 70 per cent of them keelboats. There are more than one hundred boats (almost all keelboats) presently sailing on western Long Island Sound (New York and Connecticut). Overhang is small and thus the waterline length is long for a 19-footer. The small cuddy makes possible overnight trips.

The O'Day Corporation (168 Stevens St., Fall River, Mass. 02722) now builds and sells the Rhodes 19. Frederick P. Warne (8 Larkspur Lane, Loudon Woods, Rye, N.Y.) is President of the Rhodes 19 Class Association at the time of writing. Price for the new boat is $2535; used ones sell at $1800 to $2500.

VITAL STATISTICS: L.O.A. 19'2"; waterline 17'9"; beam 7'; draft (keel model) 3'3"; draft (centerboard model) without board 10", with board 4'11"; sail area 175 sq. ft. (spinnaker used); weight (keel model) 1355 lbs., (centerboard model) 1030 lbs.; the boat can be trailed; racing crew, two or more.

ROSS 13

This 13-foot sloop is a California class which was designed by Helen Ross "to give," as a local authority puts it, "the thrills of the International 14 at the lowest possible cost. The class is a semi-open or development one, to give owners the chance to experiment with rudder, centerboard, mast location, etc., but by restricting the sail plan and shape of the hull to eliminate the cost of keeping up with major expensive changes."

The boat is nearly a foot narrower than the International 14 and is lighter in weight, but it has a much smaller sail area. Being only 4'7" wide and a planing type, she relies a great deal on human ballast for stability. There are about fifty in the class, with the principal sailing area Pomona, California. Richard Collins (1244 N. College Ave., Claremont, Calif.) is the Ross 13 Class Secretary. Builders are the Granite Company Boat Division (604 S. Garey, Pomona, Calif.) and S. and H. Sailboats (3046 S. Bristol St., Santa Ana, Calif.). Price is $695 new, $500 to $600 for used boats, $200 for kits.

VITAL STATISTICS: L.O.A. 13'2"; waterline 12'3"; beam 4'7"; draft without centerboard 4", with C.B. 3'2"; sail area 110 sq. ft. (spinnaker used); weight 180 lbs.; trailable; racing crew, two.

ROSS 13. *Courtesy Richard Collins.*

S CLASS

In these days when so many racing classes are short-lived, the history of the Herreshoff-designed S Class sloop is extraordinary. First constructed in 1919 by the Herreshoff Manufacturing Company of Bristol, Rhode Island, they continued to be built until 1930, most of them by Herreshoff and a few by Lawley—both firms noted for the quality of their work. How well the S boats have demonstrated that! While none have been built in recent years, the class remains vigorous in its various fleets and the unparalleled quality of construction and materials seem to have resulted in an almost ageless boat. The boats have planked wooden hulls, and the Herreshoff manual says they were built to last a lifetime. The first boat is still in beautiful condition and racing actively.

An authority writes:[*] "The boats were well designed, sturdily built and beautifully maintained. They were of heavy displacement, but extremely fast in light airs and, at the same time, seaworthy when the going was rough. Competition was unusually keen and interest was maintained at a high pitch because the hulls were strictly one-design and rigid rules had been drawn to restrain those who might be tempted to alter sail plan, spars or weight to their own advantage." The cockpit is large enough for six or more adults and the cabin is adequate for cruising. You can always recognize an S boat by the tilt aft of the upper part of the mast.

There are now thirty-eight boats in the Narragansett Bay fleet, twenty-five in the western Long Island Sound fleet, and some on Chesapeake Bay and at Hawaii—out of one hundred still racing, thanks to the enthusiasm of James Benfield and other devoted S skippers. Herbert L. Jamison, Jr., is Secretary of the Western Long Island Sound Herreshoff S Class (Forest Ave., Rye, N.Y.). The Cape Cod Shipbuilding Company (Wareham, Mass.) now has the building rights and plans. While no new boats have been built recently, it is reported that used ones can be obtained for $3000 to $3800.

VITAL STATISTICS: L.O.A. 27′6″; waterline 20′6″; beam 7′2″; draft (keel) 4′9″; sail area 426 sq. ft. (spinnaker used).

SAILFISH and SUNFISH

Soon after World War II two young men, Alexander ("Al") Bryan and Cortland ("Cort") Heyniger, had an idea which was destined to start a revolution in sailing. In their garage in Waterbury, Connecticut, they began the construction of a type of sailboat which later came to be described as a "boardboat," a sailing surfboard or bathing-suit boat. The two men

[*] "Reviving the S Class," by James W. Benfield, *Yachting*, May 1945.

S CLASS. *Photo by Morris Rosenfeld, courtesy William Keys.*

SAILFISH. *Courtesy Alcort, Inc.*

organized the firm of Alcort, Inc. (P. O. Box 1345, Waterbury, Conn.), and sold their boats under the trade-mark name of Sailfish. Later, they added two Super Sailfishes and a Sunfish. As the idea spread rapidly, other builders got into the act with boats under other names, some incorrectly called Sailfish by the public—no more correct, as Bill Robinson has pointed out,[*] than calling all sedans Fords. D. Bruce Connolly of Alcort is Secretary of the Sailfish-Sunfish class.

As a great many boardboats are homemade or built from kits which may or may not result in boats, no one knows how many there are. Alcort was reported to have sold 14,000 Sailfish or Sunfish by the end of 1959 and they say that the number in the world now is 25,000. It should be clear, therefore, that when we discuss in this book the number of boats in the various sailboat classes and explain that the Snipes, for example, are the largest class in the world, we are not including Sailfish, Sunfish, or any other class of boardboats.

In this section we are confining ourselves to the best-known, the Alcort Sailfish and Sunfish, though there are others in this growing market.

The Sailfish and the larger Super Sailfishes and the Sunfish all have lateen sails. Bathing suits are the accepted costumes for these wet but "self-bailing" boardboats, and youth is a considerable asset. "Paradoxically," Bill Robinson says, "despite their propensity for dumping people in the water and getting them wet even when they don't capsize, boardboats tend to inspire confidence in the neophyte, and they make an excellent trainer in the basics of handling a boat under sail.

"A novice gets aboard one already prepared to get wet and to get dumped, and there is no more fear about capsizing in one than in falling off a rubber mat in a pool"—provided the boat doesn't get carried out to sea, and provided the air and water aren't too cold. "One fanatic on the Shrewsbury [River] sails a Sailfish all winter clad in a skin-diver suit, but he has not, as yet, developed any following cult."

The boardboats accelerate rapidly and when they get planing it takes considerable agility to manage them. The smaller Sailfish usually takes a crew of one, but the larger Mark II or Sunfish often take two or three. These larger boats have shallow foot wells in place of cockpits. In the Sailfish the "cockpit" may be a nonskid painted area.

[*] "Boardboat Jamboree," by William W. Robinson, *Yachting*, December 1959.

SUNFISH. *Courtesy Alcort, Inc.*

VITAL STATISTICS: *Sailfish and Sunfish Types.*

	L.O.A.	Beam	Sail Area Sq. Ft.	Hull Weight Lbs.	Crew Capacity Lbs.	1 Hull Material	Prices
Sailfish							
Standard	11′7½″	2′7½″	65	82	300	Plwd. & F.G.	$297
Super	13′7″	2′11½″	75	102	100	Plwd. & F.G.	334
Super Mark II	13′7″*	2′11½″*	75	98	400	All F.G.	394
Sunfish							
Plywood	13′7½″	3′11½″	75	142	500	Plwd. & F.G.	395
Fiber glass	13′10″	4′½″	75	139	500	All F.G.	467
						Kits are $217 to $268.	

* Exclusive of flange

SEA SHELL. *Photo by Edward Saxe Studio, courtesy Roberts Industries.*

SEA SHELL

This is an 8-foot cat-rigged, plywood dinghy with a daggerboard. One authority says there are twenty-five hundred of them, another five thousand. By either count it is a large class. Mrs. W. R. Ledbury is Secretary of the Sea Shell Class Association (Pine Orchard, Conn.). Boats are said to be common on Long Island Sound and Narragansett Bay and on "all lakes and rivers." Roberts Industries (105 Post Rd., Branford, Conn.) is a leading builder. Price is $280 to $300 new, used $100 to $150, kits $125 to $150.

VITAL STATISTICS: L.O.A. 7′10½″; waterline 6′6¾″; beam 4′1¼″; draft without board 6″, with board 1′11¼″; sail area 41 sq. ft.; weight 65 lbs.; trailable or cartop.

SEMINOLE. *Photo by Yeatman King, courtesy Glander Boats.*

SEMINOLE

This is a new 14-foot fiber-glass sloop, designed and built by Glander Boats (5960 S.W. 78th St., South Miami 43, Fla.). It has a hard-chine, V bottom, and is said to be stiff and a good sailer. The boat is decked over and attractive. It is said to have been built as a rival of the Blue Jay class. Besides being sailed on Biscayne Bay, Miami, the boats have gone to South America and have been used by the U. S. Coast Guard for recreation. Price is $785 at Miami, including Dacron sails.

VITAL STATISTICS: L.O.A. 13′9″; beam 4′7″; draft without dagger-board 6″, with board 2′6″; sail area 72 sq. ft.

SHAMROCKS. *Courtesy Dr. William A. Bellamy.*

SHAMROCK

The Shamrock is an 11½-foot cat-rigged plywood dinghy designed in 1946 by William B. Nichols and built by his company (1401 Middleharbor Rd., Oakland, Calif.). There are sixty of them, chiefly in the San Francisco Bay area, where they are now raced actively by the Belvedere Sailing Society. Dr. William A. Bellamy (450 Sutter St., San Francisco 8, Calif.) is the Fleet Captain and recommends the Shamrocks highly. Price is $795 new, used $350.

VITAL STATISTICS: L.O.A. 11'7"; waterline 11'4½"; beam 4'7"; draft without board 7", with board 3'2"; sail area 72 sq. ft. (no spinnaker); weight 160 lbs.; trailable; racing crew, two.

SHIELDS CLASS

"Shields Does It Again" might well have been the title of an article which appeared in the New York *Times* on January 18, 1962. For it was then announced that the man who founded the famous International One Design Class in 1936 was to be the founder of a new racing class which might well turn out to be a "farm class" for the earlier boats.

"The creation of a one-design class that may become important in local, national, and international sailing competition," said the *Times,* "has been made possible through a gift to two maritime colleges by Cornelius Shields, Sr. of Larchmont, N.Y. The United States Merchant Marine Academy (Kings Point, Long Island, N.Y.) and the United States Coast Guard Academy (New London, Conn.) were the recipients of a gift to be applied towards the design and construction of twelve fiber-glass sloops, 30'2½" in overall length, to be designed by Sparkman and Stephens."

SHIELDS CLASS. *Courtesy Sparkman and Stephens.*

In addition to being used in intercollegiate competition, the yachts will be available for North American Championships when held on Long Island Sound and in the regular Yacht Racing Association of Long Island Sound Championships. Shields was the first winner (1952) of the Mallory Cup, representing the men's North American Sailing Championships, as well as one of the most noted skippers in American yachting history. At the suggestion of the cadets of the two academies the class was named the Shields class. Recently released designs show a beautiful keelboat with a tall rig and graceful lines. Stringent one-design regulations will be put into effect. Sails will be drawn by lot; new mainsails and spinnakers will be permitted only every three years, jibs every two years. Haul-outs will be limited. Besides the twelve gift boats, Shields will have one of his own. The builder is now the Sailboat Division of the Chris-Craft Corporation (Pompano Beach, Fla. 33061), who purchased the rights to the Shields class from Cape Cod Shipbuilding Company in 1964.

VITAL STATISTICS: L.O.A. 30'2½"; waterline 20'; beam 6'4"; draft (keel) 4'9"; sail area 382 sq. ft. (spinnaker used); weight 4200 to 4500 lbs.

SIX METER

While the Six Meter class has been to a considerable extent superseded by the 5.5 Meter Class on account of the expense, a number of them are still sailing and the class has too important a history to be omitted here. Like the other "meter boats" this is a development class, first launched in the United States in 1921 after many years of racing in European waters. Of the first four boats built for American use, two were designed by W. Starling Burgess and two by William Gardner. The boats were planned for international competition and some of our greatest racing sailors, including C. Sherman Hoyt, Cornelius Shields, and Briggs Cunningham, were active in the class.

The Seawanhaka Corinthian Yacht Club of Oyster Bay, New York, was the leader in sponsoring the Sixes and cooperated with four British clubs in planning for team races. While boats designed by Clinton H. Crane, such as *Lanai*, dominated early competition in the class, Sixes designed by Olin J. Stephens and A. E. Luders, Jr., came later into the picture. International competition was not limited to contests with the English; there were also races with crews from Cuba, Bermuda, Scotland, and Norway. The boats have always been considered primarily an international class. The famous Seawanhaka Cup was raced for by Six Meters as early as 1922.

During their history the Six Meter boats, being a development class under the International Rule, have undergone considerable change. "In the early days," says Bill Taylor,[*] "designers experimented with wide boats, narrow boats, deep boats, centerboard boats, long boats, short boats, light boats and heavy boats. Gradually they evolved a type from which only minor variations were considered worth experimenting with."

VITAL STATISTICS are so varied as to make an attempt to list all of them meaningless. The latest boats were in the general range of L.O.A. 37'; waterline 23'9"; beam 6'; draft 5'5"; sail area 460 sq. ft.; displacement 9500 lbs.

[*] "The 'Sixes' Sail Again," by William H. Taylor, *Yachting*, June 1947—to which I owe much of the material for this section.

SIX METER. *Booz Photos.*

SNIPE. *Courtesy Gerber's Boat Works.*

SNIPE

In March 1931 at Sarasota, Florida, the West Coast Racing Association had a meeting. It was decided that the time was ripe for a small racing sailboat which "could be carried about the State on a trailer the same as outboard race boats had been handled." The class was to be known as the Trailer class, a more distinctive name then than it is today when trailing sailboats has become standard procedure. The boat was to be not over 16 feet nor carry over 100 square feet of sail. William F. Crosby of *Rudder* was present and promised to get up the design of such a boat and publish it in his magazine. In the July 1931 issue appeared the plans of a Trailer-class boat 15½ feet long. It was to be known as Snipe, for it was the custom of this pioneer yachting publication to call all *Rudder* sailboats after sea birds. This was the beginning of what was to become the largest class of racing sailboats in the world.

Demands for the plans became so great that copies of the original *Rudder* article were soon out of print. Fourteen-year-old Jimmy Brown of Pass Christian, Mississippi, built the first one with the help of his father, and when the Snipe Class International Racing Association (SCIRA) was formed in November 1932, Jimmy's boat was given the racing number 1. Since then over 13,500 numbers have been issued. A Snipe authority estimates that about 3000 of these—or the boats they represented—have gone, and that there are now about 10,500 Snipes sailing, of which 7500 are active in the United States. There are now 538 fleets in twenty-seven foreign countries, not counting those now behind the Iron Curtain. At the 30th Anniversary World Snipe Championship in 1961 at the American Yacht Club, Rye, New York, one representative each (as allowed) from eighteen different countries raced their Snipes on Long Island Sound. The countries represented, in the order in which they finished, were: Brazil, the United States, Spain, Switzerland, the Bahamas, Norway, Bermuda, Argentina, Belgium, Denmark, France, England, Japan, Canada, British Guiana, Sweden, Italy, and Uruguay. Due to the effect of winds generated by Hurricane Esther, which fortunately missed the Sound, the going was very rough, resulting in a few mishaps, though on the whole the Snipes took it well.

Social contacts among people of many nations are among the many pleasant features of Snipe racing, resulting in some amusing episodes. William F. Crosby describes one of these.* The occasion was an invitation to British yachtsmen to race their Snipes in Northern Ireland, which ended as follows:

"Weather permitting, the Celtic twilight will be turned on at 11 P.M. each evening and the local Banshee is a very fine mezzo-soprano. Apart from local color we have many interesting and primitive customs; some of us sail our Snipes sharp end first, as we think they go faster that way; and others find the metal centerplate so handy for cutting other people's moorings that they carry it down even when going to windward. All our protests are, of course, settled with shillelaghs in front of the clubhouse, but visitors will be given choice of weapons, and their Executors may appeal to the Y.R.A."

---

* "The Snipe Story," by William F. Crosby, *Yachting*, June 1953.

SNOWBIRD. *Photo by Beckner Photo Service, courtesy W. D. Schock Co.*

The Snipe is a hard-chine sloop which will plane under certain conditions, though its weight and shape does not enable it to plane as do the modern types of planing hulls. Although it is a one-design class, it has developed considerably over the years and has been subject to much experimentation. The boom, for instance, is set high. Hulls are of wood planking, plywood-covered fiber glass, or molded fiber glass. An unusual feature for a boat of its size: spinnakers are not carried. The Secretary of SCIRA is Birney Mills (655 Weber Ave., Akron 3, Ohio). Ask him for the names of the many builders. Price range, new, is from about $1000 to $1450, used $500, kits $160 to $200.

VITAL STATISTICS: L.O.A. 15'6"; waterline 13'6"; beam 5'; draft without board 6", with C.B. 3'3½"; sail area 116 sq. ft. (no spinnakers); weight 440 lbs.; trailable; racing crew, two.

SNOWBIRD

This is a 12-foot cat-rigged dinghy designed and built by the W. D. Schock Company (3502 S. Greenville St., Santa Ana, Calif.). It is said to be one of the largest racing classes in the Pacific Southwest. Boats are of plywood or fiber glass with flotation tanks. Price with Dacron sails is $755.

VITAL STATISTICS: L.O.A. 12'; beam 4'6"; draft without daggerboard 4½", with D.B. 3'; sail area 81 sq. ft.; weight 126 lbs.

SOUTHEASTER

The 16-foot sloop Southeaster was designed in 1944 by Robert Halsey at Sarasota, Florida. It is raced primarily on Biscayne Bay, Miami. The idea was to provide a low-cost, easily built, flat-bottomed scow-like boat which would plane. The boat is variously called "Poor Man's Planer," "Toboggan with Sail," and "Sail on a Water-Ski." With its blunt bow the boat is wet and is lacking in stability, but it is said to provide exciting sailing. Douglas A. Baker (3891 Shipping Ave., Miami, Fla.) makes them—of plywood. Price is $600 to $900 new, $450 to $700 used, kits $325.

VITAL STATISTICS: L.O.A. 16'; waterline 13'6"; beam 5'5"; draft without board 4", with board 3'4"; sail area 135 sq. ft. (no spinnaker); weight 300 lbs. minimum; trailable; racing crew, two.

SOUTHEASTER. *Photo by Frank Zagarino, commodore of Southeaster Sailing Association.*

SPRITE.
*Courtesy O'Day
Corporation.*

SPRITE

The 10-foot sloop Sprite came about primarily as a result of the efforts of Dr. Norris Hoyt of St. George's School, Newport, Rhode Island, to create a small junior trainer. Dr. Hoyt enlisted the aid of naval architect Robert Baker and George O'Day and the boat was created of fiber glass. The O'Day Corporation (168 Stevens St., Fall River, Mass. 02722) is the builder and there are now over eleven hundred boats in about thirty states, where they are often adopted as junior trainers. The mast can be moved and the rig changed to that of a cat. Price is $617 new, $510 used, no kits.

VITAL STATISTICS: L.O.A. 10'2"; waterline 9'4"; beam 4'9"; draft without board 3", with board 3'5"; sail area 63 sq. ft. (spinnaker used); weight 150 lbs.

STAR

Although the famous Star class celebrated its fiftieth birthday in 1961, the real story of the Stars began fifty-five years earlier when an 18-foot class called Bug was designed in the office of William Gardner. These boats had hulls much like those which the Stars were to have. But they were considered too small and too wet, so George A. ("Pop") Corry, who had been interested in the Bugs, went to Gardner to ask for a larger version. It was Francis Sweisguth, in Gardner's office, who made the original Star drawings, and Pop Corry is called the "Father of the Stars"—the first international racing class ever to have reached its fiftieth birthday. (The North Haven Dinghies which reached their seventy-fifth birthday in 1962 are not an international class.)

It is generally agreed that the success of the Stars has been due to two things: first, to the boat itself, and second, to the remarkably efficient International Star Class Yacht Racing Association. Both seem to inspire unusual loyalty. Just as Pop was Father of the Stars, George W. Elder, who bought a Star in 1914, became Father of the class association launched at the Hotel Astor, New York, on January 22, 1922. This became a model for many other associations. Without the ISCYRA there would probably be no Stars racing today. While Corry was the first President of ISCYRA, it was Elder, taking over the Presidency in 1924, who really "put over" both the Star class and the association. His book, *Forty Years among the Stars*, written by Elder just before he died in 1954, is a classic and most entertaining to read. (Copies are available at the ISCYRA office, 51 E. 42nd St., New York 17, N.Y.)

With more than fifty years of successful racing and over forty-six hundred boats in thirty-two countries, backed by a strong organization and first chosen of the Olympic classes, the Stars are probably the best known and most influential one-design class in the world. The 1962 "log" lists 218 fleets, of which seventy are in the United States, including four in the Hawaiian Islands. There are fleets at Moscow and Leningrad, U.S.S.R. To everyone's surprise a Russian Star skipper won the Olympic Gold Medal in 1960.

While the Star hulls with their hard chine, long overhangs, and low freeboard have remained unchanged over the years, wide latitude has been allowed in their staying and rigging. Thus, the Stars have been called a semidevelopment class, not 100 per cent one-design, but with far less opportunity for variation then, for example, a 6 Meter. In the beginning a short mast carried a long gaff almost parallel to it, called a sliding gunter rig. Later a short Marconi rig was used, and now the tall Marconi rig, which makes the boat sporty to look at and exciting to sail. It is not a

STAR. *Photo by R. C. Veit, courtesy Durward Knowles.*

"family boat"—it is too low and wet, has too large a sail area and too small a cockpit for that—but a first-class keel racing machine of the displacement type with a modern rig and equipment. It is a spectacular boat to sail or to watch and it is not unusual for both members of the crew to be completely outside the boat, "clinging like monkeys to the topsides" as someone put it. Stars are kept out of water between races and their hulls shine like glass.

Recently I asked Paul H. Smart, able Executive President of the ISCYRA, if the tremendous vogue of light planing hulls had not had an unfavorable effect on Star-class development.

"Not at all," said he, and C. Stanley Ogilvy, Vice-President of ISCYRA and noted Star sailor, agreed. "More new Stars were built in 1961 than in any one year in Star history—185 of them. The planing hulls don't compete with the Stars, they are entirely different kinds of boats." Also we imagine that few planing hulls would have survived as long as the Stars. While Number 1 Star was broken up after some years on the grounds of the Manhasset Bay Yacht Club and a plaque at the bar now commemorates her, Warren Ransome of Rye, New York, still uses Star Number 7 (*Ceti*) as a day sailer. Star Number 8, built in 1912, took part in the fiftieth-anniversary regatta at Rye, New York, on May 30, 1961.

As Stanley Ogilvy has pointed out,* superiority in Star sailing is well distributed among many areas and countries, as International records show. See the association "log" for a list of the many Star builders. Prices are now from $3400 to $3900 for a new Star.

VITAL STATISTICS: L.O.A. 22'9"; waterline 15'6"; beam 5'8"; draft (keel) 3'4"; sail area 281 sq. ft.; trailable with special trailer; racing crew, two.

TALLSTAR

Designed by Robert Baker, the 14-foot Tallstar fiber-glass sloop is built and sold by Sailstar Boats (West Warwick, R.I.). A feature is the so-called "Kickerpit," an outboard-motor well which makes unnecessary any outward evidence that the skipper ever has to use outboard power. The builder describes a transom outboard bracket as "unsightly." I suspect that a more weighty objection would be one of *status*. A 210 Class champion once

* "50 Years of Stars," by C. Stanley Ogilvy, *Motor Boating*, May 1961. I owe much to this article and to Messrs. Smart and Ogilvy in person for their help on this section, though I am responsible for all unquoted opinions.

TALLSTAR. *Courtesy Sailstar Boats.*

looked with scorn at my suggestion that if he and his class mates carried an outboard on Long Island Sound they might get home to supper more promptly after a race. I gathered that he would prefer to spend all evening drifting around, though he would accept a tow with someone else providing the power.

The Tallstar has a large, roomy cockpit which can be obtained self-bailing if desired. Spars are aluminum, as are the centerboard and rudder blade, both the pivoting type. The boom provides for roller reefing. Under favorable conditions the boat will plane. There are reported to be about two hundred of these boats in the United States. Pat Gammino (12 Seaview Ave., Edgewood, R.I.) is class Secretary.

VITAL STATISTICS: L.O.A. 14′; beam 5′9½″; draft without centerboard 6″, with C.B. 3′9″; sail area 122 sq. ft. (spinnaker used); weight 450 lbs.; trailable.

TEAL

The 15½-foot sloop Teal, designed by Hindriks Bulthuis, is a duplicate in fiber glass of a popular small B M class in the Netherlands, intended for a combination family day sailer and class racing boat. There are about 115 of them in the United States. A standard feature is a mechanically operated centerboard pennant, by means of a capstan pivoting on the mast support. Unlike many other boats, the Teal's deck is nonskid. Enough Styrofoam to support eight hundred pounds is installed under the fiber-glass seats. The mast is hinged and self-locking. The Teal has a round bilge and is a very pretty boat. The U. S. Teal-class Secretary is Harold Bob Burns(14232 Ardmore, Detroit 27, Mich.).

The Teal is built by Anchor Reinforced Plastics, Inc. (1831 E. 9 Mile Rd., Hazel Park, Mich.). The price is $1375 with Dacron sails; used boats can be bought for $1075.

VITAL STATISTICS: L.O.A 15′5″; waterline 14′2″; beam 5′; draft without centerboard 10″, with C.B. 3′; sail area 122 sq. ft. (spinnaker used); weight 475 lbs.; trailable.

TEAL. *Courtesy Anchor Reinforced Plastics.*

TECH DINGHY. *Courtesy American Boatbuilding Corp.*

TECH DINGHY

This is a 12½-foot cat-rigged dinghy designed by the Massachusetts Institute of Technology for racing on the Charles River (Cambridge and Boston). It is widely used in Eastern intercollegiate racing and there are about eight hundred in the United States, one hundred elsewhere. The American Boatbuilding Corporation (Warwick, R.I.) makes them. Price is about $850 for new boats (fiber glass), $500 for used.

VITAL STATISTICS: L.O.A. 12′6″; beam 5′; draft without centerboard 8″, with C.B. 2′10″; sail area 72 sq. ft. (no spinnaker); weight 250 lbs.; trailable.

THIRTIES—The New York Yacht Club "Thirties"

One of the most famous one-design racing classes ever to round a mark, the "New York Thirties" race no more as a class. But for many years during the early part of this century the interest they created and the caliber of men who raced them placed these handsome sloops in a class by themselves. Large boats by present standards, they were once considered the smallest boats which would qualify an owner to join a New York Yacht Club cruise. Though only a few are still sailing, the story of the Thirties belongs in any account of the sailboat classes of North America.

On November 16, 1904, three members of the New York Yacht Club—William Butler Duncan, Jr., Addison G. Hanan, and Newbury D. Lawton—acting on behalf of a group of Club members, signed a contract with the Herreshoff Manufacturing Company for the construction of a new one-design racing class to be known as the New York Yacht Club Thirty-Foot Class. For some years racing men in the Club had been considering the idea of a "small" class which would not be restricted to the few who could afford to build and maintain the large boats—some over 100 feet long—which had dominated Club racing. The new class was to be 43½ feet in over-all length and 30 feet on the waterline.

Enthusiasm grew and by February 1905 eighteen boats had been ordered, with a list of owners well known in the yachting, social, and financial worlds. By the end of that year fifty-one races had been sailed by the Thirties, beginning the active and hard-driving competition that was to last for about thirty years. Efforts to develop wide interest in a class of New York Fifties, and later Forties, met with limited success, but the Thirties continued to maintain their popularity. It was not until 1935 that a new class of New York Yacht Club "Thirty-Twos," designed by Sparkman and Stephens with a modern rig, began to replace the gaff-rigged Thirties, which by that time had become scattered.

Why were the Thirties so successful? They were very narrow and uncomfortable by modern standards for boats of that size. Their cockpits were so small and their tillers so long that room was at a minimum. Their cabins were small, lacking suitable accommodations and headroom. The answers, as in many similar cases, lay in the class of men who sailed the Thirties and because the time was ripe for such a boat.*

At the time the Thirties were built a minimum 30-foot waterline length was required for voting by the New York Yacht Club. The Thirties were

---

* Facts for this section were obtained largely from "Class Will Tell," by Sam C. Slaughter, *Yachting*, November 1939, and *Sailing Craft*, edited by Edwin J. Schoettle, The Macmillan Company.

THIRTY CLASS ("New York Thirties"). *Photo by Morris Rosenfeld.*

built to this minimum and thus gave rise to several good yarns. One of them, told to the writer on what seemed like good authority, is about a leading member of the Club who had sold his much larger boat and found himself temporarily without a yacht which would qualify him as a voter. A friend suggested that a somewhat inactive Thirty might be bought for a song. The yachtless member purchased the Thirty without previous inspection, only to have his secretary discover later that his Thirty had been sunk for several years (according to one version of the story), or was a derelict (according to another version).

VITAL STATISTICS: L.O.A. 43'6"; waterline 30'; beam 8'10"; draft 6'3"; sail area about 1000 sq. ft.

THISTLE. *Photo by Beckner Photo Service, courtesy W. D. Schock Co.*

THISTLE

The 17-foot undecked sloop-rigged Thistles began sailing in 1946. There are now about eighteen hundred scattered in many parts of the United States and Hawaii and at least fifty more elsewhere. Designed by Gordon K. ("Sandy") Douglass and first built by Douglass and McLeod, the Thistle is a round-bilged plum-stemmed centerboard boat with a large sail area for her over-all length—so fast, especially when planing, that she is more than a match for much larger boats. There are now nearly one hundred fleets of this very sporty and popular class.

Ralph Wiley, the well-known Oxford, Maryland, sage, is eloquent in comparing the Thistles with other one-design classes: * "Embryo one-design classes are frequently hothouse plants. The seed is planted in carefully prepared soil, fertilized with propaganda and lightened by humus in the form of plowed-under long green. Many such seedlings cannot endure transplanting to the cold outdoors. Like the Biblical seed, a few that fall on fertile ground survive but many fall among the tares and die. The seeds of the Thistle, like those of her prickly Scotch namesake, have been broadcast by friendly breezes and, like the hardy flower of Scotland, she is tough enough to flourish and grow wherever the seeds may fall."

The Thistle open hull allows plenty of room for family sailing and there is no deck from which children can slide overboard. She is also an exciting racing boat, which has become well-known internationally. An active Thistle Class Association produces, among other things, an interesting publication called the *Bagpipe*. Mrs. Marlin ("Honey") Abramson is Secretary-Treasurer (226 E. 17th Ave., Columbus 1, Ohio). As there are too many builders to list here, the Secretary may be written for a list, or *Yachting's Boat Owners Buyers Guide* may be consulted. Boats are built of molded plywood or fiber glass and cost about $2200 new, with Dacron sails.

VITAL STATISTICS: L.O.A. 17'; waterline 17'; beam 6'; draft without centerboard 9", with C.B. 4'6"; sail area 175 sq. ft. (spinnaker used); weight 500 to 550 lbs.; trailable; racing crew, two or three.

TOWN CLASS

This is a 16½-foot wooden sloop designed and built by Pert M. Lowell of Newbury, Massachusetts, as a family boat which could also be used with an outboard motor. While not a planing type, it is said to be a good all-around sailer. Of one thousand which have been built, it is reported that about 250 are active in the National Town Class, of which Roy Larsen is Secretary (181 Azalea Drive, Norwood, Mass.). Principal sailing areas are in Massachusetts and Rhode Island. Price is about $1100 new, $400 to $700 used.

VITAL STATISTICS: L.O.A. 16'6"; beam 5'9½"; draft without centerboard 9", with C.B. 2'4"; sail area 150 sq. ft.; weight 630 lbs.; trailable; racing crew, two to four.

* "The Thistles," by Ralph H. Wiley, *Yachting*, July 1952.

TOWN. *Courtesy Ernest J. Benoit.*

TURNABOUTS. *Courtesy Harold R. Turner, Inc.*

TURNABOUT

There are now close to two thousand of these 9½-foot cat-rigged dinghies designed and built by Harold R. Turner (Parker River, Newbury, Mass.).

This is primarily a trainer for children, used chiefly on the East Coast of the United States and made of plywood, though they can be fiber-glass covered. An active National Turnabout Association guides class affairs and publishes a handbook. Bradford L. Jones is Secretary (Cloutman's Lane, Marblehead, Mass.).

It all got started late in December 1949, when some members of the Ipswich Bay Yacht Club, anxious to find a small boat fast enough to buck a 4-knot current in Plum Island Sound and safe enough to ride a tide rip, gathered to try out the first Turnabout. Mary Hogan of Andover had guaranteed to buy the first boat for her nine-year-old daughter, Polly, and had asked her noted uncle, John G. Alden, to be on hand to watch the demonstration. Alden had already made helpful suggestions to Harold Turner. The trial was a success and the career of the Turnabouts had begun.

The boat is strictly one-design and has been used in many junior programs, camps, etc. The famous brigantine *Yankee* carried a Turnabout on a voyage around the world, as a recreation boat for skipper and crew. Price is about $400 for a new boat, $300 for a used one or kit.

VITAL STATISTICS: L.O.A. 9'8"; waterline 8'7"; beam 5'3"; draft without centerboard 6", with C.B. 3'; sail area 60 sq. ft.; weight 225 lbs.; trailable.

TWELVE METER

This class is important, not because of the number of boats now active, but because it has recently been the class selected for the America's Cup Races. Though thirty-five 12 Meter boats were built in Europe between 1907 and 1914, the class was not introduced into the United States until 1928, when six boats designed in America by Burgess, Rigg and Morgan, and built in Germany by Abeking and Rasmussen, began sailing on Long Island Sound. While the 12 Meter class is a *development* class, with the opportunity of variation controlled by restrictions too complicated to attempt to explain here (even if I could), these early boats were 69'2" over-all; 42'11" on the waterline; with a beam of 12'8"; draft of 8'5"; and a sail area of 1970 square feet.

A Third International Rule was drafted in 1933 to become effective on January 1, 1936. Between 1933 and 1939 six 12 Meters were built in the United States: *Seven Seas* and *Gleam* (designed by Clinton Crane); *Mitena* (designed by L. Francis Herreshoff); *Nyala, Northern Light,* and *Vim* (designed by Sparkman and Stephens). In 1939 *Vim* was raced successfully in England, proving to be probably the fastest 12 Meter built up to that time.

TWELVE METER *Intrepid. Photo by Theodore A. Jones, courtesy One-Design & Offshore Yachtsman.*

The redrafting of the rules governing the races for the America's Cup, leading to the selection of 12 Meters, gave a stimulus to their development in 1958. Three new 12s were built in the United States to compete with *Vim* for the right to defend the Cup: *Columbia* (designed by Sparkman and Stephens), *Easterner* (designed by C. Raymond Hunt), and *Weatherly* (designed by Philip L. Rhodes and built by Luders Marine Construction Company). As all yachtsmen know, *Columbia* was selected in 1958 after a close final struggle with *Vim*, and then easily beat *Sceptre*, the English boat. *Weatherly* was selected for the defense in 1962 and won.

The following comparisons show how closely the American 12s compare in basic measurements as developed under the rules. It should be remembered that the *rated* sail area is usually considerably less than the actual sail area carried. The following are the *Vital Statistics* as they were reported in 1958:[*]

	Over-all Length	Waterline Length	Beam	Draft	Sail Area Sq. Ft.	Displacement Lbs.
Vim	69'7"	45'	12'	8'11"	1916	56,900
Columbia	69'7"	45'	12'	8'11"	1985	56,800
Easterner	65'6"	46'	12'	9'	1920	60,000
Weatherly	69'	45'6"	11'10"	8'10½"	1870	58,000

A new 12, designed by Ted Hood, was built in Marblehead for the 1962 Cup trials. She was named the *Nefertiti*, for a beautiful Egyptian queen.

Up to the 1958 Cup Races it was estimated that about ninety-five 12 Meters had been built in the world under the three International Rules since 1907, of which it was believed that about half were then in some kind of use. With the additional boats being built for the America's Cup Races of 1962, the total now must be close to one hundred, not a bad showing for boats of their size and expense—they are now the *big* boats of all racing classes and certainly as beautiful as any.[†]

210 CLASS

A later and larger sister of the 110 Class, the 29-foot 210 sloop, also designed by C. Raymond Hunt, first took the water at Marblehead, Massachusetts, on May 15, 1945, at the Marblehead Yacht Yard. Racing began in 1946. With its pointed bow and stern, well-inboard rig, flat bottom with a

---

[*] Figures are approximate, and not to be taken too literally.
[†] Thanks are due to Walter C. Hadley's "Some Twelve Meter History," *Yachting*, July 1957, and T. W. Howland's "What Is a 12 Meter Sloop," *Yachting*, September 1958.

210 CLASS. *Courtesy International 210 Association.*

hard chine and long, narrow sleek hull, it is a distinctive boat wherever it appears. Although primarily designed for racing, the cockpit, unlike that of the 110, has room enough for at least four adults comfortably. The designers planned to obtain a fast racing boat at the lowest possible price, and when the boat was launched Hunt hoped to keep it at close to $1000. Sad to say, times have changed, though it is still fairly inexpensive for its length.

While not properly classed as a planing boat, the 210 will plane under especially favorable circumstances and is considered fast among displacement boats of its size or larger. A former owner of an International One Design who later owned a 210 and has raced a great deal on both told me that he much preferred to race in the 210 as it was much easier to handle. "Everything is within easy reach. The 210 is the best racing boat there is of her size," he added. Another 210 sailor, with many championship races to his credit, points out that in heavy winds, especially on runs and reaches, the 210 is definitely faster than the International. In medium and light airs he considers it a toss-up, depending on wind angles and other conditions. (The 210 is 3 feet shorter over-all, 2½ feet longer on the waterline, and carries considerably less sail.)

There are fleets from Long Island Sound to Maine, with the largest concentration on Massachusetts Bay and Long Island Sound. There are also two fleets in Michigan and others on San Francisco Bay and in the Hawaiian Islands. Since the boats are one-design and considerable effort has been expended to keep them so, boat owners can participate in distant regattas by sailing local boats and bringing their own sails. Match races are held, "home and home" on alternate years between the Cohasset (Mass.) and western Long Island Sound fleets, the visiting crews using local boats.

The class has continued to grow until there are now reported on good authority to be about 250 active boats; another estimate places the number at over 300 but probably includes some boats which have been wrecked or destroyed. For instance, while the 1961 yearbook of the International 210 Association lists 326 numbers as having been issued, a look at the list discloses the fact that twenty-four boats have been either wrecked or destroyed by fire. The hurricanes took their toll. A good many also are reported as unassigned, meaning not built. Robert James is Secretary-Treasurer of the class (41 N. Main St., Cohasset, Mass.). The 210s are built by Graves Yacht Yard (Marblehead, Mass.), Beacon Boat Company (Holland, Mich.), and Ali Wai Boat Works (Honolulu, Hawaii). Price is $3800 to $4000. Used boats cost $1500 to $3500.

VITAL STATISTICS: L.O.A. 29'9⅝"; waterline 24'; beam 5'10"; draft (keel) 3'10"; sail area 256 sq. ft. (spinnaker used); weight 2400 lbs.; trailable on special trailer.

VIXEN. *Courtesy Ray Greene & Co., Inc.*

VIXEN

This is a 10-foot sloop-rigged fiber-glass dinghy built and sold by Ray Greene & Company (508 S. Byrne Rd., Toledo, Ohio) and used principally on the Great Lakes. It is reported that there are 380 of them. The boats have an antiskid interior, flotation in hull and inside the mast, and a "double skin sandwich construction." Price is $666 with Dacron sails.

VITAL STATISTICS: L.O.A 10′; beam 4′6″; draft without centerboard 5″, with C.B. 1′8″; sail area 80 sq. ft. (no spinnaker); weight 285 lbs.; trailable.

WAYFARER. *Courtesy Mrs. C. Dodson, U. S. Wayfarer Association.*

WAYFARER

The 16-foot Wayfarer sloop primarily is an English class, designed by Ian Proctor for coastal sailing around England, where she had to be prepared to "take it." It is claimed that two watertight compartments give the boat sufficient buoyancy to be sailed even when the cockpit is full. The boat is reported to be fast and stable, with a planing hull. The mast pivots below deck, for easy trailing and negotiating low bridges when sailing rivers or waterways. Centerboard and rudder will pivot.

It is said to be a very popular class in England, and was introduced to Canada in 1960. In 1961 it was brought to the United States. On two separate occasions a Wayfarer was sailed with a crew of two from England to Norway across the North Sea—a distance of six hundred miles. If the Wayfarer can take the waters of the North Sea and the English Channel, it would seem able to take almost anything we have to offer in the United States, except possibly a hurricane.

At the time of writing there are 25 boats in the United States, 98 in Canada, and 550 in the world. The United States Wayfarer Association is represented by Mrs. Claire Dodson, Secretary (3839 N. Greenview Ave., Chicago 13, Ill.). The class Secretary is Wally Cavill (49 Laurel Ave., Islington, Ontario, Canada), who is also Secretary of the Canadian Wayfarer Owners Association. The builder is Smallcraft (Southampton, England). Importers are Croce and Lofthouse (Westhill, Toronto, Ontario, Canada). Price is $1600; kits are $1100.

VITAL STATISTICS: L.O.A 15′10″; waterline 14′10″; beam 6′1″; draft without centerboard 8″, with C.B. 3′10″; sail area 141 sq. ft. (spinnaker used); weight 365 lbs.; trailable; racing crew, two.

WIANNO SENIOR and JUNIOR
Wianno Senior Class:

This class of gaff-rigged sloops was designed and built by the Crosby Yacht Building and Storage Company in 1914, when the original thirteen boats were built. During the winter of 1961–62 five new boats were added, bringing the total built to 116. It is estimated that in the summer of 1962 there will be approximately sixty-three boats racing in the waters of Nantucket Sound, with four yacht clubs participating, namely Wianno, Hyannisport, Bass River, and Stone Horse. Many other boats are scattered up and down Buzzards Bay and Massachusetts Bay, with about twenty-five scattered down the Atlantic Coast. The Wianno Senior Class is probably the most active of its age in the southern Massachusetts area. There is a great deal of interclub competition, with most of the activity centered around the Edgartown and Hyannisport regattas. In 1961 thirty-two starters were listed for the Hyannisport Regatta. The class has a very loyal following and comes close to the Stars in length of service, though not in numbers or world fame.

One of the original boats made in 1914 is still being sailed by the original owner, James G. Hinkle, of the Wianno Yacht Club. It is believed that this record of longevity cannot be matched by any other fleet in the southern Massachusetts area. James G. Hinkle is Secretary of the Wianno Senior One Design Committee (care of Preston, Moss & Company, 24 Federal St.,

WIANNO SENIOR. *Photo by Norman Fortier, courtesy Joseph Mattison, Jr.*

Boston, Mass.). The Crosby Yacht Building and Storage Company (Osterville, Mass.) is still the only builder. The boats are of planked mahogany and cost $5400 new, about $2400 for used boats.

VITAL STATISTICS: L.O.A. 25′; waterline 17′6″; beam 8′; draft without centerboard 2′6″, with C.B. 4′6″; sail area 366 sq. ft. (spinnaker used); it is not trailable.

Wianno Junior Class:

This class of smaller sloops was originated in Osterville, Massachusetts, with the first boats being built in 1921. As in the case of the Seniors, Crosby was the designer and builder. Although eighty-one boats have been built, many have been lost in storms or abandoned, and it is estimated that approximately fifty boats may still be afloat. Of this number, about fifteen are

WINDMILLS.
*Courtesy Winton P.
McMillen.*

raced at the Wianno Yacht Club and approximately six are sailed at the Hyannisport Yacht Club. These are the only two yacht clubs maintaining an active interest in this class.

The Wianno Junior has been used primarily by juniors, with the age limits for sailing the class being held at eighteen years. Team races are held annually between the two neighboring yacht clubs and occasionally this class has participated in the Falmouth Regatta. Though the class is small, five new boats were built in the winter of 1960–61. Price is $2570 for new boats, $1500 for used.

VITAL STATISTICS: L.O.A. 16'6"; waterline 13'; beam 6'; draft without centerboard 1'6", with C.B. 3'6"; sail area 139 sq. ft. (spinnaker used); weight 1400 lbs.; not trailable.

WINDMILL

This 15½-foot class of sloops was designed by Clark Mills of Clearwater, Florida, to take care of the young skippers of Clearwater who had reached fifteen and were therefore obliged to graduate from the Optimist Class (previously described). A Clearwater Windmill Fleet was formed about

1953 which grew to about twenty boats and then began to fade away for lack of interest until April 1958, when there appears to have been a demonstration of the power of the boating press. W. P. McMillen, now Commodore (and Measurer) of what has become the Windmill Class International Racing Association, wrote an article on the class which appeared in the April 1958 issue of *Motor Boating*. That turned the tide. The magazine received many inquiries and passed them along to McMillen, who directed the writers to Clark Mills for the plans.

Another article in *Motor Boating* by this eloquent expounder of the merits of the Windmill Class brought more inquiries, until in December 1959 the WCIRA was formed with seventy-five registered boats. By the end of 1960 there were three hundred Windmills and today 754 are registered. An amazing story and a tribute to Clark Mills and his boat as well as to W. P. McMillen! Also, *Motor Boating* is due its share of the credit.

What practical features in the boat seem to be responsible for its growth? There are plenty of other good boats of the size of Windmill. The most striking features, it seems to me, are the very low cost for a boat as long as 15½ feet, its light weight, its easy-to-build shape with the hard-chine V-bottom construction which encouraged amateurs, its generally good sailing qualities with the ability to plane well on a reach.

Principal sailing areas are in Florida, California, Texas, New York, Maryland, Canada, Georgia, and Washington. While most of the builders are amateurs, the WCIRA has a list of professional builders and one can be found in *Yachting's Boat Owners Buyers Guide*. Mrs. John Lucas (2906 Pass-a-Grille Way, Pass-a-Grille, Fla.) is the class Secretary. The Windmills are made of plywood. Price is $675 for a new one, $550 for a used boat. Plans including membership in WCIRA cost $10 and are obtainable by writing W. P. McMillen (784 53rd Ave. S., St. Petersburg, Fla.). Checks should be made out to Windmill Class International Racing Association. With these plans and specifications it is reported that boats can be built privately for $265 to $325.

VITAL STATISTICS: L.O.A. 15½′; waterline 14′10″; beam 4′8″; draft without centerboard 6″, with C.B. 4′; sail area 119 sq. ft. (no spinnaker); weight 230 lbs. rigged and equipped; trailable.

WOOD PUSSY

The Wood Pussy is a pretty 13½-foot catboat, with a modified spoon bow instead of the usual plum stem, a graceful sheer, high freeboard, and a round bilge. Wider than usual for a boat of her length, she looks like a good

WOOD PUSSY. *Booz Photos.*

family day sailer with plenty of cockpit room and stability, is fairly fast and fun to just sail or to race by either children or adults. The fact that over a thousand have been built is a good indication of the fact that a good many others feel that way about her.

Philip L. Rhodes designed the Wood Pussy shortly after World War II. During the winter of 1946–47 the National Wood-Pussy Class Association was formed to set up controls and safeguards for a true one-design class and to foster racing activities. The O'Day Corporation (9 Newbury St., Boston, Mass.) is the only franchised builder recognized by the association for the construction of fiber-glass boats of the class. Plans for wooden boats and the names of licensed builders of boats of this type can be obtained from the National Wood-Pussy Class Association (P. O. Box 169, Wall St. Station, New York 5, N.Y.). Bassett S. Winmill of the Monmouth Boat Club (Red Bank, N.J.) is Commodore of the Association, and the Secretary is Robert R. Schorn (Cold Spring Harbor Beach Club, Cold Spring Harbor, Long Island, N.Y.). National championships started in 1947, and regional championships, which started on the East Coast, are now held on the Pacific Coast and will be extended to the Great Lakes and elsewhere.

Principal areas of sailing activity are Long Island Sound, New Jersey, the Pacific Coast, upper New York State, the Great Lakes, and Massachusetts. Price new is $950 to $1100, used $250 to $750; no kits are sold.

VITAL STATISTICS: L.O.A. 13′6″; waterline 11′9″; beam 6′; draft without centerboard 7″, with C.B. 2′6″; sail area 120 sq. ft. (no spinnaker); weight 430 lbs. minimum; trailable; racing crew, two.

Y-FLYER

This 18-foot sloop-rigged scow, with a very low freeboard and every appearance of great speed, is sometimes called a "15-square-meter inland lake scow." Designed by Alvin Youngquist, an Inland Lake Class A Scow sailor of Toledo, she had her first trial on Chippewa Lake, Ohio, in 1941. The design was published in *Rudder* just as the United States got into World War II. After the war the class started in Montreal and a Canadian Y-Flyer Yacht Racing Association (46 Claude Ave., Dorval, Quebec) was organized in 1947. The Y-Flyers became one of the largest and most active classes in Canada.

Progress was slow in the United States until 1952, when the American Y-Flyer Class Association was formed. There are now about twelve hundred boats in the United States and Canada, including 525 in the United States. While there are a number of professional builders, well over half the regis-

Y-FLYERS. *Courtesy American Y-Flyer Yacht Racing Association.*

trations come from amateur "do-it-yourselfers." The same restrictions apply
to both associations, except that the Canadians allow the use of spinnakers
and the Americans don't—the Americans want to keep sailing as simple as
possible so as not to discourage the many wives who sail and race (as a lady
has explained it).

Mrs. Jessie H. Helms, Corresponding Secretary of AYFYRA (821 Pepper
St., Columbia, S.C.), although possibly not entirely unbiased (her husband
makes the boats), describes the Y-Flyer so eloquently that I can't resist
quoting her:

"The Y is wonderfully sensitive to the tiller, planes easily, and is very
stable. It is easy to trailer—get into the water—rig, and get under way. No
struggling and losing one's happy frame of mind before starting to sail. I

shall have to speak personally but we are an average example, I think. My husband likes to race and has brought left-footed me to a degree of proficiency as crew so that I can race with him. I love to joy-sail aimlessly—wherever the wind is. The Y is wonderful for both.

"I have ridden the Y at hair-raising speeds in Charleston Harbor and elsewhere. Yet, on a day that is moderately windy, our sixteen- and eleven-year-old daughters (beginners) can handle the boat with the greatest of ease. It is truly a boat that has something to offer every sailor, from the beginner to the seasoned skipper. It is not an ocean racer; however, it is widely sailed in coastal waters and with much success."

There are thirty-one Y-Flyer fleets in the United States, located in South Carolina, Georgia, Louisiana, Texas, Michigan, Ohio, Indiana, Arkansas, Missouri, Kansas, Alabama, Kentucky, Florida, North Carolina, and Illinois. Each August a National Championship Race is held. There are also International Championships (alternating with Canada). Spinnakers are not allowed in the races held in the United States; they are allowed in Canada.

Builders are well scattered and now include Jack A. Helms Company (821 Pepper St., Columbia, S.C.), Falls City Fiberglass Company (125 S. 9th St., Louisville, Ky.—fiber-glass boats), Glen Mottin Sailboat Sales (8005 Monroe St., St. Louis 14, Mo.), Gibbs Boat Company (6530 Morin Grove, Erie, Mich.), Bakker Bilt Boats (8 Sewall Ave., Clifton, N.J.), and Hiwassee Manufacturing Company (P. O. Box 305, Jacksonville, Ark.). Material is usually plywood, but some fiber-glass boats are built in the United States. Prices range from $1300 to $1800 for new boats; used $500 to $1500; kits from $500 up.

VITAL STATISTICS: L.O.A. 18′2″ (maximum), 17′11½″ (minimum); waterline 13′6″; beam 5′8″; draft without centerboard 6″, with C.B. 4′; sail area 161 sq. ft. (for spinnakers, see above); weight 500 lbs. minimum; racing crew, two in the United States, three in Canada, where spinnakers are used.

ZEPHYR

In a booklet entitled *The Origin of the Zephyr Class,* published in 1961 "as a labor of love" by Jack Greenwood, the origin of the class is explained as follows:

"On a Sunday in the spring of 1947, Ed Thrall and Pete Cole sailed down the airport channel from Alameda in two El Toros. . . . The wind, that day, was wild. It took all of the skill possessed by these experienced

ZEPHYR.
*Photo by
Signe Allen.*

skippers to keep from capsizing. They arrived at the Oakland Airport dock soaking wet—and cold.

"Huddled against the lee side of the shack on the dock, they dreamed of a boat that, like the El Toro, could be sailed single handed, but would stand up to the worst that San Francisco Bay could churn up. It would have to be a keel boat. It should be simple to build and repair . . . , easy to launch and rig . . . , trail easily. . . . Above all, it would have to be fast."

Evidently the result was a rather long jump from the Toros, which are 7′ 10″ long, for the boat Ed Thrall designed (assisted by Jack Freitag) was 20 feet over-all, and so much like C. Raymond Hunt's 110 Class (which came nearest to their requirements) that at a distance it would be difficult for the inexperienced to tell them apart. By 1949 the class had begun and the boats were racing. There are now about ninety-one of them—on San Francisco Bay. The boats are fast, though not a planing type, very narrow, and with their flat bottoms, would probably pound a bit in a short, choppy sea. The Zephyr One-Design Association was soon organized. James L. Allen is now Secretary (1274 Monterey Ave., Berkeley 7, Calif.). The official builder is Basin Boatcraft Company (601 Embarcadero, Oakland, Calif.). Boats are of plywood and cost $1500 new; used boats cost about $900, as do kits.

VITAL STATISTICS: L.O.A. 20′, waterline 18′6″; beam 4′; draft (keel) 2′6″; sail area 115 sq. ft.; weight 750 lbs.; trailable with special trailer; raced single-handed or with crew.

ZIP

In one way at least, if the claims of one of its promoters are correct, the Zip class is most unusual. Zips have been "bought and raced by such people as . . . Dwight D. Eisenhower . . . Franklin Delano Roosevelt" and other not-quite-so-noted celebrities. This is not a surprising claim so far as F.D.R. is concerned, for he was an enthusiastic sailor. I didn't realize, however, that the General had done any sailing.

The original 17-foot Zip sloops, made of wood, and in both keel and centerboard types, were designed and built by Harold Brainard of Clinton, Connecticut. This was from 1935 to 1943. In 1944 John Ek took over, to be succeeded by Zip Sloops, Inc., Ek's own company (1580 N.E. 125th St., North Miami, Fla.), which now exclusively builds the boats—in fiber glass only. John Ek and Richard M. Besola designed the fiber-glass modification, with a long, shallow keel. The modern version was shown in 1961 at the Miami Boat Show, and, it is claimed, will neither capsize nor sink, and in a calm can be sculled with the tiller (a not unusual accomplishment, we might add). The boat is a decked boat with a hard-chine bilge, and though heavy for her length, looks as though she would sail fairly well, though not a planing type.

John Ek reports that there are 925 now in the United States, with sailing activities largely on Long Island Sound (many of them are in the Madison and Clinton, Conn., area) and on Biscayne Bay, Miami, Florida. He says there are about sixty outside of the United States. Elsa Ek is Secretary of the Zip Sloop One Design Racing Association (at the same address as Zip Sloops, Inc.). Price of the last new wooden boats (1959) is $1500; used wooden boats cost $350 to $850; standard fiber-glass boats are $1795.

VITAL STATISTICS (fiber-glass boats): L.O.A. 17′; waterline 16′; beam 6′; draft (keel) 2′; sail area 130 sq. ft. (no spinnaker); weight 1000 lbs.; trailable—presumably with a special trailer.

ZIP sloop. *Courtesy John Ek.*

PART TWO
CRUISING CLASSES

INTRODUCTION

By cruising classes we mean boats which are used primarily for cruising—including day sailing—rather than for racing as a class, though some of them do race in that way from time to time. In most cases, however, when they race, it is on a time-allowance basis against boats of other classes or against those which do not belong to any stock class. Such races are apt to be under CCA (Cruising Club of America) or MORC (Midget Ocean Racing Club) rules which determine the basis of handicapping. Also, as we see it, to qualify as a cruising class the boats should have such minimum accommodations as bunks for at least two, a "head" (toilet), and a galley or stove—or at least provision for the installation of all of these.

As it is sometimes difficult to determine whether a class belongs with the cruisers or racers, let us take the two types of 22½-foot Electra sloops as examples. The Electra which we are including with the cruising group has berths for two (with two more optional), a galley, icebox, toilet, and other accommodations. The cabin (with a doghouse) is substantial for a boat of her size and the cockpit is small and self-bailing. This boat is qualified for deep-sea racing under MORC rules. We think she belongs with our cruising classes. The Electra Day Sailer, on the contrary, though the hull is the same, has a tiny cuddy for a cabin and a 9-foot-long cockpit. While there are berths for two in the cuddy and a toilet can be installed, this Electra is primarily a class racer and day sailer and obviously belongs with the racing classes.

The number of stock auxiliary cruising classes has grown so rapidly in recent years that it is impossible within the scope of this book to include them all. I would rather cover adequately a limited number of classes—giving for each the designer, purpose, history, special features, interesting facts, etc.—than give a long list with very little said about any one class. Thus we are including only classes in which at least thirty boats have been built, are on order, or are definitely scheduled for the year immediately ahead at the time of our inquiry, according to the best information we are able to obtain to date. I am sure that in future editions more classes will be added and that in this edition we shall find that we have missed a few which should have been included. If so, as Bill Taylor suggested, we'll hear from their admirers. I hope they'll let us know at the same time the number of boats in the classes which have been left out of this edition.

If anyone wants a full listing, we suggest that he obtain a copy of *The Sailing Cruisers of 1962—being a catalogue of Stock Boats from 18′ to 45′ available in U.S.A.* This was published with the February 1962 issue of *The Skipper* (2nd St. at Spa Creek, Annapolis, Md.). It has been one of our most helpful sources of information.

Explanations: The following explanations are in order:

1. *Accommodations:* In connection with each class described we are noting only the basic accommodations; a complete list is obtainable from the builder, importer, or dealer, whose names and addresses we have indicated in each case.

2. *Prices:* While the prices given are intended to include prices with working sails and it was so stated in our questions to the respective authorities for each class, we do not guarantee that this is *always* the case. Furthermore, especially with cruising classes, the number of items encompassed by the base price varies greatly. Some companies include most of what a cruising man would need. Others have a one- or two-page list of "extras" or "optional" items, many of which would be considered necessary. Thus the prices should be taken in many cases as only a rough indication of what a boat would cost. Prices are also, of course, subject to change without notice. They were, however, all based on the situation as we found it at one time—the first half of 1962—and thus should offer some basis for comparison. The *Number in a class* is also at time of writing.

3. *Sail area* covers working sails only. Among the cruising classes it can be assumed, however, that spinnakers are allowable unless we have stated otherwise. Genoas, also, are commonly used.

4. *Weights* given are approximate, and include the boat with masts, rigging, etc.

ALBERG 35. *Courtesy Northrop and Johnson.*

ALBERG 35

Designed by Carl A. Alberg of Marblehead, Massachusetts, and called "big sister" to the Alberg-designed Triton, the Alberg 35 is the largest of a very successful trio—the Electra being the smallest. Constructed by the Pearson Corporation of Bristol, Rhode Island, a subsidiary of the Grumman Aircraft Engineering Corporation, it is reported that fifty-five have already gone down the ways—a sizable number for a boat that large which has only recently come on the market. This boat is a deep-water ocean racer with six berths (6′4″ and 6′5″), a head, galley, and all of the usual accommodations for a 35-foot cruising yacht. She may be obtained in either a sloop or yawl rig. Price with sails is approximately $20,000. Northrop and Johnson (366 Madison Ave., New York 17, N.Y.) is a leading dealer.

VITAL STATISTICS: L.O.A. 34′9″; waterline 24′; beam 9′8″; draft 5′2″; sail area 535.5 sq. ft.; displacement 12,600 lbs.; Cruising Club of America; power 30-h.p. Universal Atomic Four.

AMPHIBI-CON

The 25-foot auxiliary sloop Amphibi-Con, designed and built by the Mount Desert Yacht Yard (Mount Desert, Me.), was so far as I know the first of the now-many cruising auxiliaries designed specifically with trailing in mind. Cyrus Hamlin and E. Farnham Butler (President of the company) were pioneers when in 1954 they anticipated the recent trend toward easily trailable auxiliaries. The name "Amphibi-Con" was adopted as an abbreviation of amphibious controversy—amphibious because it was to be trailered, controversy because it was to be of light displacement with a reverse sheer.

Several years ago when I sold my Dutch-built 21-foot sloop, it became very clear that the fact that she was trailable greatly enhanced the demand. For instance, the fellow who bought my *White Tulip* (on a trailer in my backyard at Scarsdale, New York) was expecting to be transferred by his company to parts as yet unknown to him. He purchased the boat not only because he liked it, but because he was reasonably sure that he could take it with him wherever he was sent, and find a nearby lake large enough for sailing it. He was right. He went to Burlington, Vermont, on Lake Champlain.

Easy trailability is one of the very important assets of the Amphibi-Con. She is a moderately light displacement yacht made of wood-strip planking, with reverse sheer and centerboard fully housed in a keel which provides shallow enough draft (2′4″ without the board) both for shoal-water cruising and trailing. Small enough for trailing and large enough to be comfortable, 110 have been built at the time of writing, of which 102 are in the United States. About 50 per cent of the present class was built from kits or partly finished by amateurs.

Despite her small size for a cruising boat, the Amphibi-Con has four 6′6″ berths in two cabins. A convertible canvas-top "doghouse" provides a cabin with over six feet headroom. This can be taken down for day sailing or racing. The cockpit is self-bailing. With a galley, head, and other facili-

AMPHIBI-CON. *Photo by W. H. Ballard, courtesy Mount Desert Yacht Yard.*

ties it is claimed that she has the accommodations of a very much larger boat. From what I have learned from an experienced member of the Cruising Club of America whose son owns an Amphibi-Con, she is all that is claimed for her and is besides a fast boat. Principal sailing activities of the class are on the Atlantic Coast and Great Lakes.

Amphibi-Cons have won many races, including those held by the Off-Soundings Club and others where the competition is tough. One of the features of the races between members of the class is that boats take part which come from widely separate waters, trailed to the racing rendezvous by their owners. An Amphibi-Con owner who keeps his boat on Long Island Sound can start a cruise, if he wants to, north of Cape Elizabeth, "where the Maine Coast really begins."

The Amphibi-Con Association, to which owners of the smaller Amphibi-Ettes also belong, provides a club which is different from most of the yacht clubs or associations of which owners of cruising boats are members. It consists of owners of the same class of boat. When the boats are raced together, no question of handicap is involved. Like many other class associations, this one has had much to do with the development and success of the class. Mrs. Henry R. Keene (79 Bates St., Dedham, Mass.) is Secretary at the time of writing. The price of the Amphibi-Con ranges from $7000 upward according to the requirements, used boats from $5000 up. The cost of kits varies considerably, from $1995 up, according to how far along a buyer wants the boat to be.

VITAL STATISTICS: L.O.A. 25′5″; waterline 21′8″; beam 7′9″; draft without centerboard 2′4″, with C.B. 4′3″; sail area 266 sq. ft.; weight 3900 to 5500 lbs.; trailable; power is outboard motor operating in a well, which contains a hinged section that swings down into place to provide a smooth bottom when the motor is removed for racing.

AMPHIBI-ETTE

The Amphibi-Ette sloop is a slightly smaller and lighter edition of the Amphibi-Con, also designed by the Mount Desert Yacht Yard (Mount Desert, Me.). Accommodations are similar, with a similar convas hood arrangement (see Amphibi-Con). Unlike her "older sister," the Amphibi-Ette has a pronounced hard chine with a slightly reversed cross-section and a more sharply angled transom. She, too, of course, is easily trailable and has a large enough keel to enable her to go to windward without the centerboard, if necessary, in shoal waters. The reverse sheer is also there, as is the outboard well. A combination cruiser and day sailer, she is said to sail well. Amphibi-Ette affairs are handled by the Amphibi-Con Association, with the same Secretary (at the time of writing, Mrs. Henry R. Keene, 79 Bates St., Dedham, Mass.). There are about thirty boats in the class. Price is $5800, kits $1650.

VITAL STATISTICS: L.O.A. 24′1½″; waterline 20′1″; beam 7′9″; draft without centerboard 2′4″, with C.B. 4′10″; sail area 225 sq. ft.; weight 3000 lbs.; trailable; power by inboard-mounted outboard motor.

AMPHIBI-ETTE. *Photo by Bill Robinson.*

ANNAPOLIS THIRTY. *Courtesy O. E. Olsen.*

ANNAPOLIS THIRTY

The Annapolis Thirty sloop was brought out by Olsen Marine Products (4th and Chesapeake Ave., Annapolis, Md.) primarily as a cruising auxiliary. At the time of writing, thirty-six have been launched or are under construction. Built of fiber glass, the boats have already spread from Chesapeake Bay to Long Island Sound (where it is expected a class association will be started), to Lake Michigan, to Massachusetts, and there is one even in South America. There are four berths, full headroom, and an enclosed head "with cosmetic shelf and full-length mirror on door for the ladies," also a galley and the usual other cruising accommodations.

VITAL STATISTICS: L.O.A. 30′2½″; waterline 22′3½″; beam 8′5″; draft (keel) 4′6″; sail area 400 sq. ft.; power 25-h.p. Palmer or Universal engine.

BARNEGAT 20

Designed by James E. Graves, the Barnegat 20, a keel sloop, was developed at Graves Yacht Yards (Marblehead, Mass.) to provide a small family boat at a low price. Planking is marine plywood. There is room for two to sleep in the cabin and two more in the cockpit under a boom tent. There is a toilet in the cabin. While the size and price necessitate modest accommodations, the boat seems to offer a good deal for the money. To date thirty-three have been built, chiefly for use in New England. Ted Garrity (108 Village St., Marblehead, Mass.) is President of the Association. Basic price is $2425 with Dacron sails, $2700 with power also.

VITAL STATISTICS: L.O.A. 20′1″; waterline 18′; beam 7′; draft (keel) 3′7″; sail area 175 sq. ft.; weight 1350 lbs.; trailable on special trailer; power a 5½-h.p. Evinrude with reverse installed under after deck.

BAY LADY

These 20-foot sloops of Sheldon design are imported by Sheldon Yacht Sales (Loch Lomond Marina, 620 Point San Pedro Road, San Rafael, Calif.). So far, it is reported that thirty-two have been sold "in the world." In this country their principal sailing area is San Francisco Bay and San Pedro. The boat is "planned," say the importers, "to accommodate 5 adults comfortably in the cockpit. Can sleep 4 adults below with adequate stor-

BARNEGAT 20. *Photo by Dike Mason, courtesy Graves Yacht Yards.*

age space for all sails and gear." Let's hope that the adults sleeping in the cockpit are very small, willing to sleep like sardines, and have not-too-high standards of comfort. (I have owned a 21-foot sloop myself.) Construction is double-planked mahogany, mast stepped in cabin-top tabernacle. This, together with the fact that it is a keelboat, helps to provide room below. The plan shows four berths, space for a pantry, head, etc.

BAY LADY. *Courtesy Sheldon Yacht Sales.*

Bud Smith is Secretary of the Bay Lady Association (2574 36th Ave., San Francisco, Calif.). Price is $2995 for new boats; used cost about $2700.

VITAL STATISTICS: L.O.A. 20'; waterline 17'8"; beam 6'4"; draft (keel) 3'10"; sail area 180 sq. ft.; weight 3000 lbs.; trailable (special trailer); power, 3- to 7½-h.p. outboard, stowed in stern hatch, attached to shaped transom.

BEAR. *Courtesy W. S. Cauchois.*

BEAR

As all yachtsmen know who have sailed on San Francisco Bay from May to August, the going can be very rough when fresh breezes of 15 to 30 miles an hour sweep through the Golden Gate. The 23-foot Bears were designed and built by Manuel Nunes and Sons (Sausalito, Calif.) to take just this. Since the early 1930s the Bears have been a familiar sight on the Bay, both as racing boats and as cruisers. Nunes not only sells the finished boats but also provides plans for amateur construction, which can be obtained through the association. Material is wood. There are now about sixty-five Bears, one of the largest classes on the Bay.

Despite the interest of many owners in racing, the Bears also are cruised a great deal, both among the maze of sloughs in the deltas of the San Joaquin and Sacramento rivers, but sometimes outside to Drakes Bay, Bolinas, and Tomales Bay.

The cabin sleeps three or four. Most of the boats have a toilet abaft the mast and adequate space for a galley. Henry A. Getz is Secretary of the San Francisco Bay Bear Boat Association (256 Los Banos Ave., Walnut Creek, Calif.). Another authority is W. S. Cauchois (315 Blair Ave., Piedmont, Calif.). Price is $6000 to $7000 for new boats, $3500 to $5000 for used.

VITAL STATISTICS: L.O.A. 23′; waterline 18′1″; beam 6′9″; draft (keel) 3′6″; sail area 268 sq. ft.; weight 5000 lbs.; not trailable. Power is optional.

BOUNTY II

The 40′10″ Bounty II, designed by Philip L. Rhodes, was the first auxiliary cruising boat of substantial size designed for fiber glass and built of fiber-glass-reinforced plastic; she was the pioneer. Starting in 1957, approximately sixty have been built, an unusually good showing for a boat of that size. I can well remember the interest the Bounty created when first exhibited at the New York Motor Boat Show. Built by Aeromarine Plastics Corporation (Sausalito, Calif.) and Pearson Corporation (Bristol, R.I.) the Bounties are sailed on the Pacific Coast, the East and Gulf coasts (including the Caribbean), and on the Great Lakes. The boat comes in sloop or yawl rig.

Accommodations include berths for six, over 6-foot headroom, galley, enclosed head, and many conveniences. Bounties have competed in Transpacific and Bermuda Races as well as in Detroit-Mackinac Races on the Great Lakes and have won a number of trophies. Price is $28,500; used boats are obtainable at from $20,000 up.

BOUNTY II. *Courtesy Northrop and Johnson.*

VITAL STATISTICS: L.O.A. 40′10″; waterline 28′; beam 10′3″; draft (keel) 5′10″; sail area 714 sq. ft. (sloop), 799 sq. ft. (yawl); displacement 18,800 lbs.; power, 30-h.p. Universal.

CALIFORNIA 20s. *Photo by Beckner Photo Service, courtesy Jensen Wenck Marine Corporation.*

CALIFORNIA 20 and 24

These two sloops, each with over ninety in its class, were designed by C. William Lapworth and are built by the Jensen Marine Corporation

(Costa Mesa, Calif.). Al Naine of Vancouver, British Columbia, also builds the 20. Both boats are constructed of fiber glass. Although the first C 20 was launched early in 1961, there are already fleets at San Diego, Newport Harbor, San Francisco, and on Alamitos Bay. The C 24s are also chiefly in California. Both classes are qualified for ocean racing under Midget Ocean Racing Club rules. The 20 has two 6'6" berths, and optional equipment includes an extra berth forward and a toilet. The 24, of course, being 4 feet longer, has more ample cruising accommodations. Both have outboard wells. The C 20 is a keelboat, the C 24 has a combined keel and centerboard.

Don Stein (279 Church Lane, Los Angeles, Calif.) is Secretary of the C 20 Association. Peter Ebeling (3424 Centinella Ave., Apt. 7, Los Angeles 66, Calif.) handles the affairs of the C 24s. Prices are as follows: C 20 $3445 (no kit); C 24 $6200 (kits $3450).

VITAL STATISTICS:

	L.O.A.	Waterline	Beam	Draft	Sail Area	Displacement	Power
C 20	20'	18'	7'	3'4"	196 sq. ft.	1600 lbs.	O.B.
C 24	24'	20'	8'	2'6"*	260 sq. ft.	3000 lbs.	O.B.

* Keel only, 2'6" draft; with centerboard 4'6"

CAP VERT

Designed for ocean cruising by Jean-Jacques Herbulot, the 26-foot cutter Cap Vert is imported from France by the Nautica Corporation (P. O. Box 26, Paramus, N.J.). Hulls are molded mahogany, or fiber glass with built-in flotation. A single-cabin model has berths for four, while the double-cabin model will take care of five. Each boat has a galley, a head, and an outboard well which will carry motors of from 5 to 10 horsepower. The boats have a reverse sheer and very little overhang. They have a combination keel and centerboard.

Like the other classes imported by Nautica, the sailing area of the Cap Verts includes particularly the English Channel, the Mediterranean, the East and West coasts of the United States, and the Gulf of Mexico. Altogether, about 150 have been built to date. Association functions are handled by Nautica. Price is $6995 up for single-cabin boats.

VITAL STATISTICS: L.O.A. 26'3"; waterline 24'; beam 8'; draft without centerboard 2'7½", with C.B. 4'7"; sail area (main, jib, and forestaysail) is 318 sq. ft.; displacement 4000 lbs.; power, 5- to 10-h.p. outboard.

CAP VERT. *Courtesy Nautica Corporation.*

CHALLENGER. *Courtesy John Alden and Co.*

CHALLENGER

The 38½-foot Challenger yawl, of molded fiber glass, was designed by John Alden & Company (131 State, Boston 9, Mass.). It is described as follows by Donald G. Parrot, President of that company, who calls it "one of the most successful class auxiliaries brought out in recent years."

"The hull is molded for us by Halmatic, Ltd., of Portsmouth, England, and the boats have been completed primarily by Paul Molich, of Hundested, Denmark; A. le Compte Company, Inc., of Jutphaas, Holland; and Halmatic, Ltd., of London, England. Some Challengers have been finished in this country by Palmer Johnson Boats (Sturgeon Bay, Wis.), Robert E. Derecktor (Mamaroneck, N.Y.), and Saybrook Marine Service (Old Saybrook, Conn.). To date, thirty-six Challengers have been built or are in process of construction. They have been sailed quite extensively in European waters, here on the East Coast from Maine to Florida, on the Great Lakes, and there is one sailing on the West Coast."

The Challengers have full headroom, with two built-in berths and two extension transoms in the main cabin and two berths in the foreward cabin. All of the other usual accommodations for a boat of that size are there. The Challenger is a very attractive yacht, and should be able to go anywhere and make an excellent showing for a boat of her size. She has a combination keel and centerboard. Price is $32,000.

VITAL STATISTICS: L.O.A. 38′6″; waterline 27′; beam 11′; draft (keel only) 4′; power, Gray Model 4-112 Direct Drive.

CHESAPEAKE 32

The 32-foot sloop is one of the growing classes of fiber-glass cruising yachts. Designed by Philip L. Rhodes, the class only got started in 1960 and at the time of writing, sixty had been built, the principal builder being Danboat, Denmark. George B. Walton, Inc. (Annapolis, Md.), imports the C 32s, which have five or six berths, in two cabins, and all of the usual accommodations for a boat of that size: enclosed head, galley, etc.

Principal cruising grounds are the U. S. East Coast and Bermuda. Price is $16,800.

VITAL STATISTICS: L.O.A. 31′9″; waterline 22′1″; beam 8′9″; draft (keel) 4′10″; sail area 464 sq. ft.; power, 25-h.p. Graymarine.

CHINOOK

This 34-foot Chinook sloop, designed by Frederick Geiger, is another fiber-glass cruising yacht. It is built by Yacht Constructors (7110 N.E. 42nd Ave., Portland 18, Ore.) and so far thirty-seven have been turned out, including two on order. This is a Pacific Coast class, with ten on the Columbia River in the Portland area, ten in the vicinity of Los Angeles, two on Lake Coeur d'Alene, Idaho, and the rest scattered from Victoria, British Columbia, to San Diego, California. Two are on the Great Lakes and one has gone to Long Island, New York.

Yacht Constructors was founded by five members of the Rose City Yacht Club, Portland, Oregon, who wanted a cruising sloop about 35 feet long

CHESAPEAKE *32. Photo by Morris Rosenfeld, courtesy Philip L. Rhodes.*

CHINOOK. *Courtesy Yacht Constructors, Inc.*

that would sleep four comfortably, have the usual other cruising accommodations and a large cockpit for day sailing. None of these men could afford a boat like this unless he built it himself. So the five got together on their building. Three of the original partners, through Yacht Constructors, are offering yachtsmen a chance to buy a fiber-glass hull, with plans for completing the boat—to be finished by the purchaser. The price of $7500 is what the boat would cost the buyer on a do-it-yourself basis, with the purchaser buying the rest of the materials and finishing the boat himself.

The Chinooks have four or six bunks, galley, enclosed head, and many other accommodations below. The self-bailing cockpit holds six comfortably. There is a combination keel-centerboard. The boat has attractive, conventional lines and is fast enough, it is reported, to have already won a number of racing trophies. Price of bare hull and plans (see above) is $2975 at Portland.

VITAL STATISTICS: L.O.A. 34'; waterline 23'; beam 9'; draft without centerboard 3'10", with C.B. 6'6"; sail area (Plan A) 530 sq. ft., (Plan B) 470 sq. ft.; displacement 12,000 lbs.; Cruising Club of America rating Plan A 24.4, Plan B 22.4; power, 25-h.p. Gray Seascout or equivalent.

Note: Yacht Constructors also has a smaller boat—the Cascade (29 feet over-all)—which is sold on a similar partly constructed basis. Price of bare hull and plans is $1775 at Portland.

COASTWISE CRUISER. *Photo by Norman Fortier, courtesy A. Donald Brice.*

COASTWISE CRUISER

Designed by John G. Alden, the first Coastwise Cruiser was built in 1938 and the last in 1944. About forty were constructed to this design, most of them by James E. Graves, Inc., of Marblehead, Massachusetts, though a few were made outside of this country. There used to be a class association under the late Richard O. H. Hill, but there is no active association today. Having had many good times cruising on one of these well-proportioned, fine-sailing, and attractive sloops, I am sorry to see them approaching the end of the road, at least so far as new boats are concerned.

The Coastwise Cruisers have proved fast boats, the winners of many trophies, as well as comfortable cruisers with four berths, enclosed toilet,

COLUMBIA 29. *Photo by Beckner Photo Service, courtesy Sparkman and Stephens.*

galley, full headroom, and the other usual accommodations. Of planked construction, the sloops originally cost $6500 but would cost about $25,000 to build today. Used boats now on the market sell for $10,000 to $12,000.

VITAL STATISTICS: L.O.A. 36′5″; waterline 26′; beam 9′9″; draft 5′3″; sail area 585 sq. ft.; power, Alden Special Model Gray 4-22.

COLUMBIA 29

The Columbia 29 sloop is a new addition to the Sparkman and Stephens-designed fleet of auxiliaries. At the time of writing twenty-seven have already been sold. The design was created for the West Coast and the boat is being manufactured by Glas Laminates (Costa Mesa, Calif.). It is also being marketed on the Great Lakes and East Coast. The construction is of fiber glass and the boat is a good-looking example of an auxiliary of her size, with moderate overhangs and a cabin with a moderate doghouse.

Accommodations include four 6½′ berths, a head, galley, etc. Headroom is 6 feet. Price of the standard boat with Dacron working sails is $9512 f.o.b. Costa Mesa, California. This includes in the standard equipment a good deal of what is sometimes included as extras.

VITAL STATISTICS: L.O.A. 28′6″; waterline 22′6″; beam 8′; draft (keel) 4′; sail area 382 sq. ft.; power either through a concealed outboard well (standard) or an inboard 8-h.p. Palmer (optional).

CONCORDIA

The first of this well-known and very successful class was designed and built in 1938. Waldo Howland and C. Raymond Hunt (then a partner in the Concordia Company), assisted by Llewelyn Howland, pooled their boating knowledge to produce a yacht that would sail well through the short seas and whistling sou'westers of Buzzards Bay, Massachusetts. After building four boats in New England, the remainder of the ninety-two built to date have come from the famous boatyard of Abeking and Rasmussen in Germany. They are sold by the Concordia Company, Inc. (South Wharf, South Dartmouth, Mass.).

Concordias are well known in many harbors along the East Coast, particularly in New England. They are also seen in California occasionally and on the Great Lakes. Some have been shipped to Europe and one sailed to Portugal from the United States via Bermuda and the Azores. They have a fine racing record. Among the Concordia yawls are a few which have been slightly modified in hull form and rig and are called Concordia 41s. There is no formal class association but I am sure from what I know of Waldo Howland, President of Concordia Company, that he and his company serve as a very good substitute.

"Concordia," says Mr. Howland, "has tried to furnish a first-class product of lasting value rather than a boat which takes advantage of special trends."

Price now is about $30,000 and I am informed that used boats are seldom offered for sale.

VITAL STATISTICS: L.O.A. 39′10″; waterline 28′6″; beam 10′3″; draft 5′8″; sail area 690 sq. ft.; displacement 18,000 lbs.; power, Gray 4-Cycle 31-h.p.

CONCORDIA yawl. *Photo by Norman Fortier, courtesy Concordia Co.*

CONTROVERSY 27 (MOUNT DESERT 27). *Photo by W. H. Ballard, courtesy Mount Desert Yacht Yard.*

CONTROVERSY 27 (MOUNT DESERT 27)

While Mount Desert 27 is now the official name, she is known to many by her former name, Controversy 27, and we are thus including our story here. Like E. Farnham Butler's other designs, this one isn't conventional and piles in an unusual amount of cruising room for its size. The first of the class, the *Rubicon* (note the "con"), took the water in 1960. While she is strip-built, her design is also suited to fiber-glass construction. There is a movable housetop, a Butler characteristic, and by using the cockpit she can sleep six, with four berths below. Besides these there is an enclosed head, a galley, and a surprising number of conveniences for a boat of this size, ingeniously planned. Her sheer is almost straight and overhang is very slight.

As usual, Butler had trailing in mind when he designed her; her beam is one inch less than the 8-foot limit for unrestricted travel on U.S. highways. She is built of wood on a semicustom basis by the Mount Desert Yacht Yard (Mount Desert, Me.) and by the Marriott's Cove Yacht Builder (Chester, Nova Scotia). Boats are also built of fiber glass in England by Miles Marine and Structural Plastics, Ltd., and imported by the Mount Desert Yacht Yard. The boat has a combination keel-centerboard.

Price of the fiber-glass model is about $9300 on the East Coast of the United States. This does not include an inboard engine costing $900 to $1100 for 10-h.p., $1300 for 25-h.p.

VITAL STATISTICS: L.O.A. 27'6"; waterline 22'6"; beam 7'11"; draft 2'10" (without centerboard); sail area 316 sq. ft.; displacement 4600 lbs.; power, 10- to 18-h.p. outboard (inboard motor optional).

CORSAIRE

According to its importers, the 18-foot sloop Corsaire is the world's largest stock class of auxiliary sailboats. With a total of fifteen hundred built to date, this estimate cannot be far off. Like the Cap Vert, the Corsaire was designed by the well-known French naval architect Jean-Jacques Herbulot, and the boats (which are built by Cidevyv) are imported from France by the Nautica Corporation (P. O. Box 26, Paramus, N.J.).

A reverse sheer provides extra cabin room, as does the fact that both mast and centerboard are taken out of the cabin, the mast being set into a tabernacle and the centerboard put inside of the keel. A raised deck with the cabin extending to the side of the boat aids in providing more space below, besides making it more comfortable for those sitting on the bunks. I once made the circuit of New England and Nova Scotia in a 26-foot raised-deck sloop and know what a difference it makes to one's comfort

CORSAIRE.
*Courtesy Nautica
Corporation.*

below. By raising the cockpit floor to make it self-bailing, Herbulot added to the boat's safety and provided extra stowage space. Flotation material also enhances safety. The Corsaire has a hard chine which adds to its stiffness, as does 330 pounds of ballast in the keel.

With two quarter-berths in the main cabin and a small V-shaped double berth forward, three adults or two adults and two children can sleep below. There is a stowable outboard bracket suitable for a 3- or 5-horsepower outboard, and space for a stove is provided. A portable or permanent head can be installed forward.

While I haven't seen a Corsaire, it would seem from the above that considerable ingenuity has been used in the design in order to give the most possible boat for its size and cost. Her sailing waters in Europe are largely in the English Channel and the Mediterranean; in the United States

CUTLASS. *Courtesy Richard D. Carlson.*

the boats are scattered along both East and West coasts and on the Great Lakes. Nautica functions as the Association. Price for the boat is $2400.

VITAL STATISTICS: L.O.A. 18'1"; waterline 16'; beam 6'3"; draft without centerboard 1'9", with C.B. 3'3"; sail area 172 sq. ft.; displacement 1210 lbs.; trailable with special trailer; power, 3- to 5-h.p. outboard.

CUTLASS

This 23'7" sloop was designed by Richard D. Carlson (Box A, Shelter Island, N.Y.) and is built to individual order by Astilleros J. Gallart of Barcelona, Spain. Carlson imports them and so far thirty-two have been built, of which twenty-two have come to the United States. Since there were only ten over here in 1961, this indicates progress. The Cutlass qualifies under the rules of the Midget Ocean Racing Club and so far its record has been very good in racing with other boats of its size. For instance, during 1961, Carlson's *Medea* won five firsts and two seconds out of seven starts on eastern Long Island Sound, while Holmes had a similar record with his *Widgeon* on Chesapeake Bay. Others did almost as well with their Cutlasses.

"Please pardon the high opinion that I hold for this design of mine," writes Carlson. "I realize it places me under suspicion as an egomaniac." He points out that "particularly to windward she normally beats (boat for boat) yachts up to 25 feet waterline and larger with ease. . . . Though of displacement type (3800 lbs. on 19′ waterline) she has logged up to 9 knots under certain conditions (not 'surfing'). This is possible, in my opinion, because of extremely easy buttocks aft which give her semiplaning characteristics."

Her accommodations include a toilet, galley, two berths (to which two more forward can be added if desired). Cockpit is self-bailing; hull is of mahogany planking. She is a keelboat.

Richard D. Carlson, at the above address, functions as an association head. He says that the design is now in production and it is expected that fleets will be established in Barcelona, Spain; western Long Island Sound; upper Chesapeake Bay; and Southern California during 1962 and 1963.

Base price is $5150 for new boats, $4500 for used; kits are $1400 and up.

VITAL STATISTICS: L.O.A. 23′7″; waterline 19′2″; beam 7′1¼″; draft 4′; sail area 242 sq. ft.; weight 3800 lbs.; trailable (special trailer); power choice of two inboard engines, 5- or 10-h.p., about $1000 extra.

DICKERSON 32

While exploring the Eastern Shore for *A Cruising Guide to the Chesapeake,* I saw a good-looking ketch riding at her moorings on the southeast branch of Fishing Creek, which leads into the Little Choptank River. I was surprised, as the low-tide channel depth shown on the chart was only two or three feet, though we were told later it was three and a half feet. William C. Dickerson soon turned up and showed me one or two of the ketches in process of construction. The boats looked well-built, simple but sound, and sensible in their interiors. When I heard the price, I was astonished. I couldn't recollect any boat of that size (32 feet), even a foreign import, which gave a family cruising man so much for his money. Dickerson has already built forty-two of them and they are sailing on Chesapeake Bay, Barnegat Bay (sailing *out of* would probably be more correct than *on,* as Barnegat Bay is very shoal), Long Island Sound, the Gulf of Mexico, and the east coast of Florida.

The Dickerson 32 ketch was not built as a racing boat but, as Mr. Dickerson says, "for the owner who wants a good family cruiser at a very moderate cost." The hull and cabin sides are of Philippine mahogany, the

DICKERSON 32 ketch. *Courtesy Dickerson Boatbuilders, Inc.*

cabin top of marine plywood covered with fiber glass. Below there is 6-foot headroom, two berths in the forward cabin and two in the main cabin, one of which is a double berth which also doubles as a dinette when not in use for sleeping. An enclosed head, a galley, hanging locker, etc., are among the usual accommodations. The cockpit is self-bailing. Dickerson Boatbuilders, Inc., is located on Church Creek Road, Cambridge, Maryland.

The Dickerson 32 comes ordinarily with a keel only, of moderate draft (4 feet), but it is also available at an extra charge with a keel-centerboard combination (3 feet without board, 5 feet with it). Auxiliary power is described below. The class Secretary is William F. Broske (1601 Summit Ave., Camp Hill, Pa.). The price of the standard model with sails is $10,800.

VITAL STATISTICS: L.O.A. 32′; waterline 26′6″; beam 10′; draft (keel) 4′; sail area 440 sq. ft.; lead keel weighs about 3000 lbs.; power is a four-cylinder 25-h.p. Universal Utility engine.

DOLPHIN

The 24-foot sloop Dolphin was designed in 1959 by Sparkman and Stephens to meet the requirements of George D. O'Day and to qualify under the rules of the Midget Ocean Racing Club. She is built of fiber glass at the Marscot Plastics Division of the O'Day Corporation (168 Stevens St., Fall River, Mass. 02722). The aim was to produce a low-cost cruising and racing auxiliary with as much room as possible for the size, a fast boat which would be seaworthy and trailable. The boats are distributed by U. S. Yachts, Inc. (Village Square, Westport, Conn.), who explain the situation, in part, as follows:

"With an eye on the excellent performance of Bill Scranton's 24-foot *Trina* in MORC competition George O'Day wanted to produce a fiberglass boat which would perform as well as or better than the famous yawl. The Sparkman & Stephens design has lived up to the O'Day requirements and has won races under the CCA, LMYRA and MORC rules. Wiki McNeil of Annapolis, Ralph Heinzerling of Port Washington, Long Island, a New London owner, and Peter Grimm of Chicago have all been big winners.

"Fifty boats have been delivered and ten are now being built to order for customers in the United States. Fifty per cent of the Dolphin owners use them solely as weekend cruisers, while the other 50 per cent are raced and cruised. We anticipate forty new owners in 1962. Three boats have been built from kits and all are sailed from Southport, Connecticut. R. Clark

DOLPHIN. *Courtesy U. S. Yachts, Inc.*

DuBoise of Fairfield, Connecticut, is in the process of forming a class association with a regular racing schedule."

Principal sailing areas are on the East Coast of the United States and the Great Lakes. The accommodations include a double berth forward and two quarterberths in the main cabin, a galley, and a head (where "privacy is obtained with curtains"). Cockpit is self-bailing. Price is $7500 for new boats; used are about $1000 less.

VITAL STATISTICS: L.O.A. 24′; waterline 19′; beam 7′8″; draft without centerboard 2′10″, with C.B. 5′2″; sail area 297 sq. ft.; weight 4500 lbs.; power, a Palmer Huskie inboard engine.

ELECTRA. *Courtesy Northrop and Johnson.*

ELECTRA

The 22½-foot Electra cruising sloop is the smaller sister of the well-known Triton, just as the Alberg 35 is the bigger sister. All three are designed by Carl A. Alberg of Marblehead, Massachusetts, and built by the Pearson Corporation of Bristol, Rhode Island. I have been aboard one of the new Electras and seen several more in the water. With their fiber-glass hulls gleaming in the sunlight, their new Dacron sails and well-proportioned lines, I think they are as beautiful as any boat of their size I have ever seen. Northrop and Johnson (366 Madison Ave., New York 17, N.Y.) is a leading dealer, among others. A City Island, New York, dealer is Sagman's Marine, Inc. (City Island Ave., New York, N.Y.).

While most of the 150 which have been built so far are cruising-racing sloops qualified for racing competition under the Midget Ocean Racing Club requirements, an Electra Day Sailer has recently come on the market. This is discussed in our section on racing classes.

The cruising version has berths for two, and optional equipment includes two additional berths forward, galley, icebox, toilet, and other accommodations needed for weekend cruising. Unlike the doghouse on some boats of her size, the Electra's doghouse blends very well in appearance with the rest of the cabin.

An association of Electra-class owners on Long Island Sound has recently been formed under the Chairmanship of Charles H. Zimmerman (4 Cottage Circle, Larchmont, N.Y.). The class will race on the Yacht Racing Association of Long Island Sound schedule as well as in overnight races. It might thus be considered on the borderline between a racing and a cruising class. However, we are including it with the latter because of its cruising attributes. Price is about $4220 with sails.

VITAL STATISTICS (cruising version): L.O.A. 22'6"; waterline 16'9"; beam 7'; draft (keel) 3'; sail area 227 sq. ft.; displacement 3000 lbs.; power is by outboard operating from a removable stern bracket.

FOLKBOAT

When two Folkboats crossed the Atlantic in the single-handed race in 1960, finishing second and fourth, American yachtsmen sat up and took notice. Though many Americans have heard of these boats, they are best known in the Scandinavian countries, West Germany, and Britain, where the class has been making a name for itself for twenty years.

F. C. Clark, Jr., tells how the class got started and some of its characteristics:*

"To better understand the boat, a brief look at her background may be in order. The Kattegat, Skagerrak, and Baltic are deep, virtually tideless waters. Seas can be short but steep, winds moderate to rail down. There are many small one-design racing classes, just as there are here, but before the war there was no one-design cruising class. Feeling the need for a

---

* "Nordiska Folkbaten," by F. C. Clark, Jr., *The Skipper*, July 1961.

FOLKBOAT. *Photo by The Jerners, courtesy Solar Boat Co.*

family sloop suitable for 'round-the-cans' competition during the season as well as for family cruising, KGSS, the Royal Goteborg Yacht Club, held a designing contest. Over sixty designs were submitted and a Danish and Swedish proposal split the price. Tord Suden, Goteborg naval architect, was selected to combine the two. In 1941 the first Folkboat slid down the ways. Twenty-five feet one inch over-all, nineteen feet eight inches on the water, she had a beam of seven feet three inches, with three foot eleven inch draft. Area of the working lowers is 258 square feet. Though she may appear a mite thin to American eyes, she is a good compromise between reasonable room below and good performance. With the short steep seas of the Baltic a beamier small boat would have been stopped when beating into a chop. With plenty of water, draft was no problem, so the stability of the deep keel was practical. Outside ballast weighs some 2200 pounds, and with a hull weight of 4750, the weight-ballast ratio runs around 47 per cent. With good winds the sail area could be kept to a modest size that is easily handled.

"Plans called for a type of construction that would be economical in small one-at-a-time yards, or in series in the larger shops. Thus, the lapstrake planking, copper fastenings, and transom stern.

"There is more than economy behind any successful class boat. Scandinavians are great sailors and they have found her an ideal all-around sloop. For summer afternoon races, she is handy and quick and provides good sport for a two or three man crew. During vacations she will sleep three, or even four (in some intimacy) for pleasant 'longshore voyaging. Naturally, with her deep keel and short rig, she is no ball of fire in light air though responsive enough and fun to sail. But when the wind begins to whistle and the water climbs the tree, the Folkboat begins to sparkle. Clawing off a lee shore into a sharp chop is her cup of tea, and she eats up the distance in a most satisfactory fashion. Off the wind, with a slop of a following sea she has a tremendous sense of security and knowing. Though no boat can be called foolproof the stout, well mannered Folkboat can withstand a lot of foolishness from an inexperienced helmsman. She's also a safe trainer for the spouse or the growing hands in the family. Her performance in last summer's Trans-Atlantic attests to her seakeeping qualities."

The Folkboats are not all built to a standard, though the different versions have much in common. Since many are homemade and built in Europe, no reliable figures can be given as to their number. However, one authority estimates that there are about fifteen hundred in Europe, three hundred to four hundred in the United States—close to two thousand in all.

George B. Walton (4th St. and Severn Ave., Eastport, Annapolis, Md.) has "evolved" a Folkboat for the American market, which is called a Nordic Folkboat. The cabin has been enlarged and a large forward hatch added. There are two berths in the main cabin and two forward, a galley, toilet, icebox, etc. Auxiliary power is also provided. The lapstrake construction with the pleasant sheer is still there. Cockpit is self-bailing. Walton is now planning to bring its Folkboat out in fiber glass.

Unlike most of the distributors who sell cruising boats, the list of extras in Walton's Folkboat is not a page or more long. They do list thirty "extras" below their price of $6950 at Annapolis, but opposite each item on this list are the words "no charge." By including all of such items as part of standard equipment, Walton is able to provide them at a lower cost than if the boat purchaser had to buy them himself at retail prices.

VITAL STATISTICS (Nordic Folkboat): L.O.A. 25'; waterline 19'8"; beam 7'5", draft (keel) 3'11"; sail area 258 sq. ft.; power (included in price), Volvo-Penta MD-1 Diesel Engine.

FRISCO FLYER. *Courtesy Herbert Hayes Yacht Sales.*

FRISCO FLYER

The 25-foot sloop Frisco Flyer is a Folkboat type modified by Arthur C. Robb, built by the Cheoy Lee Shipyard (Hong Kong, China). Roland Reed Associates (1712 High St., Alameda, Calif.) distributes the boats, which are also sold on the East Coast by Herbert Hayes Yacht Sales (Yacht Haven, Wallace St., Shippan Point, Stamford, Conn.), and in the Middle West by International Yacht Sales (14100 E. Jefferson Ave., Detroit, Mich.). Reports vary as to the number which have been sold, but the more conservative report says over sixty in the United States.

Like the Folkboats, the Flyer is reported to be a lively racing-cruising auxiliary, qualifying for ocean racing under Midget Ocean Racing Club rules. Her seaworthiness is indicated by the fact that in 1956 a prototype made a transatlantic voyage, single-handed, from Great Britain to New York and back. Accommodations include four berths, galley, "concealed" toilet, etc. As in the case of Walton's Nordic Folkboat, many of the usual "extras" (though not all, as in the other case) are included in the price of $6450. This does *not* include the engine, starter, and a few other items.

VITAL STATISTICS: L.O.A. 25′; waterline 19′6″; beam 7′2″; draft (keel) 3′11″; sail area 230 sq. ft. (350 sq. ft. in optional masthead rig); displacement 5500 lbs.; power, Volvo-Penta, MD-1 Diesel, 5-h.p. engine

HOLIDAY CLASSES

Several classes of boats are imported by Holiday Yachts, Inc. (Centerport, Long Island, N.Y.). None of them has an association, though Holiday Yachts is the principal source of information. Builders vary from time to time and occasionally dimensions are changed. For instance, I used to own a Holiday Sailer (a hard-chine fine-sailing boat, but with cramped accommodations) when they were 21 feet over-all and the builder was Van de Stadt in Holland. Now it is 24 feet long, called a Sailor, and built by another boatyard. However, while classes change and vary, the aggressive Richard A. Johnson, President of Holiday Yachts, has sold a good many of them—too many for separate descriptions here except as reported below by Holiday Yachts:

	24' Sailor	24 Jr. H.	28' Victor	30' Holiday	35' H H
1. Dimensions	L.O.A. 24'1" L.W.L. 18'6" Beam 7'7" Draft C.B. 2'3"–5" Fin 3'7"	L.O.A. 24'1" L.W.L. 18'3" Beam 7'6" Draft C.B. 2'3"–5" Fin 3'7"	L.O.A. 28'0" L.W.L. 20'0" Beam 7'10" Draft C.B. 2'9"–5" Fin 3'9"	L.O.A. 30'2" L.W.L. 23'0" Beam 8'5" Draft C.B. 3'3"–6'3" Fin 4'3"	L.O.A. 35'4" L.W.L. 28'3" Beam 9'10" C.B. 3'9"–6'11" Fin 5'5"
2. Sail area (sq. ft.)	261	261	300	368	502
3. Auxiliary Power	None	8-h.p. Palmer	22-h.p. Palmer	22-h.p. Palmer	22-h.p. Palmer
4. Number of berths	2 full berths 2 qtr. berths	2 full berths 2 qtr. berths	2 full berths 2 qtr. berths	2 settee 2 qtr. berths	6–8 berths
5. Year in which class started	1954	1954	1955	1954	1957
6. Approx. total number built	49	80	22	55	21
7. Principal Builders	Holiday Yachts, Inc. in Holland	Holiday Yachts, Inc. Holland	Holiday Yachts, Inc. Holland	Holiday Yachts, Inc. Holland	Holiday Yachts, Inc. Holland
8. Class Assoc., if any	All handicap races; no associations formed to our knowledge				
9. Price, approx. range	New $4190	New $5490	New $5590	New $9490	New $17,100
10. Principal areas of sailing	Wilamtee Sound Chesapeake Bay L. I. Sound	Los Angeles L. I. Sound Chesapeake Bay	Great Lakes East Coast	San Francisco Los Angeles East Coast L. I. Sound	West Coast East Coast

Thirty-foot HOLIDAY. *Courtesy Holiday Yachts, Inc.*

In addition Holiday has brought out a 24-foot fiber-glass sloop called Catalina Holiday (no relation to the Catalina Catamaran). This has a round bilge, keel, and transom which inclines forward. It qualifies for the Midget Ocean Racing Club. Accommodations include two single berths and one double, enclosed head, galley. Price is $7400 for the standard sloop.

VITAL STATISTICS: L.O.A. 24′; waterline 20′; beam 8′; draft 3′6″; sail area 314 sq. ft.; displacement 3350 lbs.; trailable (special trailer); power, 8-h.p. Palmer.

Twenty-four-foot HOLIDAY JUN-
IOR. *Courtesy Holiday Yachts, Inc.*

Twenty-four-foot HOLIDAY
SAILOR. *Courtesy Holiday
Yachts, Inc.*

IDLER. *Courtesy Philip L. Rhodes.*

IDLER

Designed by Philip L. Rhodes, this 25-foot class of sloops started in 1946. To date about thirty have been built: by Kargard (Marinette, Wis.) and by Estlander (Denmark). Construction is conventional wood with a fin keel and light displacement. Accommodations include two berths, galley aft, toilet, etc. Principal cruising areas are the U. S. East Coast and the Great Lakes. Price is $8000 for new boats, $4000 to $7000 for used.

VITAL STATISTICS: L.O.A. 25′; waterline 20′; beam 8′; draft (keel) 3′10″; sail area 311 sq. ft.; power, 25-h.p. Brennan Imp.

KESTREL.
*Courtesy Seafarer
Fiber Glass
Yachts, Inc.*

K 40
(KETTENBURG 40)
*Courtesy
Kettenburg Co.*

KESTREL

The 22-foot Kestrel sloop was designed by Sparkman and Stephens and is sold by Seafarer Fiber Glass Yachts, Inc. (205 E. 42nd St., New York 17, N.Y.). Thirty have already been built and twenty more have been sold, or fifty in all. Built of molded fiber glass, the boats are imported from Europe by Seafarer and are expected to be contenders in Midget Ocean Racing Club races. Her shoal-draft centerboard design makes the Kestrel trailable. Her four full-length berths, galley, head (concealed by curtain), and other accommodations make her livable, certainly for weekend cruising. Headroom is 4′7″, "unlimited under a sliding open hatch."

Price is $4790 without sails. Seafarer will arrange to have sails made by "the sailmaker of your choice."

VITAL STATISTICS: L.O.A. 22′1¼″; waterline 16′6″; beam 7′¾″; draft without centerboard 2′4″; sail area 228 sq. ft.; power, concealed outboard well for motors up to 7½-h.p., or inboard motor (optional).

K 40 (KETTENBURG 40)

Kettenburg (2810 Carleton St., San Diego 6, Calif.) is the designer and builder of the K 40 sloop. Thirty-seven have already been completed and one more is under construction, or thirty-eight in all. Made of conventional mahogany planking on oak frames, she is also conventional in her appearance—and very good-looking with her graceful profile and a doghouse which is only slightly higher than the rest of the cabin. But while the construction material and hull shape are conventional, the cabin interior, it is reported, has some new wrinkles. Says Kettenburg: "The common ladder leading from a cramped cockpit to a dark, gloomy cabin [How familiar that sounds! I have nearly broken my back working my way down such ladders] has been replaced with two broad steps providing access to a light, airy galley, chart area, and uncluttered salon." As would be expected in a boat of this size, there is full headroom below. Accommodations include six berths in two cabins, enclosed head, galley, etc.

The K 40 is reported to have a notable racing record and has a Cruising Club of America rating of 28.2. Base price of the K 40 is $21,367, including working sails, but, as in most large cruising yachts, there is a long list of extras.

VITAL STATISTICS: L.O.A. 39′11″; waterline 27′4″; beam 10′4″; draft (keel) 5′4″; sail area 556 sq. ft.; displacement 14,250 lbs.; power, Gray 4-91.

KING'S CRUISERS. *Courtesy George B. Walton, Inc.*

KING'S CRUISER

The 28-foot King's Cruiser, designed by Tord Sunden, who produced the final lines of the Folkboat, is essentially a Folkboat modification with more room due to increased over-all length and a doghouse. Until Triton sold over three hundred boats in U.S. waters, the King's Cruiser was America's largest four-berth, auxiliary one-design class. At the time of writing there are 231 in the United States and about 300 in the world. The boats are built by A. B. Telfar of Goteburg, Sweden, and distributed in the United States by, among many others, George B. Walton, Inc. (P. O. Box 1528, Annapolis, Md.). Material is African mahogany. Accommodations include four berths, toilet, galley, etc.

Principal sailing areas in the United States are on Chesapeake Bay, Long Island Sound, and the Great Lakes. There is no national association for the

LION. *Courtesy Herbert Hayes Yacht Sales.*

class, though last year twenty-seven King's Cruisers hit the line off Annapolis on the Chesapeake—a large showing for an auxiliary-class race.

When a King's Cruiser was first shown at the New York Motor Boat
Show, a number of visitors considered this the best buy in the Show among
the auxiliaries under thirty feet. Later, the fiber-glass Tritons stole the
show, capitalizing on the advantages of fiber glass. However, we are told
that the King's Cruisers continue to sell well with no decline in sight.
They are certainly beautiful boats and good sailers. Price for new boats
is $8190 (with *no* extras, in accordance with George B. Walton's policy
described in connection with the Nordic Folkboat). Used boats cost $5000
up.

VITAL STATISTICS: L.O.A. 28′; waterline 20′10″; beam 7′3″; draft
(keel) 3′11″; sail area 278 sq. ft.; displacement 4800 lbs.; power, 8-h.p.
Volvo-Penta Diesel.

LION

Like the Frisco Flyer, the 35-foot Lion was designed by the Englishman
Arthur C. Robb and built of teak by the Cheoy Lee Shipyard of Hong

MARAUDEUR. *Courtesy Nautica Corporation.*

Kong. It is sold in the United States by Herbert Hayes Yacht Sales (Yacht Haven, Wallace St., Shippan Point, Stamford, Conn.) and International Yacht Sales, Inc. (14100 E. Jefferson Ave., Detroit 15, Mich.). It is reported that about a hundred have been sold to date, a good showing for a boat of that size. Accommodations include four berths, galley, head, etc. Headroom is 6'2". The boat looks like a comfortable cruiser of conventional profile and should be a good sailer. The price seems very reasonable for a 35-footer: $15,950 plus $695 for Dacron mainsail and jib, or $16,645 with regular sails for the sloop rig. Yawl rig costs somewhat more.

VITAL STATISTICS: L.O.A. 35′2″; waterline 25′; beam 8′9″; draft (keel) 5′6″; sail area 475 sq. ft. (main and jib); displacement 14,200 lbs.; Cruising Club of America rating 21.9; power, Stuart-Turner 8-h.p., or at extra cost Universal 30-h.p.

MARAUDEUR

This 16-foot centerboard sloop is the smallest boat among our cruising classes and is a typical camping cruiser in which two people can sleep in a completely enclosed cabin. Designed by J. J. Herbulot and constructed in France of lightweight African mahogany, the Maraudeur will plane under favorable conditions. The boats are imported by the Nautica Corporation (P. O. Box 26, Paramus, N.J.), which reports that thirteen hundred have been built—by Cidevyv.

The boats have a combination keel-centerboard and, it is claimed, can go to windward in sixteen inches of water. This is a stock boat in France's largest boatyard and thus it can be sold cheaply, as the price indicates—it is the cheapest on our list of cruising classes, as well as the smallest. The Maraudeurs have flotation safety and roller reefing of both mainsail and jib which can be controlled from the cockpit.

While this isn't a boat for an extended cruise by adults, it provides enough overnight accommodation for a father and a couple of "kids," if they don't expect the unreasonable.

Price is $1425 with sails. Mattresses are extra.

VITAL STATISTICS: L.O.A. 16′; waterline 15′4″; beam 5′9″; draft without centerboard 11½″, with C.B. 3′9″; sail area 152 sq. ft.; displacement including keel ballast 440 lbs.; trailable.

MARLIN and FISH CLASS

The success of the Bull's Eye (the modern fiber-glass, Marconi-rigged version of the original Herreshoff 12) encouraged the Cape Cod Shipbuilding Company, makers of the Bull's Eye, to bring out a fiber-glass version of the Nathanael Herreshoff Fish class. The Fish class was an enlarged 12 with roomier accommodations and a small cuddy forward. The Cape Cod Marlin was built from molds of the Fish class with a cabin in which two can sleep and added length, obtained through an extension of the stern above the waterline to enable her to carry a modern masthead Marconi rig with a permanent backstay. Aluminum spars were added with roller reefing gear on the boom.

MARLIN. *Courtesy Cape Cod Shipbuilding Co.*

The Marlin sleeps two, with berths 6'6" long, toilet, galley, and other accommodations. A large hatch when open gives standing headroom at the galley, and a forward hatch with a translucent top provides light and ventilation. The cockpit is self-bailing and roomy for day sailing. The Marlin is a keel boat and is said to perform "creditably under her MORC rating."

About eighty have been built, most of them for sailing on the U. S. East Coast. There is no association. The Cape Cod Shipbuilding Company (Wareham, Mass.) is the source of information. Price is $6300 for new boats, about $5000 for used.

MAYA. *Photo by Beckner Photo Service, courtesy Balboa Marina.*

VITAL STATISTICS: L.O.A. 23'; waterline 16'11"; beam 7'2"; draft (keel) 3'3"; sail area 241 sq. ft.; weight 3300 lbs.; trailable is "doubtful but occasionally done"; power, Palmer 16-h.p. inboard engine.

MAYA

The Maya was designed by a Japanese naval architect who was obviously influenced by *Sopranino,* the small sloop (designed by the Englishman Lawrence Giles) which made a successful transatlantic passage. The boat is also built in Japan, by the Okamoto and Sons Boat Works (Yokohama, Japan). Originally imported by Getz Brothers and Company in 1956 and now by Balboa Marina (201 East Coast Highway, Newport Beach, Calif.), the Maya is one of the growing number of cruising-class sloops which qualify for the Midget Ocean Racing Club. It is also one of the most successful, with ninety-five built altogether, of which sixty-eight are in the United States. These are located chiefly on San Francisco Bay, at Los Angeles, Newport, and San Diego Bay—all on the U. S. Pacific Coast. While the boats race as a class on San Francisco Bay, where within two years about twenty-five were actively racing, elsewhere the owners seem to prefer to use them for cruising, day sailing, or ocean racing under the Cruising Club of America rule or P.H.R.F. (Pacific Handicap Racing Fleet).

With her short overhangs and beamy end sections, it is reported that the Maya is a very comfortable boat to sail, with pitching reduced to a minimum. The slight reverse sheer adds space below, where there are berths for three or four, a head, galley, and other accommodations, depending upon the requirements of the owner. While some inboard auxiliaries have been installed, the importers say that most skippers prefer a space-saving, lighter, and less expensive outboard motor.

The boats have a double-planked wooden hull with mahogany on the outside. The only "weak point" of the Maya, according to an authority, is the one "shared by most small [under 30 feet] boats that are built of wood. . . . They [the classes] are being replaced by the easy-to-maintain fiberglass boats which in many instances are inferior designs." Price is $5000 with sails; used boats cost about $4000.

VITAL STATISTICS: L.O.A. 23'; waterline (with cruising equipment) 20'6"; beam 6'7"; draft (keel) 4'1"; sail area 149 sq. ft.; weight (completely equipped) about 4200 lbs. (bare boat 3660 lbs.); trailable with special equipment; power is usually by an outboard on a bracket.

MERIDIAN

Designed by Philip L. Rhodes, the 24'9" sloop Meridian has unusual accommodations below for a boat of her size. Headroom is 5'11"; there are berths for four, a head (located in the forward cabin between berths), a galley aft, and plenty of storage facilities. She is a well-proportioned boat with a doghouse that blends well with the lower part of the cabin. Construction is reinforced plastic hull and deck. She is a relatively heavy displacement shoal-draft keelboat. The class was started in 1961, and is made

MERIDAN.
*Photo by Hein de Bouter,
courtesy Philip L. Rhodes.*

by G. deVries Lentsch, the largest yacht builders in Holland. Seafarer Fiber Glass Yachts, Inc. (205 E. 42nd St., New York 17, N.Y.), the importers, have already ordered one hundred of them. It is estimated that seventy-five have been built.

As Philip L. Rhodes put it, "The Meridian represents our effort to design a minimum-size cruising-racing sloop without in any way creating a toy or a so-called 'tabloid.' She is a husky and substantial little ship and in no sense a tub. Her displacement of 5060 pounds with her deep bilges and wide garboards not only makes possible her generous interior layout but also allows us to carry a ballast keel that weighs 2500 pounds. This is the way a small cruiser of this size should be designed: with plenty of what it takes to take care of herself and carry her sail when the going gets rough. Her underbody is of a nature that offers comparatively small wetted surface, so that with her sharp rig she will do equally well in light airs."

Her principal cruising grounds are on the East, West, and Gulf coasts of the United States, on the Great Lakes, and in northern Europe. An outboard well is provided and has a door which will be flush with the bottom and (we were told) won't leak when the boat is sailing. I went aboard a Meridian at the New York Motor Boat Show in 1962 and was much impressed with her. Price without sails is $5850.

VITAL STATISTICS: L.O.A. 24'9"; waterline 17'6"; beam 7'; draft (keel) 3'3"; sail area 274 sq. ft.; power, 10-h.p. outboard in well; Cruising Club of America rating 1961 17.8; Midget Ocean Racing Club 21.30.

MOUNT DESERT 27 (See Controversy)

NEW HORIZONS

The 25-foot New Horizons sloop at the New York Motor Boat Show gave impressive evidence of the thought given by Sparkman and Stephens, the designers, and Ray Greene & Company, Inc. (508 S. Byrne Rd., Toledo 9, Ohio), the builders, to every detail of the arrangements below. There is at least as much room on this all-fiber-glass auxiliary as I have seen on any boat of this size, including 6'2" headroom under the doghouse section of the cabin. According to calculations made by Ray Greene and Company, the use of fiber-glass plastic construction "permits an 18.1% increase in the useable interior space by elimination of frames and other parts required in wooden boats." There are two quarter-berths plus a double berth forward, a galley, enclosed head, hanging locker, built-in ice chest, etc.

Although a recent addition to the zooming classes of small cruising sloops, at the time of writing 150 have been built, all but four for sailing in the United States. Sailing areas include the Great Lakes, Eastern United States, Florida, the Bahamas, Bermuda, Alaska, Canada, and France. Besides her facilities as a good family shoal-draft keel-centerboard cruiser, she looks like a good sailer, and meets the Midget Ocean Racing Club requirements. There is no class association at the time of writing, but Ray Greene & Company is a valuable source of detailed information. Price is $9850 including Dacron mainsail and jib. Ray Greene has a very complete list of added optional equipment, including some "recommended," such as mattresses costing $290, etc. From this it is easy to figure out what the total cost would be to meet a buyer's full requirements.

VITAL STATISTICS: L.O.A. 25'5"; waterline 21'3"; beam 7'9" (within trailable limits); draft without centerboard 3', with C.B. 6'5"; sail area 324 sq. ft.; weight 6030 lbs.; trailable (with special trailer); power, 25-h.p. Universal Atomic Four.

NEW HORIZONS. *Photo by The Jaqua Company, courtesy Ray Greene & Company, Inc.*

NEW YORK 32 (*Voyageur*). *See THIRTIES, page* 195. *Photo by Morris Rosenfeld, courtesy Sparkman and Stephens.*

NOMAD. *Booz Photos, courtesy Siddons and Sindle, Inc.*

NOMAD

The Nomad is a 21-foot sloop designed and built by Siddons and Sindle, Inc. (Central Ave., Island Heights, N.J.). Thirty-seven have been constructed or are on order at the time of writing, the first twelve of molded plywood, the remainder of fiber glass. The boats have no major area of sailing concentration. There are Nomads on widely scattered sounds, bays, and lakes from the U. S. East Coast to the Middle West. As Harry R. Sindle wrote:

"The boat was conceived as a practical way for landlocked sailors to cruise for a weekend or longer. The construction and design permits easy

ORION.
*Courtesy
Sailstar Boats.*

trailing, launching from ramps or beaches, and still livable accommodations. Many of our customers, for example, live well inland, and use the boat through most of the season on small lakes, trailing it to the larger bodies on the East and Gulf coasts, for example, during their vacation period."

The Nomad has an unusual feature in two lateral ballasted bilgeboards which are streamlined for minimum resistance. According to the builders, she has a positive righting moment even if she gets a knockdown with the boards up. A self-bailing cockpit and foam flotation help to make her a safe boat. In the cabin there is full sitting headroom, and a hatch near the galley is an added asset to the cook. Two 6'6" berths are located forward with a toilet in the center underneath them. There are also two quarter-berths amidships, a galley, and other accommodations. While roomy for her size, according to reports from owners she handles and sails well.

Having no projections underneath, the Nomad can easily be put on a trailer or rolled on air rollers. She does not need a special trailer or a lift. The mast is stepped in a tabernacle on the deck and can be raised or lowered by one person.

Price with Dacron working sails, $4185 (racing sails, add $60). Cruising equipment is extra.

VITAL STATISTICS: L.O.A. 20'9"; waterline 19'; beam 7'6"; draft without bilgeboards 11", with boards down 4'6"; sail area 185 sq. ft.; displacement 1500 lbs.; trailable; power a 5- to 7½-h.p. long-shaft outboard mounted on stern bracket.

ORION

Like Maraudeur, only larger, this 19-foot sloop is another camping-type cruiser, with a two-berth cabin, and a large hatch which gives full headroom in that part of the cabin when open. A boom cover adds the cockpit to the cabin space. As the cockpit will seat six, this enlarges considerably the sheltered area. "A Racing Boat in a Pocket Cruiser" is the way Sailstar Boats, the builder and distributor, describes it. (They are at 770 Main St.,West Warwick, R.I.) The Orion was designed by Robert Baker. Although new in 1962, fifty boats have been built at the time of writing.

The mast is stepped on the cabin top, leaving the space below unobstructed, with room for a toilet and a couple of bunks or a double berth, if preferred. While the boat ordinarily comes in a centerboard model, those who want to race her in the Midget Ocean Racing Club events can get her with a keel and enclosed centerboard. The Orion is made of fiber glass, has a self-bailing cockpit, built-in flotation, and an outboard "Kickerpit" motor well. Price is $3000.

VITAL STATISTICS: L.O.A. 19'; waterline not given but almost as long as over-all length; beam 6'9"; draft without centerboard 1', with C.B. 5'3"; sail area 200 sq. ft.; weight 1100 lbs.; trailable; power, outboard in well.

POLARIS

Designed by William H. Tripp, Jr., this 26-foot fiber-glass sloop is imported by, among others, Seafarer Fiber Glass Yachts, Inc. (205 E. 42nd St., New York 17, N.Y.). A combination keel-centerboard boat, she would appear to be well-suited for poking into "gunk holes." She is reported also to be a good weekend racer and her lines are very good-looking. It is estimated that about 120 have been sold at the time of writing.

POLARIS.
*Courtesy
Seafarer Fiber
Glass Yachts, Inc.*

Accommodations include two berths in the main cabin and two more forward, which can be closed off by an (optional) folding door. The head is located in the forward cabin between the berths and is concealed by a folding cover. There is a galley aft with icebox. Headroom is 5′3″. Price is $6290 without sails.

VITAL STATISTICS: L.O.A. 27′3″; waterline 19′; beam 7′9″; draft without centerboard 2′2″; sail area 273 sq. ft.; Cruising Club of America rating about 18.5; power, concealed outboard well for outboards up to 10-h.p., or inboard 30-h.p. Universal Atomic Four (optional).

RANGER

Designed by Philip L. Rhodes and started in 1960, the 28½-foot Ranger-class fiber-glass sloop is built in Holland and Scotland and imported by Seafarer Fiber Glass Yachts, Inc. (205 E. 42nd St., New York 17, N.Y.). Rhodes calls her his "answer to the budget-minded family for the ideal cruising boat—and racer as well." He describes her as having "a fiber-glass reinforced plastic hull and deck. Light displacement, heavily ballasted keel hull." Her lines are very attractive, her headroom is 5′10″, and her accommodations include two berths in the main cabin, two in the forward cabin, which is closed off by the hanging locker door, a head (which can be fully enclosed), galley, icebox, and other facilities. It is estimated that seventy-five have been built to date. Price is $7650 without sails for the model with an outboard well; $9450 with an inboard 30-h.p. Universal Atomic Four. Used boats are $6000 to $8000.

VITAL STATISTICS: L.O.A. 28′6″; waterline 20′; beam 8′; draft (keel) 3′10″; sail area 334 sq. ft.; power is optional as indicated above.

RANGER. *Courtesy Seafarer Fiber Glass Yachts, Inc.*

SCHOCK 22. *Photo by Beckner Photo Service, courtesy W. D. Schock Co.*

SCHOCK 22 and 25

The S 22 was designed by W. D. Schock; the S 25 by Seymour Paul. These two fiber-glass cruiser-racer sloops, built by the W. D. Schock Company (3502 S. Greenville St., Santa Ana, Calif.), are very different in appearance and characteristics. The 22 has an almost straight-up-and-down bow with a short bowsprit and virtually no overhang astern; her doghouse is conspicuously high. While all of this adds to the comfort below, it does not make for a pretty boat. The 25, on the other hand, has a long overhang, no bowsprit, very graceful lines, and a small low cabin—a very attractive sloop.

SCHOCK 25. *Photo by Beckner Photo Service, courtesy W. D. Schock Co.*

Both boats are sold by the J. C. Beery Company (Aquatic Park, Berkeley 10, Calif.) and Hugh Doherty's King Harbor Boats (901 Pier Ave., Hermosa Beach, Calif.). Both have positive flotation.

The S 22 has a combination keel-centerboard, is trailable, and can be equipped with a bracket for outboard power. She has four single berths, a head between the forward berths, a galley, and other accommodations. The mast is mounted on deck and easily raised or lowered with the jib halyard. Seventy-eight have been built to date. The 22 qualifies under Midget Ocean Racing Club rules. Price is $5580 with Dacron working sails.

VITAL STATISTICS, S 22:   L.O.A. 22'; waterline 20'; beam 7'6"; draft without centerboard 2'2", with C.B. 4'6"; sail area 241 sq. ft.; weight 2100 lbs.; power is provided by outboards of 3½ to 7 h.p. using an outboard bracket.

The S 25 has a fin keel which is fairly deep for a boat of her size. The cabin is much smaller than that of the 22. The 25 has a waterline nearly 4 feet shorter than that of the 22, and she is 6 inches narrower. Accommodations include two berths in a cuddy cabin which convert into a double. Removable boards enable two more to sleep in the cockpit under a boom cover. There is a head between the cabin berths. The S 25 was designed with interclass racing very much in mind and was selected for the Mallory Cup (North American Sailing Championship) finals in 1962. At the time of writing, fifty-five of the class have been built or are on order. Price is $4800 including Dacron sails.

VITAL STATISTICS, S 25:   L.O.A. 25'; waterline 16'3"; beam 7'; draft (keel) 4'; sail area 222 sq. ft.; weight 2200 lbs.; power is provided by an outboard operating through a well which is integral with the structure and has a match-plate for a smooth seal.

SEAWIND

The 30½-foot Seawind ketch was designed by Thomas C. Gilmer of MacLear and Harris, is built by Lunn Laminates, Inc. (Oakwood Rd. and 11th St., Huntington Station, Long Island, N.Y.), and sold by Northrop and Johnson, Inc. (366 Madison Ave., New York 17, N.Y.). It is a new fiberglass class but I am informed that production plans call for forty boats a year. The boat is of a conventional shape with a long keel. Accommodations include four berths in two cabins, an enclosed head, and a galley. Price is about $14,500 with working sails.

VITAL STATISTICS: L.O.A. 30'6"; waterline 24'; beam 9'3"; draft (keel) 4'4"; sail area 448 sq. ft.; displacement 12,010 lbs.; power, a 30-h.p. Atomic Four.

SEA WITCH

The 22-foot fiber-glass sloop Sea Witch is similar in design and size to the famous 21½-foot *Trekka*, designed by J. Laurent Giles, the noted English naval architect, "to demonstrate the seaworthiness of a cambered deck, light displacement craft." The demonstration was considered successful, for the *Trekka*, manned by John Guzzwell, sailed around the world over a four-year period without an untoward incident. For his cruise, Guzzwell, a Briton, obtained the Slocum Award, named in honor of Joshua Slocum, the first sailor to circumnavigate the globe single-handed. The Sea Witch has

SEA WITCH. *Photo by Jean Lacombe, courtesy Midget Yachts, Inc.*

SEAWIND ketch.
*Photo by
Agnew Fisher,
courtesy
Northrop
and Johnson.*

a reverse sheer, a cambered deck design, and—most unusual for a boat of this type—twin keels. Her doghouse blends well with the rest of the cabin, helping to give her an attractive appearance. She qualifies under Midget Ocean Racing Club rules. Her design was a joint effort by William Shaw, Richard Ketcham, and J. M. Willis.

Accommodations include a double-cabin arrangement, with two single berths in the main cabin and one double berth forward, a galley, enclosed head, etc. Headroom is 4′7″ (doghouse); 4′1″ (trunk). The mast is stepped in a deck tabernacle, which helps to provide room below. Her twin keels avoid having a centerboard trunk in the cabin and yet they provide very shoal draft for a keel boat. The twin keels have the added advantage of allowing a grounded boat to sit upright.

The Sea Witch has only recently come on the market, and while sixteen are reported to be under construction at the time of writing, it is expected that 120 will be built during the first year. The boats are produced and sold by Midget Yachts, Inc. (75 Marine St., Farmingdale, N.Y.). The price with Dacron working sails is $4865.

VITAL STATISTICS: L.O.A. 22′3″; waterline 19′4″; beam 7′; draft (keels) 2′1″; sail area 183 sq. ft.; displacement 2800 lbs.; Cruising Club of America rating est. 18.0; power, Palmer P. W. 27 (8-h.p. Huskie).

SWIFTSURE

The Swiftsure is a 33-foot Philip L. Rhodes design which has had unusual success for a boat of its size. Only started in 1959, it is estimated that about a hundred have been built up to the time of writing. The builder is G. deVries Lentsch, of Amsterdam, Holland. The leading importer is Seafarer Fiber Glass Yachts, Inc. (205 E. 42nd St., New York 17, N.Y.). Her cruising grounds are well scattered over the United States and western Europe. Philip L. Rhodes describes her as having a "fiberglass reinforced plastic hull and deck, medium displacement, stiff, a beamy centerboarder." She is a sturdy, good-looking sloop with a conventional profile and has a combination keel-centerboard.

Accommodations include two berths in the main cabin plus two extension berths; also two berths in the forward cabin—or six in all. A galley, an enclosed head, and other facilities are included. Price is $17,990, not including sails.

VITAL STATISTICS: L.O.A. 33′; waterline 22′11″; beam 10′; draft without centerboard 3′6″, with C.B. 6′7″; sail area 508 sq. ft.; power, 30-h.p. Universal Atomic Four.

SWIFTSURE. *Courtesy Philip L. Rhodes.*

TARTAN 27 yawl. *Courtesy Sparkman and Stephens.*

TARTAN 27

The Tartan 27 is a new contribution to the class of small auxiliaries. It was designed by Sparkman and Stephens and introduced in 1961 by Douglass & McLeod, Inc., builders (Box 311, Painesville, Ohio). Dealers handling the boat include the Richard Bertram Company (N.W. 21st St., Miami, Fla.) and George B. Walton, Inc. (4th St. and Severn Ave., Annapolis, Md.). While twenty-five boats have already been built, the class growth is presently at the rate of thirty boats a year. It is made of fiber glass with teak and mahogany trim and is a displacement hull said to have "excellent capabilities to windward." The rudder is of aluminum, as are the spars.

Sleeping accommodations of three single berths and one double berth have been worked into the Tartan, a real feat for a boat of only 21½ feet waterline, though the fiber-glass construction helps considerably to this end. The centerboard trunk is entirely below the cabin floor. Headroom in the raised section of the cabin is 6 feet. Accommodations include a galley, enclosed head, etc.

A member of the Tartan class, the *Dawnell,* owned and well sailed by Harold M. Scott, Jr., of Noroton, Connecticut, won the Larchmont Yacht Club's Edlu Trophy Race in May 1962 against eighty-six other boats. The *Dawnell* was the smallest boat ever to win this trophy. She not only won the race on corrected time but beat many other larger boats on actual time.

The Tartan was designed to give a good account of herself under both Cruising Club of America and Midget Ocean Racing Club rules. She is obtainable as a sloop or yawl. Sailing activities, so far, are on Long Island Sound, Chesapeake Bay, and the Great Lakes. For information about the class, write Douglass & McLeod, Inc., at the address given above. Price is $11,750, including sails.

VITAL STATISTICS: L.O.A. 27′; waterline 21′5″; beam 8′7½″; draft without centerboard 3′2″, with C.B. 6′4″; sail area 372 sq. ft. (sloop), 394 sq. ft. (yawl); displacement 6500 lbs.; power is a Universal Atomic Four.

THUNDERBIRD

During 1958 the Douglas Fir Plywood Association came to Ben Seaborn, a Seattle, Washington, naval architect, and gave him an assignment. Seaborn's task was to design a boat to meet the following requirements: one that could beat other boats of its size in racing competition, that would be comfortable and roomy enough for a family of at least four, be reasonably easy for an amateur to build, and also be safe, dry, and not too expensive. Judging from the name of the association, it would seem reasonable to ex-

THUNDERBIRD.
*Photo by
Kenneth G. Ollar,
courtesy Stefan Thordason.*

pect that it was to be made of plywood, though we are told fiber glass may now be used on top of plywood.

The enthusiasts who have written about the boat seem to think that Seaborn's Thunderbird, as the 26-foot class of sloops came to be called, comes very close to achieving what Seaborn first called impossible. During the Tacoma Yacht Club's 1958–59 winter racing season, under the capable Douglas Sherwood, the first Thunderbird won several races, including those in light, medium, and gusty winds. In one race, according to Frank C. Beesom,[*] "she was clocked at better than 10 knots under reefed main and spinnaker on a consistent semi-plane." Seaborn credits the good sailing performance of the Thunderbird to three things: (1) the hydrofoil keel ("in the shape of a symmetrical hydrofoil in vertical section, producing a highly favorable ratio of lift over drag . . . blunt on the leading edge and feathered to a trailing edge"), (2) the hard chines, and (3) the lightweight hull.

[*] "Are You Ready for Your First Cruising Boat," by Frank Carter Beesom, *Popular Boating,* July 1961.

The boat will sleep four and seat seven below. The cabin opening flares outward toward the top so that cabin and cockpit seem like one general open unit. The hatch over the cabin is in two hinged sections which raise to provide full standing room. Privacy can be obtained by side curtains.

The success of the Thunderbird has been striking. At the time of writing, 185 boats have been registered with the International Thunderbird Class Association and the number is expected to reach 200 shortly. Since well over half are built by amateurs, there are undoubtedly some boats which are unregistered. Of the 185, 140 are in the United States, 45 in Canada and elsewhere—including Australia and Holland. The fleets in Seattle and Tacoma, Washington, were the first to organize. This is a most interesting class and the boats are attractive to look at.

Yachting's Boat Owners Buyers Guide carries a long list of builders, including several on the Atlantic Coast and Great Lakes, as well as on the Pacific Coast. Builder names and other information about the class may also be obtained from the class Secretary, Walfred J. Larson, (16151 S.E. 5th St., Bellevue, Wash.). The Douglas Fir Plywood Association (Tacoma 2, Wash.) sells plans for two dollars. Price of the boat is from about $5000 up; kits are from $300 up. If you "do it yourself," it will probably cost you $3000 to $3500.

VITAL STATISTICS: L.O.A. 26'; waterline 20'; beam 7'6"; draft (keel) 4'9"; sail area 364 sq. ft.; weight 3600 lbs.; it is not practical to trail in most cases; power is a 5- to 10-h.p. outboard operating in a well.

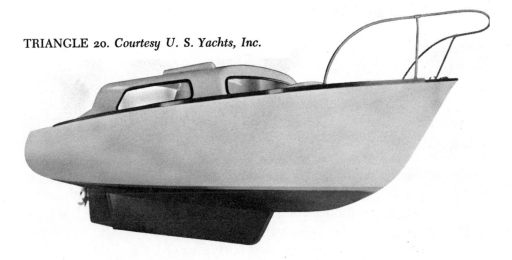

TRIANGLE 20. *Courtesy U. S. Yachts, Inc.*

TRIANGLE 20

The Triangle 20 sloop was designed by Charles Angle of the Triangle Marine Company and is sold by U. S. Yachts, Inc. (Village Square, Westport, Conn.). At the time of writing, thirty-two have already been built and forty are under construction, or seventy-two in all. This and the Triangle 32, according to Warren G. Dellenbaugh of U. S. Yachts, were "designed primarily for optimum cruising conditions, both space and sailing ability, and then everything was done to make them as fast as possible within the various racing categories that they fill. This is perhaps a reverse concept but it is one that results in probably the best compromise of two-berth and six-berth auxiliaries respectively."

There is no class association at the present time but detailed information may be sought from the Triangle Marine Company (5395 St. Paul Blvd., Rochester, N.Y.). The principal sailing areas are the Great Lakes, New England, and the Middle Atlantic states, though there is said to be interest on the West Coast.

The Triangle 20 is a keel-centerboard boat, built of fiber glass, with two berths, a small galley, and a semiprivate head. Price is $4200 with sails.

VITAL STATISTICS: L.O.A. 20′6″; waterline 16′8″; beam 7′1″; draft without centerboard 2′2″, with C.B. 4′9″; sail area 205 sq. ft.; displacement 2300 lbs.; power is outboard through a well.

TRIPP 30

The Tripp 30 was designed by William H. Tripp, Jr., and is imported from Europe by Seafarer Fiber Glass Yachts (205 E. 42nd St., New York 17, N.Y.). About thirty of these fiber-glass sloops are reported built or under construction. This is an attractive boat. Overhangs are fairly long and are characteristic of Tripp boats. Seafarer claims for her a "sensational racing record" in both Eastern circuits and on the Great Lakes.

Her regular accommodations include two berths in the main cabin and two forward, though two extra folding berths may be added in the main cabin if desired. Headroom is 6′1″. There are also an enclosed head and galley and many other facilities such as would be found on a well-designed boat of this size. She can be obtained with a yawl rig if desired.

Price is about $13,000 without sails.

VITAL STATISTICS: L.O.A. 30′4″; waterline 20′; beam 8′6″; draft (keel) 4′6″; sail area (sloop) 369 sq. ft., (yawl) 394 sq. ft.; power, 30-h.p. Universal Atomic Four.

TRIPP 30. *Copyright photo by Van Oudgaarden, courtesy Seafarer Fiber Glass Yachts, Inc.*

TRITON. *Courtesy Pearson Corporation.*

TRITON

With 355 Tritons "out now" according to the Pearson Corporation (Bristol, R.I.), this is by far the largest class of "full-sized" cruising-racing auxiliaries which we have ever had in the United States. Designed by Carl A. Alberg and built by the Pearson Corporation, this 28½-footer is the intermediate boat in a trio of Alberg-Pearson molded-fiber-glass craft, of which the Alberg 35 is the largest and the 22½-foot Electra the smallest member.

Introduced at the 1959 New York Motor Boat Show, Triton came along at a time when sailing yachtsmen were becoming much interested in fiber-glass boats in the cruising auxiliary class, and when a demand was growing for a boat in which two couples or a family of four could cruise in comfort at a moderate cost of boat and upkeep. It was the right boat at the right time and the response has been sensational for an auxiliary of that size. Good looks has a great deal to do with the success of a boat in which the whole family takes an interest. The Triton has that, as well as a good turn of speed.

The Triton is available with either a sloop or a yawl rig and is reported to be a good sailer. Accommodations include four berths, divided between two cabins; an enclosed head; a galley, and many other facilities. We know several Triton owners and each speaks highly of the all-around qualities of his boat. While there is no association covering all Tritons, a Triton Association of Long Island Sound (with over sixty members at time of writing) was recently organized. Jerome Farmer (Room 727, 350 Fifth Ave., New York, N.Y.) is Secretary-Treasurer. Triton sailing waters so far are principally on Long Island Sound, Chesapeake Bay, and the Pacific Coast. Price is about $11,500 with sails. Northrop and Johnson (366 Madison Ave., New York 17, N.Y.) is a leading dealer.

VITAL STATISTICS: L.O.A. 28′6″; waterline 20′6″; beam 8′3″; draft (keel) 4′; sail area (sloop) 371 sq. ft., (yawl) 382.5 sq. ft.; displacement 6930 lbs.; power, 30-h.p. Universal Atomic Four.

WEEKENDER

The Weekender of Sparkman and Stephens and the Coastwise Cruiser of John Alden, comparable in dimensions and coming along in the 1930s, marked the beginning of a era of offshore and 'longshore cruising in stock auxiliaries of moderate size and price. Following after the New York 32s, these boats were good all-around sailers and racers. Thirty-nine Weekenders were built. Other cruising auxiliary classes came along later, most of them

WEEKENDER. *Photo by Morris Rosenfeld, courtesy Sparkman and Stephens.*

smaller in size and many of them larger in number, but the Weekenders and the Coastwise Cruisers were among the pioneers.

Built originally by the well-known Lawley, no Weekenders have been constructed in recent years, though the familiar W E is still seen on Long Island Sound and elsewhere. Used boats can be bought at about $10,000.

VITAL STATISTICS: L.O.A. 35′; waterline 27′; beam 9′5″; draft (keel) 5′6″; sail area 368 sq. ft.; weight 6250 lbs.; power, Gray Sea-Scout.

PART THREE
CATAMARAN CLASSES
Including One PROA

INTRODUCTION

On April 10, 1877, a letter from Nathanael Herreshoff appeared in the New York *Herald*. In it the man who came to be known as the "Wizard of Bristol" (R.I.) described the reasoning which led him to design and build the famous *Amaryllis,* one of the earliest American catamarans to make conventional yachts look like ice wagons.*

"In the fall of 1875," said Herreshoff, "I was thinking and thinking how to get great speed out of single-hulled boats, or the kind in common use. To get great speed, thought I, one must have great power. To have great power one must have great sail, you must have something to hold it up, and that something must be large and wide, and have a large sectional surface, and also a great deal of frictional surface. These properties in a hull to give stability are not compatible with attaining great speed. Indeed, the more one tries to make a stiff, stable hull the less speed will be attained, even if corresponding additions are made to the sail. So, then, there are two important principles of speed which constantly work against each other. If we increase the power to get more speed we must increase the stability of the hull correspondingly. An increased hull has more resistance, both from sectional area and surface friction. So what we would fain gain one way we lose in the other. . . .

". . . A wide boat cannot have great speed, apply what power you will to her, so the next thing that has to be done is to decrease the sectional area and the frictional area. I thought I would raise the heel and the center line of the boat, and make the bilges project downward and outward from it— such a thing as a Dutchman might build. . . . I kept on following this principle, getting the keel higher and higher, when lo and behold! There was a double boat! Nothing else to be done but take a saw and split her in two, spread it apart a little way and cover all with a deck and there you are. That was the rough road which I travelled, and having arrived thus far I abandoned my ill-shaped hulls and in their place substituted two long, narrow, very light boats and connected them at the bow, stern, and middle.

* This letter was found when I was browsing around among the valuable collection of scrapbooks in the library of the New York Yacht Club. My purpose was to obtain background information for my *Block Island to Nantucket,* published by D. Van Nostrand Co., Inc., in April 1961. The story here is gleaned largely from that book, as it seemed especially appropriate for the section on catamarans.

"The extreme length of the hull [of *Amaryllis*] is 24 feet 10 inches. . . . The width [of each hull] is 20 inches in the widest place and 18 inches on the waterline."

The *Amaryllis* was launched in May 1876. During a trial in which she was going at about 18 miles per hour, her backstay parted in a puff. Herreshoff added: "Sailing in a catamaran is an entirely new sensation, and it has everything in a recreation to recommend it, safety being one of its chief attributes. There is no shifting of ballast, no hanging on with tooth and nail up to windward. I am sure that a half day's sail in the *Amaryllis* would spoil anyone for the old fashioned sailing."

It took over eighty years for catamarans again to occupy an important place on the American yachting scene. The occasion was at *Yachting's* One-of-a-Kind Regatta at Biscayne Bay, Miami, Florida, starting on February 21, 1959. With forty boats competing, including those from the fastest single-hull classes in the country, catamarans took first, second, and fourth on corrected time: respectively, the *Tigercat** (17′), the *Cougar* Mark I (17′9″), and the *Shearwater III* (16′6″). The only interruption to this string was the third-place 17-foot canoe with a sliding seat. On a boat-for-boat basis the first two catamarans were beaten only by a 38-foot Class A Inland Lake Scow, over twice their length.

Since that time catamarans and catamaran classes have grown so rapidly in number that I can do no more here than attempt to catch on the wing a few of what are considered the leading catamaran classes at the time of writing, or those that have what seems to be sufficient promise. They are probably typical of others which will follow. The classes considered here are racing and day-sailing classes. Stock classes of cruising catamarans are at too early a stage of development for us to include any of them in this book.

As will be noted in the discussions of catamaran classes which follow, most of the catamarans now have certain points in common: identical narrow hulls; twin centerboards and rudders; aluminum spars which rotate, including usually a "luffspar" on the jib for easy furling; usually more sail for their length than a single-hull craft. Usually, also, they are less comfortable than most single-hull boats and wetter at maximum speeds, though said to be drier at normal single-hull speeds.

All catamarans are not fast sailers, as I know from personal experience. In 1950, after experiencing the thrill of sailing at 18 or 20 knots in Woodbridge ("Woody") Brown's *Manu Kai* off Waikiki Beach, Honolulu, I took what proved to be an unfortunate chance and imported a 20-foot Hawaiian-built catamaran. I had not had a chance to try her out and depended upon

---

* *Tigercat* was the name of the prototype boat which won this regatta. The class which followed is called Tiger Cat.

a recommendation from someone who had. She turned out to be useful chiefly as a swimming float which moved slowly under favorable conditions and which my daughters enjoyed more than I did. Her centerboard box between the hulls dragged; her hulls were too wide and had square sections which neither sliced well through the water nor planed; she was too heavy and while we didn't engage in formal races, every boat we met beat us. Once, a borrowing friend tipped her over. I was lucky to sell her at not too big a loss and fortunately haven't seen since the man who bought her. So I learned that there is also a wrong kind of catamaran.

I have been told, on excellent authority, of at least seven catamaran classes which have not been successful. The margin between success and failure in catamaran design is sometimes a narrow one. To quote an article in *Tiger Tails*, official publication of the Tiger Cat Association: "All good catamarans satisfy *all five* of these basic requirements: (1) Proper hull shape; (2) proper size; (3) proper lateral plane; (4) proper sailpower; (5) light weight. Fail to satisfy any *one* of these requirements, and you'll have a 'dog' instead of a 'cat.'"

A great deal has been learned about catamarans since my experience in 1950. Apparently, I had the right idea but the wrong boat. As Bob Bavier pointed out in *Yachting* (May 1959), properly designed catamarans have some points in common with the fastest of the single-hull planing types. These include particularly the following:

(1) *Narrow hull.* The two types of boats which made the best showing against the catamarans in the One-of-a-Kind Regatta were the International Decked Sailing Canoe and the Inland Lake Scows. The former has a very narrow hull which is kept upright by the man on the sliding seat. The scows have in effect a narrow hull when they heel.

(2) *Power.* The catamarans, sailing canoes, and scows all acquire power by enabling the crew to get up to windward and hold the sails up to the wind. So does a planing hull with a man on the (flying) trapeze.

(3) *Light weight.* A common characteristic of most of the fastest boats, catamarans and otherwise, is their light weight.

Carleton Mitchell describes so well why catamarans suddenly began to "click" that I should like to quote from some of his remarks[*] made shortly after the One-of-a-Kind Regatta:

"If there is a secret to the sudden transformation of this ancient type into an unbeatable craft both to windward and leeward, it probably lies in the combination of lighter weight and improved stability, lessened wetted surface, and the ability to add lateral plane by means of centerboards. This, plus rigs and sails almost aerodynamically perfect, including pivoted alumi-

[*] "The Cat Leads a Revolution," by Carleton Mitchell, *Sports Illustrated*, March 9, 1959.

num masts, luffspars on jibs, and full-length main battens, all adds up to speed.

"But cats do not 'plane' by getting on top of the water in the same sense as planing monohulls. They lack the supporting surface of beam and flat hull sections. Thus there is no 'hump speed' where the boat's own bow wave must be surmounted. Instead, they are more like destroyers, very narrow in relation to their length, consequently easily driven and of low wave-making resistance.

"How fast will catamarans sail, and how may they be rated in competition against conventional craft? There seems little doubt that a good cat under favorable conditions can travel at approximately five times the square root of her waterline length, as opposed to about 1.3 in a displacement hull. In other words, a 16-foot catamaran should be capable of sailing at 20 knots. At the same time, a nonplaning boat of the same size would be plugging along at 5.2 knots. Thus, even adding the length of the two hulls together and calling a 20-foot cat 40 feet long for rating purposes would not overcome the difference in speed, lending some credence to the remark of an enthusiast: 'You can't establish a formula to match an oxcart and a Ferrari. Cats will have to race as a separate class.'

"The regatta did not prove all catamaran designers had achieved the breakthrough, and there is danger the market will be flooded with basically bad boats, both sail and power. As Roland Prout has written, 'There is more to catamaran design than twin hulls.' This was proved in the majority of races, when the catamarans divided into two widely separated groups, so far apart it was hard to believe they had started together. Of eight twin-hulled craft, four were consistently in the leading division; the remaining four were mostly back in the ruck. . . .

"No one who watched catamarans knifing through Biscayne Bay will question that sailing one is the nearest earthbound approach to jet flying—silent, responsive to the touch and with a feeling of exhilaration only the sensation of extreme speed can bring. A new dimension has been added to small-boating."

Since the One-of-a-Kind Regatta, racing by catamaran classes and between catamarans of different types has developed rapidly. For instance, we have seen a 1962 "Catamaran Racing Schedule for the Eastern Part of North America" which lists sixteen events from May to September and from Quincy Bay, Massachusetts, to Washington, D.C.—plus a regatta on Lake St. Louis, in Quebec, Canada. A North American Catamaran Championship (300 sq. ft. sail area) was scheduled for August 19–21 at the Beverly Yacht Club (Marion, Mass.), to be followed by "Trials for the British Challenge Re-Match (300 sq. ft. S.A.)." The catamarans have arrived.

AQUA-CAT. *Courtesy American Fiberglass Corporation.*

AQUA-CAT

This is one of the smallest, simplest, lightest, and least expensive members of the fast-growing catamaran family. Designed in 1959 by Arthur Javes in Norwalk, Connecticut, thirty were reported sold in 1960, 467 sold to date.

The exclusive builder is the American Fiberglass Corporation 132 S. Main St., South Norwalk, Conn.). Connecticut, Long Island Sound, and Cape Cod are the principal sailing areas, but these "cats" are reported to be already in twenty-nine states and seven foreign countries. Aluminum bars hold the twin fiber-glass hulls together and support a canvas deck which sags with the weight of the crew—a fact that adds to the sitting comfort except perhaps when spray collects there. We have seen only boats with the canvas stretched across between the hulls. With a single nylon sail, the rig is of the felucca type. Each hull has a daggerboard and a rudder.

The boats are very versatile geographically and functionally. They can be trailed easily or cartop carried, and they serve not only as fast sailboats or as outboard-driven boats, but also as family swimming floats. The Aqua-Cat Catamaran Sailing Association, recently formed, has Charles Gray as Secretary (P. O. Box 297, S. Norwalk, Conn.). Price of the Aqua-Cat is $782 complete (f.o.b. factory), no extras.

VITAL STATISTICS: L.O.A. 12'2"; waterline 11'10"; beam 6'; draft without daggerboards 5", with boards 2'; sail area 78 sq. ft. (standard), 90 sq. ft. (racing); weight 127 lbs.; trailable and cartop carried.

CATALINA CATAMARAN

Designed by Seymour Paul for the W. D. Schock Company (3502 S. Greenville St., Santa Ana, Calif.), this attractive sloop-rigged all-molded fiber-glass catamaran has a good-sized self-bailing cockpit with contoured seats. The boat has a hinged aluminum mast stepped on deck, an aluminum luffspar for a roller-furling jib, a roller-reefing main with full battens, twin pivoted centerboards, and twin tilt-up rudders. The fiber-glass decks and cockpit surfacing are nonskid and the boat looks very much like one or two of the most sucessful catamarans. This is a new class and it is too soon at the time of writing to size up how far it will go. However, the fact that Seymour Paul is an experienced catamaran designer and W. D. Schock an experienced builder of many types of boats should make its success probable. Of course, all well-designed and well-built catamarans should benefit by the tremendous growing interest in "cats." Price (Schock) is $2425 with Dacron sails, f.o.b. Santa Ana.

VITAL STATISTICS: L.O.A. 17'6"; waterline 16'; beam 7'11½"; draft without centerboards 8", with boards 3'2"; sail area 234 sq. ft.; weight 565 lbs.

CATALINA CATAMARAN. *Photo by Beckner Photo Service, courtesy W. D. Schock Co.*

COUGAR CATAMARAN. *Photo by Sam Chambliss, courtesy of Rebcat.*

COUGAR CATAMARAN—MARK III One-Design

Back in 1952 Roland and Francis Prout, of Essex, England, after considerable experimenting with twin-hulled boats, developed the original Shearwater, a 16½-foot catamaran design which grew to an international class of over a thousand boats. One of the owners of a Shearwater, Richard E. Brown, a U. S. Navy Commander on aviation duty in England, asked the Prouts to design a larger version for the United States. The new 17'9" craft was called the *Cougar* and was finished just in time for the 1959 One-of-a-

Kind Regatta at Miami, Florida. As most yachtsmen know, the first place over-all on corrected time was won by *Tigercat. Cougar,* sailed by Roland Prout, was second out of forty racing boats of forty different classes.

Retiring from the Navy, R. E. Brown went into the boat business. Rebcats (R. E. Brown Catamarans) was organized and began importing Prout-built Cougars. Later, an improved Cougar was developed which is 18'9" long and is known as the Cougar Mark III, imported by Rebcats (2727 29th St. N.W., Washington 8, D.C.). Late in 1961 the International Cougar Catamaran Association was formed (11067 Champagne Point Rd., Kirkland, Wash.). Miss Ann M. Cotter is Secretary.

The Cougar Mark III has a sloop rig, full battened mainsail, rotating mast with hinged step, roller-furling jib on a luffspar, pivotal and removable centerboards, pivotal rudders. The hull is of fiber glass, the decks and cockpit of mahogany plywood. At the time of writing there are ninety boats in the United States and about twenty elsewhere. Reported are a "sprinkling" on Midwest rivers and lakes; boats on Long Island Sound, Chesapeake Bay, in Florida, Denver, Seattle, and in England. Rebcats, the importer, has a long list of dealers for the boats, which will be furnished to those interested. Price is $2285 complete f.o.b. U. S. East Coast. Used boats cost $1700 to $2000, kits $1800.

VITAL STATISTICS: L.O.A. 18'9"; waterline 17'2"; beam 7'11"; draft without centerboards 5", with boards 2'6"; sail area 225 sq. ft.; weight 510 lbs.; trailable.

DC-14

Designed by Robert B. Harris and Frank MacLear, the DC-14 was tested on Long Island Sound late in 1960 and production-built boats were sailed during 1961. They are produced at Branford, Connecticut, by Duncan Sutphen (342 Madison Ave., New York 17, N.Y.). Abercrombie and Fitch sells them in New York City. Fiber-glass hulls are decked over by plastic-surfaced marine plywood. The bridge is of solid mahogany and mahogany plywood. The rig is lateen with a mainsail only. Bench seats rising above the cockpit floor give a comfort some small catamarans lack. A motor bracket for outboards is obtainable. She has the usual twin centerboards and twin flip-up rudders. Eighteen have been sold at the time of writing and a number of others are under construction. Price f.o.b. Branford, Connecticut, including sail, is $975. Duncan Sutphen reports that it is planned to build a DC-14 Special with sloop rig and 133 square feet of sail.

DC-14. *Courtesy Duncan Sutphen, Inc.*

VITAL STATISTICS: L.O.A. 14'2"; beam 6'8", draft without center-boards 6", with boards 2'2"; sail area 100 sq. ft.; weight without sail and rig 299 lbs. complete; trailable or cartop carried.

MALIBU OUTRIGGER
Unlike the other classes described in this section, the two hulls of the "Proa" Malibu are *not* twin hulls; one of them is an outrigger, shorter and

MALIBU OUTRIGGER. *Courtesy Ethel (Mrs. William) Buck.*

much narrower than the main hull that carries the only daggerboard and rudder used. A primary consideration with her designer, Warren Seaman, was to develop a boat which could be easily beached and hauled up. There are few good harbors on the California coast and Seaman had this very much in mind as the following comments indicate. These are by the Malibu Boat Company (Malibu, Calif.), which sells the Malibu-class boats:

"The outrigger meets the challenge of the Pacific coastal sailing. She is light, fast, easy to handle in the surf, and can be beached anywhere. She accelerates quickly, a characteristic which is the key to navigating hazardous surf. She is particularly ideal for enthusiasts who live in a locale where shoal water or surf dominate an otherwise good sailing area.

"The home of the outrigger is the Malibu Yacht Club in Malibu, California. There are no moorings, no slips, just a large private beach facing the ever-present surf. We are often dubbed 'The Malibu Lot Club.' Most of the boats are kept high on the beach at the club or on residential beaches in the area. We have no bottom paint worries, no teredo worm threats, but we do have gophers. Our gophers are evidently delighted with manila; it is not uncommon to lose several feet of a mainsheet overnight. Here is a unique problem for a unique boat.

"However, about 700 sets of plans have been sold all over the world . . . in the United States, from Maine to Hawaii, from Florida to Alaska, and in 14 foreign countries including New Zealand, the Philippines, Japan, Finland and Brazil. She has met with much interest and has passed the test of the surf, the open ocean, and the 'conventional' sailor.

"The rig is a modified lateen type which is quite flexible and thus excellent in gusty air. A daggerboard extends the draft from five inches to a maximum of four feet, making possible an extremely good performance to windward. The flexible rig and 'arms' enable her to span swells and stiff chop with ease. She is wet, but exhilarating to sail in a rough sea."

Although a Malibu made a poor record in *Yachting's* One-of-a-Kind Regatta in 1959 (finishing thirty-eighth while leading catamarans finished first, second, fourth, and seventh), she was the winner in the first Pacific Coast One-of-a-Kind Race, on both actual and corrected time. She obviously meets a need not only in Southern California, her principal sailing waters, but elsewhere, for 810 have been sold at the time of writing, of which 200 are sailed outside of the United States. Next to California, the Malibus are most frequently to be seen in Florida. Price is $1800; used boats can be bought for $500.

VITAL STATISTICS: L.O.A. 18'10"; waterline 17'; beam 11'8"; draft without daggerboard 5", with board 4'5"; sail area 192 sq. ft.; weight 400 lbs.; trailable; racing crew, two.

PACIFIC CATAMARAN

A predecessor of this all-fiber-glass catamaran was the second boat to finish out of three hundred entries in the Newport (Calif.) to Ensenada Race of 1960. She was sailing unofficially, as catamarans sometimes have

PACIFIC CATAMARANS. *Photo by Beckner Photo Service, courtesy Newport Boats.*

had to do, and covered the 130-mile course in a little over twenty-three hours. Designed by Carter Pyle, the present Pacific Catamaran is built by both Newport Boats (P. O. Box 1741, Newport Beach, Calif.) and Mobjack Manufacturing Company (Gloucester, Va.). At the time of writing there are thirty-eight Pacific Catamarans in the United States. A Pacific Catamaran Class Association has been formed. The Secretary is Peter Ferguson (11295 Havelock Ave., Culver City, Calif.).

The Pacific Catamaran has a double cockpit, one in each hull, permitting the crew easily to sit out to windward. The mast is a rotating and hinged aluminum spar and the twin centerboards and rudders kick up. There are

SCAMPER. *Photo by Morris Rosenfeld, courtesy Patterson Catamaran Corporation.*

six watertight compartments giving nine hundred pounds of buoyancy. As in the case of other catamarans, the jib is set on a revolving luffspar and can be quickly furled. The price is $2664, including Dacron mainsail and jib.

VITAL STATISTICS: L.O.A. 18'9"; waterline 17'11"; beam 7'11"; draft without centerboards 7", with boards 2'11"; sail area 267 sq. ft. (spinnaker permitted); weight 540 lbs.

SCAMPER

The Scamper was designed by George W. Patterson as a small, simple, lightweight catamaran, easy for one person to sail, and trailable. The builders are the Patterson Catamaran Corporation (25 Diaz St., Stamford, Conn.) and Marine and Industrial Fiberglass Products, Ltd. (P. O. Box 6, Lachine, Quebec, Canada). "Our racing record against other cats in our class range," Mr. Patterson reports, "is an excellent one: division II winner Eastern Multihull Regatta 1961; division II winner and over-all winner on elapsed time of all boats 14' and under at Sea Cliff Invitational Catamaran Regatta 1962. Besides being a small high-performance racing cat, the Scamper sails and handles well with a crew weight of over 300 pounds for just plain sailing fun.

"Incidentally," adds Mr. Patterson, "after the Sea Cliff Regatta, two Scampers were sailed across the Sound from Sea Cliff to Stamford, a distance of close to 18 miles, at an average speed of 10 m.p.h., which is not bad, in choppy water, for a little 12-foot boat."

A class association has been formed, with headquarters care of Patterson (133 Buttery Rd., New Canaan, Conn.).

The Scamper is produced in a sloop rig, with the usual twin centerboards and rudders which tilt up. The number built at the time of writing is thirty-three, most of which are on Long Island Sound. Hulls are of fiber glass, decks and cockpit of marine plywood. Price complete with sails is $955; in kit form it costs $735.

VITAL STATISTICS: L.O.A. 12'; waterline 11'6"; beam 6'; draft without centerboards 7", with boards 2'2"; sail area 90 sq. ft.; weight (fully rigged) 165 lbs.; trailable.

SHEARWATER III

The 16½-foot Shearwater is by far the largest class of catamarans in the world. Since the first Shearwater took to the water in England, over a thousand have been built, spread out among several countries, consti-

SHEARWATER III. *Photo by Maurice J. Mervis.*

tuting what has been called a truly international class. If the optimistic predictions of Kenneth R. Duniface, in his *Newsletter #11* to Shearwater owners, come true (though the number of Shearwaters in the United States is still small), the organization of the International Shearwater Catamaran Association "should make us the largest catamaran association in the U.S. at least until the resignations begin pouring in." Mr. Duniface is editor of the *Newsletter* and a leading source of information and enthusiasm about the class. (His address is 461 S. Brevard Ave., Apt. 18, Cocoa Beach, Fla.)

On April 9, 1962, he wrote: "As we are a restricted class, there is considerable variation among the boats. We are now in the throes of defining our own class rules. So far we have been following the British rules, which don't seem to work too well over here. I believe we will wind up with the requirement that the hulls be built by Prout (G. Prout and Sons of Essex, England, designed the first Shearwater in 1952)."

Those interested in evidence that catamaran ideas are moving almost as fast as the boats themselves will be entertained, as I was, by reading the above-mentioned *Newsletter*. A British newsletter follows along similar lines and suggests an ambitious program. It was addressed "To Shearwater Sailors in British Guiana, Canada, Canvey Island, Eire, England, France, Guernsey, Germany, Hong Kong, Italy, Mauritius, New Caledonia, New Zealand, Nigeria, Norway, Nyasaland, Orkney, Salem, South Africa, Scotland, Sweden, Switzerland, Trinidad, U.S.A., Wales."

As already explained in connection with the Cougar Catamaran, the original Shearwater was developed by two Englishmen, Roland and Francis Prout, who first brought it out in 1952. They were also the designers of Shearwaters II and III. According to Robert B. Harris, the Shearwater III "has reached speeds up to 21 knots."

Shearwater III is the American class boat and is distributed in the United States by McNichols Boat Sales (1617 E. McNichols, Detroit, Mich.). The boat is of molded fiber glass, with an aluminum mast, boom, and luffspar for roller-furling the jib. The twin centerboards, rudders, and tillers are of aluminum alloy. Price with sails, etc., f.o.b. East Coast dock, is $1750 plus local sales tax. Kits are $1225 plus sales tax.

VITAL STATISTICS (Shearwater III): L.O.A. 16′6″; beam 7′6″; draft without boards 7″; sail area 160 sq. ft.; weight including rig 350 lbs.

TIGER CAT

First on corrected time and second boat-for-boat to the Class A Inland Lake Scow, which is more than twice as long, the *Tigercat*,* closely followed by the Cougar Catamaran, made history in *Yachting's* 1959 One-of-a-Kind Regatta. The modern era of catamarans really began. The original *Tigercat* and the Tiger Cat class which followed were designed by Robert B. Harris. He and William S. Cox—a noted racing yachtsman with many championships to his credit—were the men who created the original *Tiger-*

---

* *Tigercat* was the name of the boat raced at Miami, the prototype of the Tiger Cat class.

TIGER CAT. *Courtesy Pearson Corporation.*

cat and were leaders in getting the class started. Mrs. William S. Cox (30 Point O'Woods Rd., Darien, Conn.) is Secretary of the Tiger Cat Association. At the time of writing there are 173 Tiger Cats in the class, of which three are sailed outside of the United States. Principal sailing waters are on the U. S. Eastern Seaboard, in Texas, on Lake Pymatuning (along the Pennsylvania-Ohio border), and on various other lakes.

As reported by *Tiger Tails* (official publication of the Association), during 1961 Tiger Cats won six out of the seven "open" regattas in the Eastern United States and Canada in which they participated. At the National Championship twenty-five Tiger Cats took part, making by far the largest group of one-design catamarans up to that time ever to cross a single starting line in the United States.

The Tiger Cat hulls are identical, rounded, and narrow in section, fine forward but with fairly round sections aft. Like other leading catamarans, they are fitted with twin pivoting centerboards, twin rudders, and full-length battens in the mainsail. A feature is a cockpit tent which serves as a portable cabin. This is obtainable from Hard Sails, Inc. (204 Main St., Islip, N.Y.).

Following the success of the wooden *Tigercat* at Miami, the construction of a class of these boats was assigned exclusively to the Pearson Corporation of Bristol, Rhode Island, where, in May 1876, Nathanael Herreshoff had launched his famous catamaran, *Amaryllis*. The boats are built from two molds of fiber glass throughout with a vinyl rub rail on a flange which is widened forward to form integral spray deflectors on both sides of both hulls. The mast, boom, and jib luffspar are of aluminum alloy and grooved to hold the sail bolt ropes. Both mast and luffspar rotate. The cockpit is self-bailing, as water drains through the centerboard boxes. Price, including Dacron mainsail with full-length battens, jib, and toe-straps, is $2511. Used boats cost $2000 to $2200; there are no kits.

VITAL STATISTICS: L.O.A. 17′; waterline 15′10″; beam 7′11½″; beam of each hull at waterline 1′3¾″; draft without centerboards 7½″, with boards 3′1″; sail area 235 sq. ft.; weight 585 lbs.; racing crew, two.

TIKI II

Designed by Robert B. Harris, the Tiki II is a new boat at the time of writing, with fifteen already built and many more expected. The earlier Tiki, of which eighty-six boats were built, is no longer in production. The builder of Tiki II is the Catamaran Corporation of America (2324 Summit, Kansas City 8, Mo.). So far, the principal areas of sailing are at Kansas City, Missouri; Wichita, Kansas; and Spofford Lake, New Hampshire. For information about the class, write David Halperin (4812 Black Swan Drive, Shawnee, Kan.).

The boat is of molded fiber glass, including the self-bailing cockpit, which

TIKI II. *Courtesy Catamaran Corporation of America.*

has a mahogany dash and coamings. Among other features are aluminum grooved spars, sealed for floating mast, rotating mast step, roller reefing, swing-up rudders and centerboards, foam flotation, full-batten Dacron sails. The boat is designed for easy conversion to outboard power, adequate for pulling water skiers. A mosquito-proof ventilated camping shelter is furnished for $90 extra, and there is also a custom-designed trailer at $175. Thus, every effort seems to have been made to have as versatile a boat as possible.

R. L. Anderson of Spofford Lake, New Hampshire, wrote to Mr. Halperin as follows (April 22, 1962) regarding the performance of his Tiki II on the lake: "While there was a fine 12- to 15-mile breeze most of the afternoon, we sailed very cautiously with a 90-pound crew (a child) in extremely cold water with occasional 20-miles per hour puffs and not another soul on the lake. In spite of the excess caution Tiki went remarkably well. The sails are top notch. We did not drive the boat hard at any time except during lulls, but she shows no sign of requiring pampering. Best recorded speed was 9 miles per hour on a broad reach, but we may have done better than this at times. . . . I can't get over the readiness with which Tiki tacks."

Price is $1395 complete, including mainsail and jib.

VITAL STATISTICS: L.O.A. 14′; waterline 13′; beam 7′; draft without centerboards 5″, with boards 3′; sail area 155 sq. ft.; weight 245 lbs.

WILDCAT II

The first thing to explain about the Wildcat II class of catamarans is that this class is *not* the same as the Californian catamaran of that name, designed by Seymour Paul, which was selected to represent the United States in the 1961 races for the International Catamaran Challenge Trophy and was then badly beaten by the British *Hellcat*. The Wildcat of those races was 21 feet over-all. The new Wildcat II-class boats are 17′9″ long. The Wildcat II class was designed by Seymour Paul and Dan Sanderson. She is sold by the J. C. Beery Company (Aquatic Park, Berkeley 10, Calif.) and built by S and H Sail Boats (3034 S. Bristol, Costa Mesa, Calif.). Mrs. Dan W. Sanderson is class Secretary (279 Del Mar Ave., Costa Mesa, Calif.). It is reported that there are thirty registered Wildcat owners at Newport Harbor, near Los Angeles, and at Berkeley in the San Francisco Bay area. Construction is fiber glass and mahogany. Price is about $2200 including sails, used $2000.

* *Note:* Robert B. Harris, leading American catamaran designer, has written a book which is highly recommended to those who want to delve further into the catamaran story than has been possible herein. It is called *Modern Sailing Catamarans* and is published by Charles Scribner's Sons, New York. Another book, *Sailing and Racing Catamarans* by Commander Edward F. Cotter (U.S.C.G.), was published by the Chilton Company in 1962.

WILDCAT II. *Photo by William Wainwright, courtesy John C. Beery Co.*

VITAL STATISTICS: L.O.A. 17'9"; waterline 16'; beam 8'; draft without centerboards 7", with boards 3'7"; sail area 228 sq. ft.; weight 430 lbs.; trailable; racing crew, minimum* of two.

SUPPLEMENT OF
NEW CLASSES

INTRODUCTION

To list every boat that has started a new class or begun the "latest trend" in yacht racing would be a nearly impossible task. Sailing is increasing in popularity at a faster rate than any other phase of boating; new boats and classes have developed by the score. The great majority have been excellent boats, conceived to fill a need, follow a new trend, or take advantage of a new building technique. Some of these have prospered, but others have unaccountably failed. A few boats have been ill-conceived, or at least they have failed in some important way to interpret trends or use new materials. For the most part, these have not flourished.

In a way, this is a book about success. In the long term, a book of this nature should be about those boats that have left a favorable impression on yacht racing. To write about boats that have failed would be a pointless exercise; their virtues—even their class names—would be lost. It is easy to discard classes that have come and gone. It is something else to identify those that will endure out of those that have just arrived.

Fessenden Blanchard was gifted with an astute awareness of the qualities that comprise excellence in sailboats. From the many classes in existence in 1963 he was able to pick, with amazing accuracy, those that would be around today. There are many more now, but we do not have the advantage of his wisdom to judge them.

The task of updating *The Sailboat Classes of North America* has fallen to me, and I trust that my crystal ball is not clouded. I can only hope that my judgments will be as valid five years hence as Fessenden Blanchard's are today.

The choice of which classes to list is strictly mine and is based primarily on popularity as evidenced by numbers. It has been particularly difficult to choose among the many cruising boats. Basing a listing strictly on numbers has the disadvantage that some promising new boats will be overlooked. I have tried to avoid this by mentioning such promising designs as the Morgan 45, the Chris-Craft Comanche, and the Ohlson 41, but I may also have overlooked boats that turn out to be more successful. If so, I apologize to both the reader and the hard-working manufacturer who are thus slighted.

The original ground rules as set forth in the Introduction have been followed. The only exception is the elimination of any reference to cost. Prices change so drastically that they soon become meaningless. An axiom in boatbuilding is that boats cost by the pound. As a very general rule-of-thumb, the heavier boat will also be the more expensive, regardless of over-all length and other "size" factors.

The breakdown of class types is the same: single-hull racing classes, cruising classes, and catamarans. The first two categories need no special introduction; they are simply an updating of the original sections. Catamarans, however, have developed in an unusual way, and some specific comments are called for.

THEODORE A. JONES

34 Burchard Lane
Rowayton, Connecticut

RACING CLASSES

FIREBALL. *Courtesy One-Design & Offshore Yachtsman.*

FIREBALL

Peter Milne's Fireball design was introduced to North America in a very impressive fashion when it placed second in its class in *Yachting* magazine's 1963 One-of-a-Kind Regatta. She was well sailed by England's Jack Knights, beating such outstanding high-performance boats as the Flying Dutchman.

Originally the class rules called for plywood construction, but fiber glass was approved in 1967 with the provision that fiber-glass hulls must be built by a licensed builder from an official class mold. The plywood construction allows building by amateurs. It consists of a stressed skin of

$\frac{3}{16}$-inch and $\frac{1}{4}$-inch marine mahogany plywood sheets glued together. Four watertight bulkheads insure buoyancy.

The average husband/wife team makes an ideal crew for the Fireball, provided the husband can convince his wife to use the trapeze. Actually, those who have tried the trapeze find it easy and fun as well as a more effective hiking device. Low cost and high performance are other factors that have contributed to the popularity of the Fireball, which now numbers more than 2000 internationally and more than 400 in North America. Mrs. Marilyn Olliff (1011 N. Ashley St., Valdosta, Ga. 31601) is the class Secretary.

VITAL STATISTICS: L.O.A. 16'2"; waterline 13'3"; beam 4'8½"; draft 4'½" (centerboard); sail area 123 sq. ft. (no spinnaker); weight 175 lbs. maximum; trailable; normal racing crew, two.

FLIPPER

Californians Carter Pyle and Joe Quigg designed the Flipper in 1965 as a trainer for children as young as six or seven. She is a proprietary design built only by Newport Boats. The idea of the Flipper was to simulate a high-performance singlehander such as a Finn, but in a size that a child could handle. The Flipper has a bendy rig, center lead mainsheet with an adjustable traveler, boom vang, hiking straps, and all the accouterments to make a child feel at home when he grows bigger and graduates to a Finn. The Flipper will plane readily with one child aboard. She does not turn over easily, although her name implies that she will. When she is capsized, she floats high on her side and can be flipped upright with a quick pull on the centerboard. Even with a heavy adult she performs well, and she is used for frostbiting in Chesapeake Bay. Her cockpit self-drains through either the daggerboard case or an aft bailing plug.

Everything in the Flipper's construction is either plastic or stainless steel. Foam blocks built into the area between fiber-glass hull and deck moldings provide flotation in the event of a hull puncture. The rudder, tiller, daggerboard—even the spars—are made of fiber glass for minimum upkeep.

No class organization had been formed, but plans were being drafted for class specifications and by-laws in early 1967. At that time there were more than 500 Flippers distributed throughout the United States. Newport Boats, Gloucester, Virginia 23061, should be addressed for more information.

FLIPPER. *Courtesy Newport Boats.*

VITAL STATISTICS: L.O.A. 8'; beam 3'11"; sail area 37 sq. ft.; weight is about 70 lbs.; the hull will fit in the back of the average station wagon.

FLYING SAUCER. *Courtesy the O'Day Corporation.*

FLYING SAUCER

It was inevitable that someone name a class after the common term for unidentified flying objects. In this case it is particularly apt, for the Flying Saucer is everything that the name implies, from her flared hull to her planing speed. She was designed by Andrew T. Kostanecki—an industrial designer by vocation and a Finn sailor by avocation.

The concept of the Flying Saucer is an interesting one, and the class has the potential of being nearly as popular as the "boardboats" from which it is derived. The idea was to produce a singlehanded boat with the same basic appeal of a Sunfish, only larger, faster, and more demanding. It is not a boat for beginning juniors, but is intended for adults and accomplished teen-agers. The Flying Saucer will plane in as little as eight knots of wind. In a screaming breeze it will provide all the thrills anyone could want, yet its foam-filled, molded-fiber-glass hull provides both self-bailing and positive flotation.

The original Flying Saucer, when it was introduced at the 1966 National Boat Show, had a sophisticated single-sail lateen rig set from an offset mast. This rig developed several problems, not the least of which were comments from boat-show kibitzers asking, "Hey, mister, did you know the mast's not in the middle?" After extensive testing and soul searching, the rig was changed to a more conventional sloop. The jib is rigged with a self-tending club to make the boat easier to handle when tacking or jibing.

The O'Day Corporation owns the Flying Saucer design and is the sole builder. Production was begun in January 1967, with more than 200 boats active almost immediately in the Great Lakes and on the Eastern seaboard. Inquiries regarding a class organization should be addressed to James H. Hunt (the O'Day Corporation, 168 Stevens St., Fall River, Mass. 02722).

VITAL STATISTICS: L.O.A. 15′0″; beam 5′2″; draft 3′3″ (centerboard down); sail area 108 sq. ft.; weight 195 lbs.; can be trailed or car-topped; normal crew, one.

420

Fifteen minutes' conversation with Dr. E. C. Van Valey, president of the United States 420 Association, will convince you that the 420 is the best small sailboat in the world. Dr. Van Valey's organization is one of the most active of its kind in the country—it was the only class displaying its own boat (without the sponsorship of a manufacturer) at the 1966 and 1967 National Boat Shows—and its supporters are the most enthusiastic sailors one is likely to meet. They have an excellent boat to be excited about.

420. *Courtesy Major Frank Willett.*

The aim of the French designer, Christian Maury, who designed the 420 in 1960, was to create a high-performance sailer that would be a good trainer for juniors, inexpensive to purchase and maintain, versatile, and safe. She is an excellent junior trainer, offering snappy performance without becoming too much of a handful. She carries a large jib and spinnaker, giving kids valuable experience in handling these sails. A trapeze is allowed (but not necessary for the boat's performance) in junior events, providing exposure to this popular hiking device. The 420 can also be converted to a cat-rigged singlehander by stepping the mast in the forward step.

Class rules strictly control the uniformity of all boats. Hull shape, sails, spars, even the position and types of hardware are carefully specified. Fiddling with expensive gadgets is eliminated, although the history of the class shows a general feeling of open-mindedness toward changes that will improve the boats and keep them up to date with other classes.

Construction is of fiber glass, with one licensed builder for each country. In Canada, 420s are built by Grampian Marine, Oakville, Ontario. Lindh Boat Company, Newport, Rhode Island 02840, was licensed in 1967 as the United States builder.

The 420 is relatively new to North America. Out of the phenomenal number of 11,000 active boats world-wide in six years, this part of the world boasts only 350. However, the class is growing rapidly, and Dr. Van Valey predicts that "the 420 will be the most active racing class in the United States, as it is now in the rest of the world."

The United States class Secretary is Major Frank Willett, who may be addressed in care of the United States 420 Association, 9 Rockefeller Plaza, Room 2229, New York, New York 10020. The Canadian 420 Association is at 9 Charkay Street, Ottawa 5, Ontario.

VITAL STATISTICS: L.O.A. 13'9"; waterline 13'2"; beam 5'5"; draft 3'2" (centerboard down); sail area 110 sq. ft. (spinnaker 95 sq. ft., cat rig 85 sq. ft.); minimum weight 216 lbs.; trailable; normal crew, one or two.

LS 13 AND LS 16

Two boats that diverge from the present trend toward high-performance planing boats are the LS 13 and LS 16. This is not to imply that they are dull sailers. Both are spirited, fast boats, although they could not be considered ready planers. The accent is on comfortable family day sailing and racing.

LS 13. *Chrysler Photographic.*

Masochistic Finn sailors may scoff at the LS 16's molded-in padding on the side decks, but it is both practical and comfortable. The twin bilge-boards are completely enclosed in trunks beneath the seats; they are out of the way, giving the cockpit the spaciousness of a keel boat.

The real impact of the LS 13 and LS 16 will be made by the great number of people they introduce to sailing—and eventually to racing. The boats have been distributed primarily through Chrysler Boat Company's powerboat dealers. They are going to families who probably would not have thought of owning a sailboat. Of the 1350 LS 13s sold since 1964, 150 are actively racing; and of the 650 LS 16s sold since 1965, 130 are actively racing.

Both boats were designed by Thomas Faul Associates and naval architect Charles Wittholz. They are built of fiber glass.

Class Secretaries are the following: LS 13, Norman Watkins (1324 Comanche Dr., Richardson, Tex. 75080) and LS 16, Forrest A. Garb (2501 Cedar Springs Rd., Dallas, Tex. 75201).

VITAL STATISTICS:

	L.O.A.	Waterline	Beam	Draft (cb down)	Sail Area
LS 13	13'1"	11'5"	5'1"	3'0"	93 sq. ft.
LS 16	16'0"	14'2"	6'1"	2'10"	160 sq. ft.

Both boats are trailable.

M-20. *Larson Photo, courtesy One-Design & Offshore Yachtsman.*

M-20

A surprise winner in the 1963 One-of-a-Kind Regatta was Buddy Melges' M-20 in the class for scows and trapeze centerboarders. Not that there was anything unusual about Melges' winning—he was already acknowledged as one of North America's top sailors. What was unusual was that

Buddy and Bill Bentsen, both E-Scow sailors back home in Wisconsin, showed up with a new tunnel-hulled scow-type boat called an M-20. She was the only scow in the regatta, and she was named the outstanding boat of all the class winners.

Buddy Melges' father, Harry Melges, Sr., designed the M-20. He combined the best features of the several scow classes that exist under the Inland Lake Yachting Association rules to come up with a fiber-glass one-design (the ILYA scows are not one-designs and do not lend themselves to the series production necessary for fiber glass).

The M-20 is better in light air than most scows of its size. The tunnel hull can be heeled to reduce the amount of hull surface in contact with the water. As the wind increases, the M-20 accelerates rapidly, and the transition from displacing water at low speed to planing at high speed is smooth and effortless.

The Melges Boat Works, Zenda, Wisconsin 53195, has built close to 200 M-20s. Melges is the sole builder and should be contacted for information.

VITAL STATISTICS: L.O.A. 20'0"; beam 5'8"; draft 3' (bilgeboards down); sail area 270 sq. ft.; trailable; racing crew, two.

ROBIN

Philip L. Rhodes designed the Robin for the P. Evanson Boat Company in 1962. The Robin association was formed in 1963, and national championships have been held every year since 1964.

As with several other new boats in this size range, the Robin can be converted from sloop to cat rig by stepping the mast forward and leaving the jib home in its sailbag. This is a nice feature, especially with beginners, as it allows them to gain confidence with the cat rig before switching to the more complicated and spirited sloop.

Robins are available in either molded plywood or fiber glass. There are just over 200 boats, distributed primarily along the East Coast. John Radtke, (Box 275, Masonville, N.J. 08054) is the class Secretary.

VITAL STATISTICS: L.O.A. 10'10"; waterline 10'3½"; beam 4'8"; draft 3'0" (centerboard down); sail area 80 sq. ft.; the Robin is easily cartopped or trailered.

ROBIN. *Courtesy P. Evanson Boat Company, Inc.*

SABRE SCOW. *Courtesy Sabrecraft Ltd.*

SABRE SCOW

The Sabre Scow is a new and, so far, local class. It sprang into prominence, however, when it was chosen as the boat for the Mallory Cup finals (North American Men's Championship) in 1967.

Canadian Roger Hewson, a construction engineer, designed the Sabre Scow to combine the best features of existing scow classes into a fiber-glass boat. In size, she most nearly resembles the E-Scow, but unlike the E she is a one-design class with rigid regulations controlling the variables that affect speed.

The Sabre Scow features a tunnel hull similar to the M-20's. It is interesting to note that this hull form was first developed by the Canadian yacht *Dominion* in the late 1800s.

Like all scows, the Sabre Scow will be more at home in sheltered lakes and harbors than in rough open water. The class has grown rapidly on Montreal's Lake St. Louis, where she originated, so rapidly in fact that designer Hewson had to give up his construction business to devote full time to producing Sabre Scows.

Information regarding class rules may be obtained from Sabrecraft Ltd. (4424 St. Catherine St. West, Montreal 6, Que.).

VITAL STATISTICS: L.O.A. 26'0"; beam 6'6"; draft 4'0" (bilgeboards down); sail area 272 sq. ft. (spinnaker, 400 sq. ft.); weight 840 lbs.; Sabre Scow is trailable; normal racing crew, three.

SAN FRANCISCO PELICAN

The S. F. Pelican is an unlikely-looking boat for one so new and so successful. She was designed in 1959 by Captain William H. Short to teach his family to sail on the rough waters of San Francisco Bay. The basis of the design was the Banks dory, but the dory shape was truncated fore-and-aft and made into a pram shape. If the lines were drawn out to a full dory, the S. F. Pelican would be about 19 feet instead of 12 feet. The rig is comprised of a lug mainsail, laced to the spars, and a large overlapping jib tacked to the end of a 5'7" bowsprit. The net result is an unusual, but not unpleasant, appearance. She's a boat with great character.

The performance of Captain Short's boat in rough going attracted the attention of Bay sailors. Before long, several sisters were building in the area, and Captain Short was in the boat-plans business, selling complete sets for $7.00.

SAN FRANCISCO PELICAN. *Photo by Karl H. Riek.*

There are now approximately 2500 S. F. Pelicans spread throughout North America; most are built in their owners' basements and garages. They have what amounts to a national championship when S. F. Pelicans gather for an annual race across the Bay from Sausalito to San Francisco and back over six miles of rough, windy water.

The class Secretary of the S. F. Pelican Racing & Cruising Association is Mrs. Muriel Short (203 Hawthorne Ave., Larkspur, Marin County, Calif. 94939).

VITAL STATISTICS: L.O.A. 12'2½" (not including bowsprit, which adds another 3'); waterline 10'6¾"; beam 6'2½"; draft 4'0" (centerboard down); sail area 105 sq. ft.; weight 325 lbs. (minimum all-up); trailable; racing crew, two.

SIGNET. *Courtesy Robert S. Obrig.*

SIGNET

The internationally well-known English dinghy sailor, spar builder, and yacht designer Ian Proctor designed the SigneT for the London *Sunday Times*. The idea was to provide plans for a low-cost, high-performance sailboat that could be built at home with relative ease.

The class came to North America in 1962, when a group of forty South Shore Long Island sailors banded together on a building project. "They lived up to their British billing," wrote the late Ev Morris in *The Skipper*, "boats so simple that amateurs could build them, so safe a child could handle one, so inexpensive that anyone could afford to buy into the class, and so sporty that experienced sailors would enjoy racing them."

World-wide, the class numbers more than 400 boats, with 200 in North

America; the East Coast has 100, Canada 40, and the Midwest and West 30 each. The first SigneT builder in the United States was Robert S. Obrig. He is also the class Secretary and may be addressed at 307 Little East Neck Road, Babylon, New York.

VITAL STATISTICS: L.O.A. 12′6″; waterline 11′6″; beam 4′9″; draft 3′4″ (centerboard down); sail area 88 sq. ft.; weight 190 lbs.; racing crew, two.

SUPER SATELLITE. *Courtesy Gerry Inman.*

SUPER SATELLITE

Primarily a California and Southwestern States class, the Super Satellite was designed in 1959 by Ted Carpentier. The hull is fiber glass, the mast and boom are anodized aluminum, and the rudder and daggerboard are anodized aluminum castings. An unusual feature is a vinyl covering over the stainless-steel standing rigging.

The class rules prohibit the use of either trapezes or spinnakers and place extreme limits on rigging changes, all of which tends to keep the cost of racing to a minimum. About 600 are racing.

The first Super Satellite fleet was formed at the Redondo Beach Yacht Club in 1960. The National class association was formed in 1962. Gerry Inman (1606 Todd St., Mountain View, Calif. 94040) is the class Secretary.

VITAL STATISTICS: L.O.A. 14'0"; waterline 13'0"; beam 6'0"; draft 4'0" (daggerboard down); sail area 130 sq. ft.; trailable; racing crew, two.

WIN'ARD SABOTS. *Photo by the Falkards, courtesy Hamilton Barhydt.*

WIN'ARD SABOT

This 8-foot plywood pram dinghy developed from the Naples Sabot. The two boats are identical except for their boards—the Naples Sabot uses lee-boards, whereas the Win'ard Sabot has a daggerboard. The latter was developed for rough-water sailing. Although construction is somewhat more difficult, the Win'ard Sabot has proved to have generally superior sailing capabilities, and the class has grown to more than 1000 boats, mostly home built. The principal fleets are in Southern California, Missouri, Nevada, Oregon, and Virginia. Hamilton Barhydt (8211 Billowvista Dr., Playa del Rey, Calif. 90291) is the class Secretary.

VITAL STATISTICS: L.O.A. 7'10"; beam 3'10"; draft 1'10" (daggerboard down); sail area 38 sq. ft.; weight 95 lbs.; can be car-topped and will fit inside most station wagons; normal crew, one.

CRUISING CLASSES

ALBERG 30. *Courtesy Whitby Boat Works, Ltd.*

ALBERG 30

The Alberg 30 is just big enough to be a minimum full-size cruising boat eligible for most offshore racing. The design was commissioned by Canadian builder Whitby Boat Works. Designer Carl Alberg relied on his considerable experience with fiber-glass boats of this size and type (the Electra, Triton, and Alberg 35) to refine the Alberg 30 into a comfortable, fast, family boat.

That he was successful is attested to by more than 225 owners. There are Alberg 30 one-design associations on Chesapeake Bay and Lake Ontario (Toronto) and budding organizations on Long Island Sound, in New Jersey, and in Chicago.

The Alberg 30 has complete accommodations for four adults and includes an enclosed head, a full galley, and ample lockers.

Requests for class information should be addressed to the builder, Whitby Boat Works, Ltd., 570 Finley Avenue, Ajax, Ontario.

VITAL STATISTICS: L.O.A. 30'3½"; waterline 21'8"; beam 8'9"; draft 4'3" (keel); sail area 410 sq. ft.; displacement 9000 lbs.; CCA rating 21.2'.

BERMUDA 40

More than sixty-five boats have come from the Bermuda 40 mold since she was designed in 1959 by William H. Tripp, Jr. The design was originally commissioned by a group of eight owners who wanted a fiber-glass hull with the interior trim and warmth of a traditional wooden boat. The boats were so successful that Henry Hinckley's yard has been producing Bermuda 40s to customers' orders but on a production-line basis ever since.

Bermuda 40s have never raced as a one-design class, but often seven or eight have competed in the same class in long-distance races. The boats have raced in practically every major offshore event in the world, from Transatlantic to Transpac, Bermuda, Fastnet, Southern Ocean Racing Conference, Miami-Montego Bay, and countless lesser events. They have won at least class silverware in most of them.

The hull shape is along the lines of the popular moderate-displacement centerboarders favored by the CCA Rule. Inside, she has comfortable accommodations for six with an aft galley, a large enclosed head, and particularly well-thought-out locker and storage space. Auxiliary power is either gasoline or diesel engine.

Henry R. Hinckley & Co., Southwest Harbor, Maine 04679, should be addressed for particulars. Other Hinckley-built boats include the 35-foot Pilot, the Hinckley 41, and the Hinckley 48.

VITAL STATISTICS: L.O.A. 40'9"; waterline 27'10"; beam 11'9"; draft 4'1" (centerboard up); sail area 725 sq. ft.; displacement 19,000 lbs.; CCA rating 26.5'.

BERMUDA 40. *Courtesy Henry R. Hinckley & Company.*

CAL 28. *Courtesy Jensen Marine.*

THE CAL BOATS

When Fessenden Blanchard wrote the original edition of this book, the Cal 24 and the Cal 20 had just finished one-two in the cruising division of *Yachting* magazine's One-of-a-Kind Regatta. Both boats were designed by the West Coast's light-displacement advocate C. William Lapworth and built by Jack Jensen's Jensen Marine Corporation.

Since 1963 Bill Lapworth and Jack Jensen have teamed up to produce seven new Cal classes. Rather than capitalize solely on their success with the Cal 20 and Cal 24, they have garnered further glories with their new boats. The early success of the small Cals pales almost to insignificance when compared to the subsequent record of the Cal 40, which has won the Southern Ocean Racing Conference twice, the Transpac Race, the Bermuda Race, first in class in the Transatlantic Race, and placed in every major offshore event on the East and West coasts. The Cal 28 duplicated the feat of its smaller sisters by winning the same division in the 1966 One-of-a-Kind. If the Cal 25, Cal 30, Cal 34, Cal 36, and Cal 48 have less spectacular race records, it is only a matter of degree. Each has done well and each threatens to become one of the most popular classes of its size and type.

As an example, the Cal 34 was put into production early in 1967. In May there were thirty-five boats sailing, and orders were being taken for January 1968 delivery. Because of the success of previous Cal models, the Cal 34 was a guaranteed success almost before its introduction.

The entire Cal line follows one philosophy: light weight (light displacement) means maximum speed and livability for minimum cost. To keep to the light-displacement concept, Jensen has had to build the boats carefully. He is one of the few builders to avoid overbuilding, as insurance against careless workmanship.

Write to Jensen Marine Corporation, 235 Fischer Street, Costa Mesa, California 92627, for the name and address of the Secretary of each class.

VITAL STATISTICS:

Class*	L.O.A.	Water-line	Beam	Draft	Sail Area Sq. Ft.	Displace-ment Lbs.	CCA Rating	No. in Class
Cal 25	25'0"	20'0"	8'0"	4'0"	286	4,000	—	200
Cal 28	28'0"	22'5"	9'0"	4'6"	355	6,000	25.7'	200
Cal 30	30'0"	24'6"	10'0"	4'6"	420	8,200	27.5'	125
Cal 34	33'3"	26'0"	10'0"	5'0"	515	10,000	29.5'	35
Cal 36	35'6"	27'0"	10'4"	5'8"	600	11,200	32.4'	80
Cal 40	39'4"	30'4"	11'0"	5'7"	700	15,000	35.8'	120
Cal 48	47'9"	35'0"	12'0"	6'6"	1,040	25,000	43.0'	22

* See page 235 for Cal 20 and Cal 24.

CHRIS-CRAFT "INDIANS"

When the Chris-Craft Corporation, well-known builders of powerboats, decided to enter the sailboat market in 1962, they produced a comfortable motor-sailer type. Chris-Craft had been opposed to racing their powerboats, and so it was natural that this policy should carry over to their sailboats, but when sales of their 35- and later 30-footers sagged below their market potential, they realized that what made good policy for powerboats wasn't necessarily also good policy for the sailboat market. In 1966, Chris-Craft unleashed their considerable engineering and boatbuilding skills, coming out with a new racing-oriented fleet designed by Sparkman & Stephens. The results are the 32-foot Cherokee, 37-foot Apache, and 42-foot Comanche—the Chris-Craft "Indians."

In addition, the Capri 26 and derivative Capitan, which are popular cruiser/racers and the Shields One-Design, which they now manufacture, make Chris-Craft a major manufacturer of racing sailboats.

Each boat in the line is built of fiber glass. Each incorporates several unique features—such as molded simulated teak decks and the latest fin-keel/blade-rudder shapes—which distinguish them from other stock auxiliaries.

The smallest boats in the line, the Capri 26 and Capitan, are Midget Ocean Racing Club type boats, sleeping two to four. The Capri has a larger cabin with a doghouse, while the Capitan is a combination day-sailer and cruiser built on the same hull as the Capri. Both have self-bailing cockpits and qualify for MORC racing.

The Apache 37 was the first of the "Indians" to be developed, and the Comanche and Cherokee designs are derived from it. The hull form is unusual for a boat of this size in that the fin keel is a separate bolted-on iron casting rather than an integrally molded part of the hull. The Comanche has the same shape but a conventional one-piece fiber-glass hull with lead ballast.

All the Chris-Craft boats are sloop-rigged and with the exception of the Comanche have masthead fore-triangles. The Comanche departs from the current trend with a seven-eighths fore-triangle.

Information may be obtained from the Sailboat Division, Chris-Craft Corporation, Pompano Beach, Florida 33061.

CHEROKEE 32. *Courtesy Chris-Craft Corporation.*

VITAL STATISTICS:

Class	L.O.A.	Water-line	Beam	Draft	Sail Area Sq. Ft.	Displace-ment Lbs.	CCA Rating
Capri 26 & Capitan	26′3″	19′0″	8′2″	4′0″	301	3,920	21.5′ (MORC)
Cherokee 32	32′0″	22′6″	9′0″	5′1″	434	8,000	23.9′
Apache 37	37′0″	26′3″	10′2″	5′9″	606	13,600	30.0′
Comanche 42	42′0″	30′4″	10′10″	6′6″	740	—	33.0′

CORONADO 25. *Courtesy John Linskey.*

CORONADO 25

In less than two years of production more than 500 Coronado 25s have been built. While this is not a record, it is certainly an indication of extreme popularity and success, made more remarkable by the fact that in this size of auxiliary the Coronado 25 has many competitors. One of the reasons for this success may be that designers Frank Butler and Ed Edgars avoided the popular but often unattractive raised-deck style often used to gain extra room inside. Butler and Edgars compromised nicely by giving the Coronado 25 a wide doghouse/trunk cabin combination which, in effect, provides all the room below afforded by the raised deck but retains the traditional appearance of a trunk-cabin type. Aside from this concession to aesthetics, the boat is thoroughly modern, with a masthead sloop rig, fin keel, and spade rudder.

The accommodations below are for five, with a convertible dinette, three fixed berths, a galley, and an enclosed head. John Linskey heads a very strong class organization, which lists approximately 300 active racers. Mr. Linskey's address is P. O. Box 125, Hermosa Beach, California 90254.

VITAL STATISTICS: L.O.A. 25'1"; waterline 20'3"; beam 8'0"; draft 3'8" (keel); sail area 298 sq. ft.; displacement 3800 lbs.; MORF rating 20.3'.

MEDALIST AND NORTHEAST 38

Adolf LeComte is an engaging fellow, but also a very busy one. When he isn't in his shipyard in Holland supervising the construction of the several stock and custom fiber-glass boats his company builds, or when he is not in his New Rochelle, New York, sales office operating his marina, he is either extolling the virtues of his boats to a customer or flying between Amsterdam and New York. He might even combine the latter two activities, doing both at once.

One would think that so busy an executive would not have time to worry about details, but rather than rely on the plentiful supply of off-the-shelf parts, 'Dolf designs and his yard builds most of the hardware—winches, cleats, roller reefing, stanchions, special turning blocks—as well as the fiber-glass hulls. He has a compulsion to build his boats *his* way. As might be expected, the LeComte boats are beautifully finished both on deck and below.

William H. Tripp, Jr., designed the Medalist in 1960 and the Northeast 38 in 1962. He also designed a 52-foot custom boat for LeComte. A unique

MEDALIST. *Photo by Morris Rosenfeld & Sons, courtesy A. LeComte Company, Inc.*

feature of the original Medalist is her streamlined doghouse and raised deck. A later model with a conventional trunk cabin provides more headroom forward. The Northeast 38 has a modern trunk-cabin deck arrangement.

Both boats sleep six, with more room below in the Northeast 38 than in the Medalist. Nevertheless, the Medalist has considerably more apparent room below than her 33-foot length would lead one to expect. She also has a very roomy cockpit.

Both boats have done well in handicap racing. There is no class association, but information may be obtained from A. LeComte Company, P. O. Box 117, New Rochelle, New York 10805.

VITAL STATISTICS:

Class	L.O.A.	Water-line	Beam	Draft (Keel)	Sail Area Sq. Ft.	Displace-ment Lbs.	CCA Ratings
Medalist	33'3"	24'1"	10'0"	5'2"	467	10,000	24.2'
Northeast 38	38'2"	26'8"	10'11"	5'4"	622	13,000	29.5'

MORGAN

Charlie Morgan entered the yacht business as a sailmaker. He established a fine reputation for building race-winning sails and quickly turned his hand to yacht designing. His first triumph was *Paper Tiger*, which he designed for Jack Powell. *Paper Tiger* won the Southern Ocean Racing Conference her first year out, and Charlie was launched on another career even more successful than sailmaking.

The Morgan Yacht Corporation was born out of Charlie's dissatisfaction with designing boats for other builders. In some instances he was frustrated in not being able to see engineering details through to conclusion. Starting with the Morgan 34, Charlie brought design, construction supervision, deliveries, customer relations, and sailmaking under his direct supervision. His company is unique in this regard and, though barely three years old, evidently successful.

The Morgan 34 is a development of the moderate-displacement centerboard type, which traces its roots back through *Paper Tiger* ultimately (but remotely) to the famous *Finisterre*. The 34s have won a number of important races on Long Island Sound and other widespread parts of the country. In mid-1967 more than 140 had been built.

MORGAN 24. *Courtesy Morgan Yacht Corporation.*

The interior of the 34 is unusually attractive for a stock boat. All rough edges of fiber glass are covered with fiber-glass liners. There are several optional arrangements, all sleeping six.

The Morgan 24 followed the 34 and has been in full production less than a year at this writing, when ninety had been built. The 24s have been doing well in MORC events in their home waters on Tampa Bay, Florida, and there is every reason to expect them to do well when they start racing in other parts of the country.

The 24 is also a centerboarder, but she has an unusual spade rudder, which is not attached to the keel but is suspended below the hull well aft. She has the fine interior finish of her bigger sisters and sleeps four.

The Morgan 45 went into production in early 1967. She has a modern, rakish, low cabin—almost a flush deck. Unlike the other Morgan boats, she has a keel rather than a centerboard. The rudder is attached to the keel. Her most interesting feature is a well-thought-out interior handsomely finished in formica and teak.

The Morgan Yacht Corporation can supply additional information. They are at 2501 72nd Street North, St. Petersburg, Florida 33710.

VITAL STATISTICS:

Class	L.O.A.	Water-line	Beam	Keel Draft	Sail Area Sq. Ft.	Displacement Lbs.	CCA Ratings
Morgan 24	24'11"	21'6"	8'0"	2'9"	310	5,000	21.8'
Morgan 34	34'0"	24'9"	10'0"	3'3"	550	12,500	25.7'
Morgan 45	45'8"	31'5"	11'0"	6'1"	895	25,000	35.0'

MUSTANG

The Mustang was designed in 1965 by Martin Bludworth for plastics engineer Andy Green of the PlasTrend Corporation. Andy wanted a sophisticated racing sloop for hot-shot one-design sailors who needed overnight family accommodations but who still wanted to enjoy the excitement of high-speed planing. So far, there is a small but growing and loyal band of forty Mustangers whooping around various racecourses.

The Mustang is a fiber-glass, raised-deck sloop with a centerboard housed inside a fin keel. She is very light, displacing only 2000 pounds with a ballast weight of 750 pounds. She will really plane, not just surf as some light cruising boats will, and she provides practically all the thrills of a hot day sailer.

MUSTANG. *Courtesy PlasTrend Corporation.*

Mustangs have won the Miami Columbus Day Regatta, the Chesapeake Bay High Point Series Trophy, the Galveston Bay Cruising Association Series (twice), and the Atlanta Yacht Club's Lake Lanier Fall Series.

There is no organized Mustang one-design racing yet, but Joyce Green, Route 2, Box 935, Forth Worth, Texas 76135, handles class matters.

VITAL STATISTICS: L.O.A. 22′0″; waterline 17′0″; draft 2′4″ (centerboard up); sail area 247 sq. ft.; displacement 2000 lbs.; ratings, 19.9′ CCA and 18.4′ MORC; Mustangs can be trailed and are shoal enough to be launched from a ramp.

OFFSHORE 36. *Courtesy Roland Reed Associates.*

OFFSHORE 36

Detroit yachtsman Maury Declercq designed and built a boat for his own use. She was completed in 1966 and named *Flying Buffalo*—and fly she did. She won or placed in every race she entered that year and was the combined winner of the Chicago and Port Huron Mackinac Races.

The Offshore 36 is the fiber-glass production version of this design. It is the first of the many Choy Lee Hong Kong-built sailboats to be racing-oriented, and it features the unique combination of fiber glass and teak used on their popular cruising boats. The Offshore 36 has teak decks, teak cabin trunk, and teak joiner work on a fiber-glass hull.

About thirty boats are actively sailing on both coasts and the Great Lakes.

Requests for information should be addressed to the General U. S. Representative, Roland Reed Associates, Inc., 1712 High Street, Alameda, California 94501.

VITAL STATISTICS: L.O.A. 35′10″; waterline 25′7″; beam 10′0″; draft 4′8″ (keel); sail area 555 sq. ft. (sloop); displacement 15,750 lbs.; CCA rating 25.1′.

OHLSON YAWLS AND SLOOPS

Swedish 5.5-meter designer and builder Einar Ohlson designed the Ohlson 35 in 1949. She was very successful in her own country and Europe, but it wasn't until 1958 that Ohlson 35s began appearing in North America. During 1959 a few Ohlson yawls were being raced with consistently good results on Long Island Sound and in Southern California waters. Since then they have spread to the major cruising centers of the United States, with more than thirty cruising and racing on Long Island Sound, ten in New England waters, twenty in Chesapeake Bay, and twenty on the West Coast.

Contrary to the popular trend, Ohlsons are still built in wood. They are now one of the only series-produced wooden boats of this size. This has been both an asset and a deterrent to their success. While Ohlsons appeal to the traditionalist who likes the "warmth and feel" of a wood boat, the increasing popularity of fiber glass has turned others away. Rather than being locked into a particular hull form with a rigid fiber-glass mold, Ohlson has been able to refine and develop his designs to keep them up to date—hence the existence of Ohlson 35s (the original), Ohlson 36s (introduced in 1964), and Ohlson 37s (introduced in 1967). These are basically the same boat, with subtle improvements each year.

The layouts are conventional, with a forward stateroom, enclosed head and hanging lockers, four berths in the main cabin, and a galley aft. The 35s originally had berths for five but were later expanded to sleep six, as do both the 36 and 37.

In late 1967 there was a rumor that the Ohlsons would be produced in fiber glass. This would be an Ohlson 38, but none had been seen in the United States when this was written.

All the Ohlsons have been available with either sloop or yawl rigs. Also

OHLSON 36. *Photo by Morris Rosenfeld, courtesy Campbell/Sheehan, Inc.*

a smaller Ohlson 26 is built in Sweden, but only a few have found their way into North America. They are so popular in Europe that few are available for export. A limited number of Ohlson 41s have been built. All are keel boats.

Write to Campbell/Sheehan, Inc., 22 Boston Post Road, Larchmont, New York 10538.

VITAL STATISTICS:

Class	L.O.A.	Water-line	Beam	Draft	Sail Area Sq. Ft.	Displacement Lbs.	CCA Rating
Ohlson 26	26'0"	20'0"	8'0"	4'1"	338	6,500	—
Ohlson 35	35'6"	25'0"	9'6"	4'10"	545	12,800	27.9'
Ohlson 36	36'3"	25'6"	9'8"	5'0"	576	12,850	28.4'
Ohlson 37	36'9"	26'3"	10'2"	5'3"	590	13,500	28.9'
Ohlson 41	40'9"	28'7"	11'0"	6'1"	730	18,800	30.6'

OUTLAW. *Courtesy the O'Day Corporation.*

OUTLAW

Every once in a while someone comes up with a new twist to an idea that's been kicking around for a while. The sages wonder why they didn't think of it, it's so obvious. The need that the Outlaw fulfills was for a minimum cruiser that didn't attempt to cram the hull full of berths but concentrated on outdoor living—which is where most of us in North America do our sailing anyway—on deck. Many boats force one to spend the day crammed into a minuscule cockpit while oodles of space go unused below.

Phil Rhodes found the solution with the Outlaw design in 1965. The Outlaw is larger than the average "minimum" cruiser. She has a nice comfortable cockpit, big enough for four adults to lounge in without crowding either at anchor or under sail. There are four berths below, a small galley, and a place for a head. The accommodations aren't commodious, but they're adequate for weekending.

The Outlaw is the largest boat in the O'Day line. There is no organized class activity, but individual Outlaws have raced in MORC races with excellent success. The East Coast and Canada boast about sixty-five boats.

Write to James H. Hunt at the O'Day Corporation, 168 Stevens Street, Fall River, Massachusetts 02722, for more information.

VITAL STATISTICS: L.O.A. 26'0"; waterline 19'0"; beam 8'0"; draft 4'3" (keel); sail area 291 sq. ft.; displacement 5000 lbs.; ratings, 20.4' CCA and 19.8' MORC.

RAWSON 30

The Rawson 30 design came from the talented and prolific drafting pencil of Seattle yacht designer William Garden. Mr. Garden is best known for his character cruising boats, and this is one of the few racing classes he has designed. The combination of a cruising heritage and racing ability has been brought off quite successfully. Most unusual for a boat of this size is the high toe rail, a bulwark almost, that completely encloses the deck area. The cockpit coamings are also high, providing an exceptionally roomy, deep, comfortable cockpit.

Rawson 30s race as a class in the Seattle area. One of the features of their regattas is the insistence that each boat be in cruising trim. There are 122 boats active, mostly in the Pacific Northwest.

The hull is of conventional fiber-glass construction. Mahogany trim is used on the exterior and interior. The spars are aluminum.

RAWSON 30. *Photo by Harry Merrick, courtesy Robert Camber.*

The Seattle-area Secretary is Dr. Robert Camber (3515 W. Laurelhurst Dr., Seattle, Wash.). Either he or the builder—Ron Rawson (15014 N.E. 90th St., Redmond, Wash.)—may be addressed for particulars.

VITAL STATISTICS: L.O.A. 30′6″; waterline 22′0″; beam 9′0″; draft 4′9″ (keel); sail area 410 sq. ft.; displacement 12,000 lbs.; CCA rating 21.3′.

SANTANAS. *Courtesy W. D. Schock Company.*

SANTANA

One of the most phenomenal success stories in stock cruising boats is that of the Santanas. The first of these good-looking fiber-glass mini-cruisers was launched in February 1966, and the 130th boat was launched one year later. Part of the reason for their success is the fact that they won several important races early in 1966. Designer Gary Mull must be credited not only with producing a winning design; he also created an attractive boat with plenty of room inside for cruising. One should not expect luxury in this size, and the Santana is no different. However, she does have four berths, provision for a workable galley, and head.

An interesting feature of the Santana is that she is available as either a fin-keel boat or a combination keel/centerboarder. Her construction is of fiber glass, with teak trim and aluminum spars.

Most of the more than 150 actively sailing Santanas are on the West Coast, where they are built, but some boats have found their way to most other sailing areas.

The class Secretary is John Leavitt (1612 San Antonio, Alameda, Calif. 94501). Santanas are built by W. D. Schock Company, 3502 South Greenville Street, Santa Ana, California 92704.

VITAL STATISTICS: L.O.A. 22'0"; waterline 18'9"; beam 7'0"; draft 4'4" (keel), 2'6" (centerboard model with board up); sail area 217 sq. ft.; displacement 2600 lbs.

SHARK

For a description of the Shark, imagine first a large, powerful ocean racer surging along under spinnaker at almost 10 knots. It is blowing thirty on Lake Ontario, more in the gusts, and the crew is satisfied they have put their competition safely behind. They are the largest boat in the fleet, and surely no other could overtake them now, not in this weather. But look! There astern is a sail. Gradually it grows bigger until finally a little 24-foot boat flies past with a great burst of planing speed. It must be going over 11 knots, and there is nothing the big boat's crew can do but watch in frustration as the little boat goes by to win the race.

This is no fairy tale. What's described above has actually happened, not once but three times. The little boat is George Hinterhoeller's Shark, and when the wind blows there isn't another cruising boat under 40 feet that can sail down wind as fast. On the three different occasions referred to, Sharks have sailed entire racecourses at average speeds in excess of 10 miles per hour.

George Hinterhoeller started building Sharks in his garage in Niagara-on-the-Lake, Ontario, in 1959. The first boats were built of molded plywood, but production soon shifted to fiber glass. Sharks are now built in a large, modern plant.

There are more than 500 Sharks sailing. They are governed by a strong class organization, which strictly controls hull and keel weights, sail area,

SHARK. *Courtesy R. G. Moggridge.*

rudder shape, and overall construction specifications. In addition to competitive class racing, Sharks have done well in CCA and MORC races on Long Island Sound and Chesapeake Bay as well as on Lake Ontario. Sharks were used as the North American Junior Championship boats in 1967.

R. G. Moggridge, 77 Simpson, St. Catherines, Ontario, is the Shark Association Secretary. Licensed builders are situated in eastern and western Canada.

VITAL STATISTICS: L.O.A. 24'0"; waterline 20'0"; beam 6'10"; draft 3'0" (keel); sail area 190 sq. ft.; displacement 2200 lbs.; CCA rating 22.0', MORC rating 20.5'.

SOVEREL. *Courtesy Emily Soverel.*

SOVEREL 28

Retired Navy Commander William Soverel designed the Soverel 28 in conjunction with Dan McCarthy in 1961. Their idea was to produce a comfortable cruiser to be built by Soverel in South Florida. From a modest beginning, the boat has steadily been improved and updated. Well over eighty have been built, and Soverel recently introduced a second boat, the Soverel 36, as well as a "day-sailing" version of the 28.

The Soverel 28 has had an excellent racing record in CCA and MORC events, particularly under the command of former Flying Dutchman champions Pat and Jack Duane.

Fiber-glass construction is used in the hull and deck, and she has aluminum spars. Below the doghouse there are berths for four, plus a nice galley and an enclosed head. The day-sailing model does not have the doghouse—therefore it has less headroom—but it also sleeps four.

Most Soverel activities center in the Miami area, but there are also a growing number of boats in most other East Coast sailing centers.

Emily Soverel, 2225 Idlewild Road, North Palm Beach, Florida 33403, should be addressed for full particulars.

VITAL STATISTICS: L.O.A. 28'9"; waterline 24'0"; beam 8'4"; draft 3'0" (centerboard up); sail area 500 sq. ft; displacement 7000 lbs.; CCA rating 25.0', MORC rating 24.0'

CATAMARANS

In 1962 a group of English catamaran sailors challenged their counter-parts in the United States to a match race. It was suggested that boats be designed to very loose limits, namely: L.O.A. 25', maximum beam 14', and sail area 300 sq. ft. The challenge was accepted, and boats were built in both countries. The English won the first match for the International Catamaran Challenge Trophy. Subsequent challenges by the United States and Australia have failed to defeat the English, and the event has become popularly known as the "Little America's Cup."

The success of these boats, which have been clocked at over 25 mph, and the rapid development made possible by the broad limits led to the establishment of open catamaran classes. The "Little America's Cup" boats became Class C, with the additional limitation that they be sailed with a crew of two. Classes A, B, and D were outlined and were given international status by the International Yacht Racing Union. The limits are the following:

	L.O.A.	Beam	Sail area	Number in Crew
Class A	18'	8'	185 sq. ft.	one
Class B	20'	10'	235 sq. ft.	two
Class C	25'	14'	300 sq. ft.	two
Class D	32'	20'	500 sq. ft.	three

Many of the new catamaran classes have been built specifically to one of these class limits. Most of the Class C boats are one-offs designed for competition in the "Little America's Cup." Very few Class D boats have been built, but several are planned. Under proper conditions a well-designed and -built Class D boat should be able to exceed 30 mph—faster than any contemporary water-borne sailboat has ever traveled.

A LION. *Courtesy American Fiberglass Corp.*

A LION

In 1964 Dave and Jerry Hubbard, who had designed the United States challenger for the "Little America's Cup," designed a boat to be built as a community project by a group of friends and business associates. Eight catamarans were built that first year in a rented store in Fairfield, Connecticut. The hulls were symmetrical—built from a common mold. They were extremely light for fiber-glass construction and particularly graceful for catamarans, heretofore not known for their good looks.

The design, to the limits of Class A, proved to be as successful as promised. While the Hubbard brothers have designed many catamarans since, many people consider the A Lion to be their outstanding design.

About fifty boats were built by Mobjack Manufacturing Company as Sealion 18s, and about half that number have been built under license in England. The United States manufacturing rights were bought by American Fiberglass in 1965, and the class name was officially changed to A Lion.

The A Lion is as sporty as they come. It is sailed singlehanded. It has an efficient, high-aspect ratio marconi sail. Hiking is assisted by a sliding seat. Olympic medalist and singlehanded Finn sailor Peter Barrett, after sailing an A Lion on a particularly blustery day, exclaimed that it was one of the most exciting boats he had ever sailed.

Jackie Hubbard, 149 Ocean Drive West, Stanford, Conn. 06902 can be addressed for information.

VITAL STATISTICS: L.O.A. 18'0"; beam 8'0"; draft 2'6" (centerboards down); sail area 185 sq. ft.; racing crew, one; trailable.

B LION. *Courtesy American Fiberglass Corp.*

B LION

Dave and Jerry Hubbard designed the B Lion for *Popular Boating* magazine as a fast catamaran that could be built by an amateur and that qualified for racing in International Class B. The design was an instant success, a prototype being built before the plans were published and winning the North American Catamaran Championships Class B in 1965.

Impressed by the B Lion's performance, the American Fiberglass Corporation purchased the fiber-glass manufacturing rights and built more than 160 boats in the first year of production. They are now built by Mc-Nair Marine.

The original plans call for plywood construction. More than a hundred sets of plans were sold in the first year. Many amateur boats were built, and a home-built plywood boat won the first North American Championships sailed in 1966.

The B Lion is sailed by a crew of two. The hulls are connected by two aluminum pipes, which are hinged in the middle to allow trailing without special permits (under 8-foot width). A trapeze is used by the crew for maximum hiking effect. The rig is that of a sloop with a small jib to aid in coming about.

Don McNair, Higganum, Connecticut 06438, is the B Lion class Secretary. Plans are available from the Ziff-Davis Publishing Co., 1 Park Avenue, New York, New York 10017.

VITAL STATISTICS: L.O.A. 20'0"; beam 10'0"; draft 2'6" (centerboards down); sail area 235 sq. ft.; racing crew, two; trailable.

CATFISH. *Courtesy Alcort Inc.*

CATFISH

George Patterson designed the Catfish for Alcort, builders of the voluminously popular Sailfish and Sunfish, in 1962. She was conceived to meet the demand for a small, sporty catamaran—one that could be easily car-topped, launched from a beach, and sailed singlehanded. The Catfish is all fiber glass, with aluminum spars and rudders.

The rig is that of a modern marconi cat. She has conventional wire standing rigging, and the mast steps on its own cross-beam forward.

Rick Crolius is the class Secretary. His address is Box 1345, Waterbury, Connecticut 06720. More than 1300 boats have been built.

VITAL STATISTICS: L.O.A. 13'2"; beam 6'0"; draft 2'0" (centerboard down); sail area 105 sq. ft.; racing crew, one.

SHARK. *Courtesy Jack Schuh.*

SHARK

Rod MacAlpine-Downie, who designed the successful English defenders of the "Little America's Cup" in 1963, 1964, and 1965, designed the Shark in 1963. It is very fast and has an active class association boasting eighty members. There are a total of 225 boats in the United States, distributed mostly in the New York area, Florida, and California.

The Shark qualifies for Class B in all respects except sail area. She was designed before the Class B rules were established. Nevertheless, Sharks race actively as a one-design class.

As with most modern catamarans, no spinnakers are allowed. The rig is that of a sloop with a moderately large jib and a full-battened mainsail. The hulls are of fiber glass, with either fiber-glass or plywood decks. The spars are aluminum.

Jack Schuh is the American Shark Association Secretary. He should be addressed at 631 North East 119th Street, North Miami, Florida 33161.

VITAL STATISTICS: L.O.A. 20'0"; beam 10'0"; draft 3'3" (centerboards down); sail area 272 sq. ft.; racing crew, two.